Portuguese Americans
and
Spanish Americans

This is a volume in the Arno Press collection

Hispanics in the United States

Advisory Editor
Carlos E. Cortés

See last pages of this volume for a complete list of titles

Portuguese Americans
and
Spanish Americans

Carlos E. Cortés, editor

ARNO PRESS

A New York Times Company

New York • 1980

Publisher's Note: This book has been reproduced from the best available copy.

Editorial Supervision: Brian Quinn

Reprint Edition 1980 by Arno Press Inc.

Copyright © 1980, Arno Press Inc.

HISPANICS IN THE UNITED STATES
ISBN for complete set: 0-405-13150-X
See last pages of this volume for titles

Manufactured in the United States of America

Library of Congress Cataloging in Publication Data
Main entry under title:

Portuguese Americans and Spanish Americans.

(Hispanics in the United States)
Reprint of 11 articles originally published
between 1892 and 1969.
CONTENTS: D'Eça, R. The Portuguese in the United
States.--Bigelow, B. M. Aaron Lopez.--Vorse, M. H.
The Portuguese of Provincetown.--Poage, G. R. The
coming of the Portuguese. [etc.]
1. Portuguese Americans--Addresses, essays,
lectures. 2. Basque Americans--Addresses, essays,
lectures. 3. Spaniards in the United States--
Addresses, essay, lectures. 4. United States--
Ethnic relations--Addresses, essays, lectures.
I. Cortés, Carlos E. III. Series.
E184.P8P67   973'.04691   79-6233
ISBN 0-405-13180-1

Acknowledgments

"Aaron Lopez: Colonial Merchant of Newport" by Bruce M. Bigelow, has been reprinted from *New England Quarterly*, Vol. 4, October, 1931, by permission of the editor

"The Coming of the Portuguese" by George Rawlings Poage, has been reprinted from *Journal of the Illinois State Historical Society*, Vol. 18, No. 1, 1925, by permission of the editor

"The Portuguese in California" by Frederick G. Bohme, has been reprinted from *California Historical Society Quarterly*, Vol. 35, No. 3, 1956, by permission of the editor

"The Portuguese Element in New England" by Henry Lang, has been reprinted from *Journal of American Folklore*, Vol.5, No. 16, 1892, by permission of the American Folklore Society

"Traditional Ballads Among the Portuguese in California" by Joanne B. Purcell, has been reprinted from *Western Folklore*, Vol. 28, Nos. 1 & 2, 1969, by permission of the California Folklore Society

"Spanish Immigration to the United States" by R.A. Gomez, has been reprinted from *The Americas*, Vol. 19, No. 1, July, 1962, by permission of the editor

"Basque Settlement in Oregon" by Ione B. Harkness, has been reprinted from *Oregon Historical Quarterly*, Vol. 34, No. 3, September, 1933, by permission of the editor

Contents

Harkness, Ione B.
BASQUE SETTLEMENT IN OREGON (Reprinted from *Oregon Historical Quarterly*, Vol. 34, No. 3) Salem, Oregon, 1933

Altroochi, Julia Cooley
THE SPANISH BASQUES IN CALIFORNIA (Reprinted from *Catholic World*, Vol. 146) 1938

Bieter, Pat
RELUCTANT SHEPHERDS: THE BASQUES IN IDAHO (Reprinted from *Idaho Yesterdays*, Vol. 1, No. 2) 1957

Introduction: Portuguese Americans and Spanish Americans

Most U.S. citizens of Iberian ancestry trace their Portuguese and Spanish heritages via their Latin American roots. However, there are also more than 700,000 people in the United States who either immigrated directly from Portugal or Spain or are descendants of such immigrants from the Iberian peninsula. The 1970 census, for example, reported over 240,000 first- and second-generation Portuguese Americans and 155,000 first- and second-generation Spanish Americans, figures which do not include those of third-or-more generations.

The first seven articles in this anthology examine Portuguese Americans, beginning with a brief 1939 overview of Portuguese-descent people in the United States. This is followed by a revealing look at one Portuguese immigrant, Aaron López, who came to the United States in 1752 and became a leading merchant of Newport, Rhode Island. The next three studies discuss the experiences of Portuguese immigrants and their descendants in three widely separate locales — Provincetown, Massachusetts; Jacksonville, Illinois; and California. Finally, the last two articles examine the fascinating subject of Portuguese culture, as it developed with distinctive characteristics in New England and California, particularly as reflected through such means of cultural expression as music, poetry, drama, and legends.

The last four articles in the anthology explore the experience of persons of Spanish heritage in the United States. First appears a 1962 overview of Spanish immigration into the United States. The anthology is concluded with three articles on one unusual ethnic group, Basque Americans, who blend Spanish, French, and their own unique Basque heritage. These three articles provide comparisons of Basque experience and culture in three states — Oregon, Idaho, and California.

Among Hispanics in the United States, persons of Latin American extraction dominate numerically and receive the most public and scholarly attention. Yet, as the articles in this anthology demonstrate, Portuguese Americans and Spanish Americans have also participated in U.S. history. Moreover, they should become increasingly important in the nation's future. This anthology contributes to a better understanding of their special experiences and should help generate additional and much needed future research on these two ethnic groups.

Dr. Carlos E. Cortés
University of California, Riverside

The Portuguese in the United States

Raul d'Eca

The Portuguese *in the* United States

By Raul d'Eça

Division of Intellectual Coöperation, Pan-American Union

VERY little has been written, and very little is generally known, in regard to the contribution of the Portuguese to the ethnic complexion of the American people. The small number of the Portuguese immigrants in proportion to the whole stream of foreign population flowing into the United States, their humbleness, and the inconspicuous participation in the life of the communities where they live have, no doubt, contributed to this absence of studies on this folk. Recently, however, a systematic study of foreign elements in this country has been undertaken by one of the agencies of the federal government, and whether large or small, the Portuguese element is of interest if we are to have a picture, as complete as it is humanly possible to draw, of the American people. The present writer, wishing to contribute to this study, has put together in the paragraphs that follow a few scraps of information which he has gathered on this subject while pursuing studies of related character.

When did the first Portuguese immigrants enter the United States? The answer may be found, if at all, in some old custom house records of one of the New England harbors, particularly the Massachusetts towns from where, after 1765, ships engaging in the whale fishery sailed to the edge of the Gulf Stream, Western Islands (Azores),

and the Brazilian Banks. For some reason or other, the masters of the American whalemen soon got into the habit of carrying away from the Western Islands, where they invariably stopped to revictual, boys to serve as foremast hands or to work in the steerage. These boys were shipped for little or nothing as regards remuneration, scarcely anything being said about the matter on either side; but the captains, if generous, would make them a liberal allowance upon their ships' return to America. When these Portuguese boys became expert seamen, they were usually signed up by the captain at an American consulate in any foreign port where the ship might stop during her protracted voyage in the pursuit of the whale, and as seamen they would enter the United States.

There were various reasons why these youngsters preferred to leave their humble homes for a life of hardships at sea. The always dreaded compulsory military service in Portugal, poverty and lack of opportunity to improve their lot at home, ambition, and the spirit of adventure, were, no doubt, among those reasons. They were generally strong and able-bodied and made good working-hands. In time a great many of these Western-Islanders found employment in American whalemen, and one author, writing in the fifties, declared that "almost every

365

vessel sailing from New Bedford carried more or less of them." In the opinion of the same author, they were "a quiet, peaceful, inoffensive people, sober and industrious, penurious, almost to a fault, and . . . invariably excellent whalemen."

Upon coming to America, many of these boys, if still quite young, were sent to school and brought up as other American boys. Some grew up and prospered in their life work as seamen, a few attaining even to the rank of ship masters. Not infrequently, these boys were raised as sons by some New England family, taking the name of the family, although keeping their Catholic religion.

1851-1860	1,055
1861-1870	2,658
1871-1880	14,082
1881-1890	16,978
1891-1900	27,508
1901-1910	69,149
1911-1920	89,732
1921-1930	29,994
1931-1933	880

The trend of this immigration, as to intended place of residence in America, has changed considerably since those early days of whale fishing. More of these Portuguese have come to the United States to devote themselves to agricultural and industrial work than to seafaring. The following table shows the declared principal destination of Portuguese immigrants admitted into the United States since 1898:

	1898-1900	1901-1910	1911-1920	1921-1930	1931-1932
California	1,055	9,840	12,172	4,243	160
Connecticut	127	859	1,331	1,419	51
Massachusetts	5,672	40,817	50,674	13,340	228
New Jersey	3	50	1,020	3,021	122
New York	266	4,012	7,282	4,024	188
Rhode Island	758	6,441	8,902	3,920	76
Pennsylvania	17	72	1,079	1,179	25

How many Azoreans came to America in this manner is now impossible to ascertain. Statistical data, prior to 1819, are not easily available and when available are seldom reliable. Seybert says that in 1771 American vessels engaged in the whale fishery totaled 304 employing 4,059 seamen. Although the War of 1812 wrecked the American merchant marine, by 1818 Massachusetts alone sent 72 vessels to the pursuit of the whale, employing 1,330 men. Among these men there were, undoubtedly, many Portuguese, but what number the present writer has not been able to find out. From 1820 to 1933, however, the numbers of immigrants from Portugal and Portuguese territories legally admitted into the United States were as follows:

1820-1830	180
1831-1840	829
1841-1850	550

How many of these people left the United States temporarily or permanently prior to 1908 is not possible to tell. The table below indicates the number of Portuguese who have left this country since 1908:

1908-1910	2,620
1911-1920	22,690
1921-1930	30,114
1931-1940	1,412

According to the reports of the Bureau of the Census, the following are the numbers of Portuguese residing in the United States at the time of the various censuses since 1850, when for the first time the census included the nativity of foreign population:

1850	1,274
1860	5,477
1870	8,976
1880	15,779
1890	25,735
1900	40,376
1910	77,634
1920	114,321
1930	118,242

The table below indicates the various states where the Portuguese population totaled more than 1,000 in 1930:

States who are of Portuguese descent either through one or both parents, we find a total Portuguese stock of 269,316

	1850	1860	1870	1880	1890	1900	1910	1920	1930
California	109	1,459	2,508	4,705	9,859	12,068	22,539	33,566	36,343
Connecticut	74	265	49	165	230	568	707	2,191	3,271
Massachusetts	290	988	735	1,161	3,051	13,453	26,437	54,485	48,942
New Jersey	16	14	37	23	20	62	145	1,124	4,411
New York	194	353	237	295	284	362	660	2,652	7,758
Rhode Island	58	86	146	210	833	2,545	6,501	12,949	12,766
Pennsylvania	34	90	89	175	131	124	225	1,073	1,563

This table, unfortunately is most incomplete, at least so far as the years prior to 1920 are concerned, since the *Reports of the Census* included under the general head of "all others" the Portuguese immigrants coming from the Azores, Madeira, and Cape Verde Islands prior to that year. But it serves, nevertheless, to show the general trend of Portuguese immigration during the last eighty years. In this connection, it is interesting to note that in proportion to the total population of each state, Rhode Island had in 1930 the largest percentage of Portuguese, 4.9 per cent.

Examining the total of the Portuguese population in the United States according to the Census of 1930, we find that 69,886 were males and 48,356 females; that 85,769 lived in towns, 18,698 in rural-farm districts, and 13,775 in rural-non-farm districts.

The following were the cities of 100,000 or more population where there were 1,000 or more Portuguese in 1930:

New Bedford, Mass. 13,795
Fall River, Mass. 9,783
Oakland, Calif. 4,698
New York, N.Y. 3,998
Providence, R.I. 2,609
Cambridge, Mass. 2,186
Newark, N.J. 2,088
Boston, Mass. 1,686
Somerville, Mass. 1,530
San Francisco, Calif. 1,103

If to the number of individuals born in Portugal and Portuguese territories who resided in the United States in 1930 we add the natives of the United

distributed in the following manner, including only states where there are at least 1,000:

Massachusetts 108,896
California 100,646
Rhode Island 29,573
New York 9,361
New Jersey 5,700
Connecticut 5,238
Pennsylvania 2,269
Illinois 1,096

As shown in the table above, the bulk of the Portuguese population in the United States is to be found at the present time in Massachusetts, California, and Rhode Island. In California, where the Portuguese first went in the middle of the 19th century, the first settlers were largely of the sailor class. Later followed farmers who went to the West Coast directly from the Azores, Madeira, and Cape Verde Islands, as well as from continental Portugal, or indirectly after having lived in the Hawaii Islands. Others, in more recent years, have moved to the Pacific Coast from New England. These people have engaged mainly in agriculture, usually as laborers for their countrymen already established there, rather than as tenant-farmers. Some have been able to save enough to buy land. The great majority of them are to be found in central California and within 100 miles of San Francisco. A large number engage in dairy farming, while others raise vegetables and potatoes. "The Portuguese are excellent farmers," says the *Report of the Immigra-*

tion Commission of the Senate for 1911, "and frequently, while improving their land, obtain two or three crops from the same field in the course of the year. In their thrift, investment of savings in more land, in the character of their housing and standard of living, they are very much like the Italians. In some instances, however, their housing is of a distinctly better type."

In Massachusetts and Rhode Island most of the Portuguese work now in factories, although there are many engaged in fishing, in farming, and in other skilled and non-skilled occupations. Thus, for instance, in the towns of Gloucester and Provincetown, Massachusetts, there are large groups of fishermen who are either Portuguese or of Portuguese descent; and in Portsmouth, Rhode Island, and parts of Cape Cod, Massachusetts, a large proportion of the farmers and rural laborers are also Portuguese. To Portsmouth, the Portuguese came about 1872, and as late as 1885 there was only one Portuguese landowner there. However, in 1923 there were 194 Portuguese families in that town, and more than half of them were landowners. In fact, the Portuguese landholding there was increasing so rapidly that it was feared by some that if the tendency continued Portsmouth would soon not only be a community of Portuguese people but also be Portuguese-owned. A great many of the Portuguese who work in the cranberry bogs of Cape Cod came originally from the Cape Verde Islands and are commonly called "Bravas." They are to be distinguished from the Portuguese coming from other sources in the fact that they are mostly of the African race.

On the other hand in New Bedford and Fall River, Massachusetts, and in a few other communities of the eastern United States, there are many Portuguese industrial workers. Until as late as 1889, few Portuguese, if any, worked in the cotton mills of New England. By 1899, however, there were many Portuguese millworkers, and their number has increased ever since. In fact, in 1915 there were 22,118 industrial workers of Portuguese nationality in Massachusetts alone.

What manner of people are these Portuguese? In 1894 the Probation Officer of New Bedford, Massachusetts, stated before the state's commission on the unemployed: "They [the Portuguese] are generally very prudent and good citizens"; and another witness from New Bedford declared that they are very thrifty. Summing up the results of his investigation regarding the Portuguese of two New England communities, Dr. Taft wrote as follows: "Everyone agrees that the Portuguese are capable farmers and good farm laborers. Testimony to this effect comes not only from the inhabitants of Portsmouth, but from those who have observed them on the farms of Cape Cod and elsewhere. They are in the fields as long as it is light and employ the labor of every member of their families old enough to wield a hoe. Being, in addition, exceedingly frugal, and understanding intensive farming, they are successful on New England farms where the native farmer has either failed or found more lucrative employment in the city."

Many other similar opinions could be cited and, what is more interesting, these opinions seem to be borne out by statistics so far as this can ever be done. Thus, for instance, in 1919, of a total number of arrests in Fall River, the Portuguese contributed only 14.1 per cent (347 cases in a total of 2,468 arrests), the percentage of Portuguese males from 20 to 44 years of age in that city being at the time 20.2 of all males. In Portsmouth, another community where the Portuguese element abounds, in 120 arrests from

January 1, 1916 to September 21, 1919, only 16 (13.3 per cent) were Portuguese or of Portuguese descent, whereas the proportion of Portuguese men between 15 and 44 years of age was 38.4. Among prisoners committed to jails and houses of correction in Massachusetts in 1898, the Portuguese contributed only 14 individuals. Considering that the Portuguese population of that state was 12,298 in 1895, the percentage of Portuguese criminals (10.5 in 10,000) was remarkably small, especially if compared with those of other aliens as, for instance, the French (93.5), the Swedes (98.1), the Poles (122.3), and the Irish (288.2).

In a study covering six months (December 1, 1908 to May 31, 1909), made of cases receiving public charity in 43 cities of the United States, it was found that the Portuguese had only 50 cases involving 247 persons, or 0.2 per cent of all cases. In fact they came at the bottom of the list, just above the Finns, who had the same number of cases, but a smaller number of persons involved (only 186).

As to the thriftiness of the Portuguese, it is confirmed by the fact that in a list of 17 different nationalities (excluding the older immigration peoples) inhabiting the United States, the Portuguese came in fourth place as home-owners.

On the other hand, it is shocking to find that these peaceful, laborious, and thrifty people had the highest illiteracy percentage among all aliens admitted into the United States (68.2 during the 12-year period from 1899 to 1910); one of the highest infant mortality rates in the whole country (201 in the City of New Bedford in the 1915-1920 period); and the lowest percentage of naturalized citizens of the United States (18.7 in 1930), the latter two conditions being, undoubtedly, consequences in great part of the former. It would be fitting to conclude these remarks by calling the attention of the social agencies which aim at correcting human deficiencies such as those just indicated, to the Portuguese in the United States, who otherwise seem to be worthy raw material for American citizenship.

Aaron Lopez

Bruce M. Bigelow

AARON LOPEZ:
COLONIAL MERCHANT OF NEWPORT

BRUCE M. BIGELOW

O LD Newport abounds in forgotten persons of distinction, for historians seem to overlook the commercial nabobs of this "city by the sea." The story of
its merchants is the story of the rise, the growth, and
the decline of the Rhode Island-West Indian trade. It
is a tale of sloops and ships, wharves and warehouses.
It is a story of smuggled goods, of trade with the enemy,
of Odyssean voyages, of prosperity and poverty. The
old wharves of Newport to-day are crumbling monu-
ments of this former activity. They are memorials of
days before the square-rigged vessels were replaced by
excursion steamers; before the coffee-houses became
chain drug-stores; before the homes of farmers gave
way to the marble palaces of millionaires. The Revolution, the decline of the West Indian trade, and the age
of iron all combined to seal the fate of commercial Newport. Too frequently the persons in this story have been
ignored. Following is a narrative of the career of the
immigrant, Aaron Lopez.

A biographical sketch of this Portuguese Jew almost
epitomizes the commercial history of Newport in its
golden age just before the American Revolution. This
merchant adventurer, with a younger brother David, arrived in Newport on October 13, 1752,[1] when Aaron

---

[1] The date 1752 is taken from the Naturalization Papers of Aaron
Lopez. These were made out in Taunton, October, 1752. Before the

was only twenty-one years of age. An older half-brother, named Moses, had been residing in Newport since the middle forties. The three brothers had all come from Portugal, where they had lived openly as Christians but secretly as Jews. Even their names were Christian. In Portugal, Moses was known as Jose, Aaron as Edward, and David as Gabriel. The Inquisition had made them uncomfortable, and Moses had even been in danger of imprisonment. Therefore he left the country, first going to England and thence to New York, where he was naturalized in 1741.[2] Later he moved on to Newport and soon became well known as a merchant.[3] Aaron, on his own arrival a few years later, had the good fortune to learn New England business directly from his brother.

Evidence of Aaron's early start as a merchant is scant. Apparently his beginnings were modest, for even at the period of the Seven Years' War he does not seem to have been active. Probably Lopez started, as did many other merchants of the day, by buying, selling, and exchanging in Newport and Providence alone.[4] In 1756, he was

Superior Court of that county Lopez swore that he settled in Newport on the 13th day of October, 1752. Ezra Stiles gives the date of his arrival in Newport as "about 1754." F. B. Dexter, Ed., *The Literary Diary of Ezra Stiles* (New York, 1901), III, 24. [Worthington C. Ford, Ed.,] *Commerce of Rhode Island, 1726-1800* (Boston, 1914), I, 65, *note* 2, gives the date as 1750. See an important letter on Lopez and Rivera genealogy printed in the *American Jewish Historical Review*, II, 101-106.

[2] Max Kohler, "Jews of Newport," in *Publications*, American Jewish Historical Society (1897).

[3] A William Ellery ledger in the Newport Historical Society shows a sale of 11 hogsheads of molasses made to Moses Lopez, Merchant, on March 20, 1746.

[4] Newport Historical Society, Lopez Letters, MS. Book 626. Letter of April 8, 1755. Paul Tew of Providence informed Lopez that Captain Brown wished to exchange spermaceti candles for tea. On October 15, 1755, the bargain was completed. Tew frequently supplied Lopez with goods.

in regular correspondence with Henry Lloyd of Boston.[5] At this time, however, his chief interest was in the spermaceti candle business, and Lloyd merely acted as a middleman between the whalers in Nantucket and the merchant in Newport.[6]

It is significant that Aaron Lopez did not enter the West Indian trade until 1767. He was conservative, generally making careful preparations for every new venture. Frequent reports of failure in West Indian trade during the Seven Years' War, and the combination of harsh enforcement measures in 1763, with the Sugar Act of the following year, probably decided Aaron Lopez to confine himself to candles. When, in 1765, there came a chance for expansion, he naturally looked to Europe for it rather than the Caribbean. Before 1765, his shipping had been mostly coastwise: to Boston, New York, Philadelphia, and Charleston — and the invoices usually listed boxes of candles.[7] Although he had already been carrying on a small regular correspondence with William Stead of London,[8] the European port he selected for his new scheme was Bristol, England. His correspondent there was Henry Cruger, Jr., son of Henry Cruger of New York City;[9] his plan was to dispatch vessels to Bristol, and then draw bills of exchange

[5] *Ibid.* See also letters printed in *Commerce of Rhode Island*, I, 67-72.

[6] These whalers were Joseph Rotch and his son, William. In 1765, the family moved to Bedford-in-Dartmouth, later called New Bedford. A partner with Lopez in the spermaceti candle business was his father-in-law, Jacob Roderique Rivera.

[7] Newport Historical Society, Invoice Book of Aaron Lopez. The book has a list of the out-going invoices, February 25, 1763, to December 15, 1768.

[8] Newport Historical Society, Lopez Copy Book, 1764-1765, in Lopez Miscellaneous Papers.

[9] *Ibid.*

on that port when the vessels actually sailed. Lopez at that time was contracting for the building of new brigantines and ships, and was hoping to load them all with log-wood, mahogany, building lumber, and oil for the English market. If possible, the vessels were to be sold, along with the cargo, in Bristol, and English drygoods and hardware were to be shipped back to Lopez.

In May, 1765, the plan was agreed on, and the brigantine *Charlotte* sailed for Bristol. In June the ship *America* followed; in August the *Friendship*; and in October the *Newport Packet* and then the *Charlotte* again.[10] All five ventures were consigned to Henry Cruger, Jr., and were at the entire risk of Lopez. The plan was daring, for five adventures in one year to a new port, and a distant one at that, would have been hazardous in ordinary times, but in the post-war depression prevailing everywhere the backer seemed to be inviting his own ruin. But he was confident of success. He felt the intense competition in New England for the sale of European goods, and he knew that such goods might be bought in Bristol more cheaply than London. Accordingly he wrote young Cruger in August, 1765:

My Commanding Branches I follow of the Whaling, Fishery, Spermty Works etc. and from the advantage of being the only Trader that undertakes a Steady Commerce with Bristol that I made my address to your House worthy some Notice.[11]

Lopez would have been luckier if his vessels had never sailed for Bristol that year, for they all met a very bad market. "Trade is as much at a stand in England

[10] Newport Historical Society, Lopez Invoice Book, 1763-1768.

[11] Newport Historical Society, Lopez Copy Book, 1764-1765, in Lopez Miscellaneous Papers.

as in America; [wrote Cruger on October 4, 1765] my friends in London write me, they know not what to do with their Ships; here also is the same stagnation."[12] Continuing in the same letter, Cruger may have led Aaron Lopez to try his fortune in the West Indian trade: "Suppose, Sir, you was to keep one, or more Ships in this trade, load them with the most valuable Cargo Rhode Island produced, send them sometimes to Carolina, or the West Indies . . . the Produce of these places always meet [sic] a ready sale here." Cruger apologized for making the suggestion, but the discouraged Lopez was already convinced that his plan of an extensive trade with Bristol could not succeed. He determined on a diversification of his commerce.

Conditions had improved by 1766, when the general economic depression showed signs of passing, and the disturbance caused by the Sugar Act and the Stamp Act was corrected.[13] ". . . the Confusion of the times now begins to be rectified," Cruger wrote encouragingly in March, "and like Mud in troubled Waters to subside."[14] Nevertheless the English trade had been disappointing, and Lopez made other plans — not, entirely, however, because of the failures in Bristol and London. Already in 1765, he had joined with his father-in-law, Jacob Rodriques Rivera, in two African ventures in the brigantine *Africa* and the sloop *Betsy*, both voyages being unsatisfactory.[15] Although he undertook three ventures

[12] *Commerce of Rhode Island*, I, 125. Original in the Wetmore Collection, Massachusetts Historical Society.

[13] Cruger himself had spent several weeks in London lobbying for the American interests.

[14] *Commerce of Rhode Island*, I, 147.

[15] Newport Historical Society, Lopez Copy Book, 1764-1765, in Lopez Miscellaneous Papers: Letter to William Stead, July 22, 1765.

more to the Slave Coast, and three to Bristol, in 1766, he sent four vessels directly to the West Indies.[16] This was the beginning of new business.

In order to make this commerce profitable, the trader adopted a new form of marketing: he employed a regular business agent, or factor, to reside in the West Indies. Dealing with the West Indian planters was always a ticklish problem for a northern merchant, and Lopez knew that a good bargain could be struck more quickly by a shrewd factor than a stupid captain. The wise policy was to have one's own man on the spot to make acquaintances among the leading planters and merchants, sell the cargoes of livestock, provisions, and lumber direct, and secure early return shipments of sugar and molasses. A half-brother, Abraham,[17] then living in Savana la Mar, Jamaica, was offered the position, but refused, being very pessimistic about the outcome of his ambitious brother's schemes: "These parts are so distress'd in general and so deeply involv'd," he warned, "that there would be no putting any dependance on the payments."[18] Aaron sent his son-in-law, Abraham Pereira Mendes, but the lethargic atmosphere of the Caribbean was too much for this youth, who soon forgot both business and wife.

Although Mendes was of no account and markets were not promising, Lopez was sufficiently confident to send out nine vessels to the West Indies in 1767.[19] In that same year he wrote to Henry Cruger, Jr.:

[16] Newport Historical Society, Lopez Invoice Book and also Lopez Letter Book for 1766.

[17] Abraham was a full brother to Moses. With his family he emigrated from Portugal to Jamaica in the middle of the century.

[18] *Commerce of Rhode Island*, I, 175. Original in the Newport Historical Society.

[19] Newport Historical Society, Lopez Letter Books and Invoice Book.

Hope propitious Heaven will Bless the Event of my new Plan of Trade, that our Connections may prove as beneficial to your good self as they are agreeable and obliging to me and at same time avert my incurring in painful censure of that want of punctuality too conspicuous in the Character of my American Neighbours. By dear bought experience I have learnt that the method of making remitances from these parts thro' the Guinea Channell, as also that of sending New Ships to the English market, have proved very disheartening of Late Years. There-fore I have timely alter'd the course of my Business and adopted the old Track of remiting by way of our West Indies, a trade where my Spermaceti, and Oil Connexions will afford many peculiar advantages not common to other people and having this year Launched largely into it, have reason to expect (Deo volente) that I shall have it in my power to make you next Summer and Fall some Considerable returns on the arrival of my Jamaica men.[20]

This optimism was dampened as the year 1767 rolled on and it became obvious that Mendes was making little profit in Jamaica, and the masters who had managed their own cargoes were having difficulty finding markets at other Caribbean ports. Captain James Potter, for in-stance, had sailed the brigantine *Diana* for St. Anns, Jamaica, on February 13, 1767, with a cargo which in-cluded 10 horses, 103 sheep, 54 turkeys, 23 geese, 55 barrels of flour, 30 barrels of oil, 20 barrels beef, 98½ barrels alewives, and 87 barrels of menhaden — not to mention spermaceti candles, tar, and lumber.[21] In April, he advised Aaron Lopez of the bad markets, concluding with the postscript: "I can't Inform you of the Price of produce as thair is none Shiped as yet. Nither Cann I advise Sending a nother Vessel as the Island is Gluted

[20] Newport Historical Society, Lopez Copy Book. Letter of February 17, 1767, to Henry Cruger, Jr.

[21] Newport Historical Society, Lopez Invoice Book. Alewives and menhaden were poorer grades of fish frequently shipped to the Caribbean.

mutch with our Produce."[22]   In June the discouraged
captain was still in Jamaica and expected to be there till
the last of August.[23]

Yet Lopez, always optimistic, was not disheartened.
He had learned at the end of that year that his debt to
Henry Cruger alone was £10,514. 10s. 5d. sterling[24] —
an enormous sum for the finances of the time, and explained his own difficulty in collecting debts owing him
from his American neighbors, "whose characters," he
added, "are so well distinguished by your own Experience."[25]

. . . How can I do other ways than bitterly lament my grieving
Situation at a Time when I am hearing the best of Correspondents . . . [is] . . . overwhelmed with difficulties of which
I am partly an Instrument and not to have it in my power to
extricate him at once from that piercing anxiety which honest
breasts must feel when unable to comply with your requisi-
tions. . . .

The situation improved when Lopez replaced his in-
efficient son-in-law with Captain Benjamin Wright, recommended by his half-brother, Abraham, as one of the
shrewdest traders in the Caribbean.[26] This "Presbyterian Old Yankee" — as he liked to call himself — was
no ordinary sea captain. Not only did he know ships but

[22] Newport Historical Society, Lopez Letters, MS. Book 623: Letter of
April 2, 1767.

[23] *Ibid.*; Letter of June 30, 1767.

[24] Newport Historical Society, Lopez Copy Book, MS. Book 72: Let-
ter to Henry Cruger, Jr., May 19, 1767. In MS. Book 630, letter of
George Rome to Aaron Lopez, December 23, 1767, it is stated that
Lopez also owed William Stead of London £5619.17s. sterling.

[25] *Ibid.*, MS. 72: Letter of Amy [May] 9, 1767.

[26] Newport Historical Society, Lopez Miscellaneous Papers: Abraham
Lopez to Aaron Lopez, April 30, 1767.

he had an extraordinary knowledge of the needs of planters, the packing of cargoes, their sale in Jamaica, collecting debts, and the best means of getting a load of sugar, molasses, and rum for the return voyage. Just at this time, even the agile Wright found markets glutted in the West Indies, and therefore he warned Lopez not to send too many vessels. The £10,000 debt in Bristol, however, was bothering the conscientious merchant at Newport, and he pushed his commerce all he could. In 1768, five vessels sailed for the West Indies, four to Europe, one to Africa, and thirty-seven down the coast.[27]

The first vessel of his that Wright sailed was the *America.* Cruger had secured £1,250 sterling insurance at Bristol in the autumn of 1767, and in November the *America* set sail for Savana la Mar, Jamaica,[28] with Lopez, Rivera, and Wright as backers. She arrived in nineteen days, but the market was glutted, provisions being plentiful. On January 2, 1768, Captain Wright wrote discouragingly: "I can't give any encouragement to send any more Vessels to this Island this Year."[29] Rum and molasses, moreover, were dear. Nevertheless, the cargo of the schooner *Ranger* which Lopez, Rivera, and Wright had sent down, also in November, had been nearly all sold, and the captain, William Bardin, had done well at raising cash.[30] But there was still another cargo to be disposed of. The schooner *Betsy Ann,* Thomas Tillinghast, master, sailed from Newport

[27] Newport Historical Society, Lopez Invoice Book.
[28] *Ibid.*
[29] *Commerce of Rhode Island,* I, 217. Original in Massachusetts Historical Society.
[30] *Ibid.,* 216 and 223: Letter of February 29, 1768: Benjamin Wright to Aaron Lopez.

on January 8, the trusting Aaron Lopez having consigned part of the cargo to his first factor, Abraham
Pereira Mendes, at Kingston. Another part was consigned to the master himself, and a third part, belonging to Lopez, Rivera, and Wright, to Captain Wright at
Savana la Mar.[31] At Kingston part of the cargo was
sold, and at Savana la Mar the remainder went to
Wright, who secured the return cargo, although the
price of rum and molasses had risen — to his bitter disappointment. "The price of [West Indian] produce
here," he wrote home, "is at last broke, and can assure
you my heart is allmost broke with it."[32]

But Captain Wright sensed the ambition and persistence of Lopez; he knew that he had debts to pay in
Bristol and London, and he was well aware of the danger of failure in another Jamaica venture. To save his
own conscience he warned his Newport backer that failure might come, but that if he were determined to send
the *America* to Jamaica again in the autumn he should
carefully fill the cargo memorandum that he was sending back to him.[33] The warning did not frighten Lopez,
for the brig *Diana* was loaded in April and dispatched
to Jamaica. Captain Wright was to return home in the
America; so Lopez consigned the *Diana's* cargo to the
master, James Potter. In March, a cargo for Surinam
was placed on the brig *Dolphin* and consigned to the
master, Joseph Dean, and in June the brig *Hope*, Nathaniel Hathaway, master, was dispatched to the same
market. In the summer Benjamin Wright returned to
Newport and agreed with Lopez to make another at-

---

[31] Newport Historical Society, Invoice Book.
[32] *Commerce of Rhode Island*, I, 229. Letter of March 8, 1768.
[33] *Ibid.*, 225.

tempt in Jamaica. In August Benjamin Allen was sent
in the schooner *Ranger*, and Benjamin Wright himself
followed in October with the ship *Jacob*. Business at
the Lopez wharf in Newport was active even though
the Jamaican profits were not so encouraging as could
have been expected. In November another vessel sailed
for Surinam and still another in December, for the Mole
St. Nicholas on Hispaniola.

Meanwhile Henry Cruger was being dunned by his
English creditors, and he continued to write Lopez that
he must have more remittances. "Oh God! at times it
half kills me," he wrote in April, 1768, "but I'll say no
more, as I am sure it must hurt you." Again, in August
he resumed: "you have buoyed up my hopes with Ex-
pectations of a Remittance from Mr. Mendez, and I
amused my friends with that Phantom about a twelve-
month — alas! The dream is out, and none of us here
the richer — cruel, hard fate, *not a line nor a Penny
from Mr. Mendez*, perhaps 'tis his fault alone."[84] But
Lopez was just as much distressed as Henry Cruger.

By 1769, the clouds began to break: golden days were
soon to shine on the house of Lopez. A rare combination
of business talent was now at work in Newport and Jamaica: Aaron Lopez was an ardent and imaginative a
merchant as could be found in North America. Like
all successful traders he had made mistakes — the Bristol
episode was one — but he had a good memory and an
ingenious mind. Seldom did he repeat an error, and he
was always ready to try an experiment. This was the
kind of man who brought its golden age to Newport.

[84] *Commerce of Rhode Island*, 239, 245, and 260. Also see several letters written by Cruger to Lopez in 1768 and 1769 in the Newport
Historical Society.

Down in the Caribbean, Benjamin Wright showed an almost uncanny ingenuity. The old Yankee sensed every need of the West Indian planter, almost read his very thoughts, and with a facile pen, he communicated these wants to his friend. The skilful captain had a ready wit and a sharp tongue. The same letter probably made the recipient smile and frown at his pungent wit and his caustic censure. Captain Wright was particularly insistent on excellent cargoes. Time and again he scolded Lopez about bad fish, knotty lumber, or scraggy horses. He put his business policy into one paragraph:

Am of opinion you have Masters in your Imploy more suitable then I am to Despose of any article that was not good as I would be Verry sorry to Recommend any article which was not good therefore Chuse to stick to the plan I have set out on — to deceave no person, and give me liberty to give you this piece of advice that you will for Ever be the sufferer by your Cargoes this way prevoiding [*sic*] Every article is not of the best Kind the people heare will not buy reffuse and they will not stick at a good price for a good thing.[35]

It was one thing for the captain to demand the best; it was another thing for Lopez to get it. In order to do so he inspected hundreds of barrels of shad and mackerel, thousands of feet of lumber, and horses, turkeys, geese, and hogs without number. In spite of his best efforts, bad cargoes occasionally arrived in the West Indies — and Wright's vituperations by return mail. In general, however, the letters of the agent were filled with praise, wishes for the best of health, and prayers that "the almighty impart blessings in proportion to your boundless generosity."[36]

[35] Newport Historical Society, Lopez Letters, MS. Book 630: Letter of February 27, 1769.

[36] *Ibid.*, MS. Book 634: Letter of April 7, 1773.

Captain Wright spent the between-season period making the acquaintance of the planters and merchants, gaining their confidence, and accepting their advice; and when the busy harvesting season was on, he had the sugar, molasses, and rum for his cargoes all acquired and a market for his Northern provisions practically assured. He knew all the tricks of the trade; his aim was always to have a Lopez vessel back in Newport first. With considerable pride, in March, 1770, he announced a typical victory:

... there was a plan laid by Messr Wanton's Captains four in Number to dispatch one of their Vessells the first from this Island and not withstanding they have given all their assistance Old Yankey has been to [sic] quick for them. They will not get one of their Vessells away till 10th April by which time Sloop *George* will be well on her Passage if no accident happens.[37]

It would be untrue to say that the Lopez West Indian trade began to thrive immediately upon the arrival of Benjamin Wright, for such was not the case. The confusions and disorders of 1765, 1766, and 1767 continued for two years more, and it was really not until 1770 that prosperity came in abundance.

Lopez had waited a long time for good markets. Now at last he realized a number of profitable ventures, by which time he had so extended his commerce that his vessels could be seen at Jamaica, Hispaniola, Surinam, Honduras, Newfoundland, England, Holland, Africa, Spain, Portugal, the Azores, and the Canaries. Wright gave his attention chiefly to Jamaica; Pierre Rolland and

[37] Newport Historical Society, Lopez Letters, MS. Book 631: Letter of March 30, 1770.

a partner named Zarzedas found means of evading the
French decrees and traded with Lopez vessels on Hispaniola.[38] Captain John Dupee, a Rhode Islander of
French descent, frequently acted as the Newport merchant's factor there.[39] Honduras was as precarious as
Hispaniola but it was an important trade, for the log-
wood and mahogany of the Bay usually found a market
in England.[40] A steadier commerce was that with the
Dutch at Surinam and St. Eustatius. During the sixties
the Lopez whalers in southern waters would sometimes
pick up a few casks of Bohea tea sent to St. Eustatius by
John Turner and Son, the Lopez correspondents in Holland,[41] and smuggle it into Newport. The regular Surinam trade was steadier and became more profitable.
Captain Nathaniel Hathaway was the master usually
employed in these waters.[42]

Lopez continued his trade with Europe. The firm of
Hayley and Hopkins, organized in 1769 and dissolved
in 1774, acted as chief correspondents; its aid was im-

[38] Newport Historical Society, Lopez Letters, MS. Book 624: Zarzedas
to Lopez, March 30, 1773, and April 22, 1773. Rolland to Lopez,
March 30, 1773. Lopez Letters, MS. Book 634 and 635: Rolland to
Lopez, April 7, 1773, and September 12, 1773. Lopez Shipping Book:
Bill of Lading, April 23, 1773. Lopez Letters, MS. Book 625, all in
Newport Historical Society.

[39] Ibid., MS. Book 635: Letter of Captain John Bourke to Aaron Lopez,
September 26, 1773.

[40] Newport Historical Society, Lopez Invoice Book, 1766-1768: Lopez
Miscellaneous Papers in Newport Historical Society: Letter of June 8,
1770; Commerce of Rhode Island, I, 306, 344. A number of interesting
letters from Captain John Newdigate to Lopez are in the MS. Books 631,
632, and 633 in Newport Historical Society. Others from Newdigate on
the logwood trade are in Commerce of Rhode Island, I.

[41] Newport Historical Society, Lopez Copy Book, 1764-1765, in Lopez
Miscellaneous Papers: Letter of February 14, 1765.

[42] Newport Historical Society. A number of letters on the Dutch trade
are in Letter Books 624, 632, 633, 634, and 635.

measurable.[43] Lopez captains entered the Mediterranean, where fish, rum, rice, flour, wheat, kidney beans, and staves were exchanged for salt, wines, fruit, and even mules.[44] George Sears managed the North American end of this business as Lopez factor at Newfoundland.[45] Lopez was not so much interested in the Guinea trade as his father-in-law, Rivera. He usually sent out no more than one vessel a year to the Slave Coast,[46] for the trade in "black ivory" was probably too much of a gamble for him. The merchant prince of Newport was making money, and when prosperity came he did not forget his friend in Bristol who had advanced so much credit to him in 1765. In 1767 Lopez owed Henry Cruger, Jr., £10,514; by 1773 the debt seems to have been practically erased. Cruger at that time was owed money by other Americans, and he made a special trip to this country in order to investigate their solvency. But his only interest in seeing Aaron Lopez was the de-

[43] William Stead and William Robertson were other correspondents. Many letters to Lopez from Hayley and Hopkins are in the Newport Historical Society: see particularly MS. Books 631, 632, 633, 638, and 639; and *Commerce of Rhode Island*, for letters in the Wetmore Collection of the Massachusetts Historical Society.

[44] Massachusetts Historical Society, Wetmore Collection, III: Captain Osborne to Aaron Lopez, January 1, 1761; also Newport Historical Society, MS. Book 633: letters of March 1, 1772, and April, 1772, May 5, 1772, August 4, 1772, and August 29, 1772; and MS. Book 634: letter of January 12, 1773. The accounts of Zebediah Story's ventures for mules are particularly interesting.

[45] In the Newport Historical Society, there are many letters giving prices current in Newfoundland. See Lopez Letters, MS. Books 634, 635, 636, 637, and 638. George Sears corresponded with Lopez frequently, and most of his letters for 1773 and 1774 are extant.

[46] Newport Historical Society, Lopez Invoice Book. Several letters on the Lopez Guinea trade may be found in the Newport Historical Society: Lopez Letters, MS. Books 628, 629, and 633 and also Lopez Miscellaneous Papers. Copies of some original Lopez slave papers are in the *Newport Historical Society Bulletin*, No. 62 (July, 1927).

sire to shake his hand. As he wrote from Boston, July 4, 1773:

I long for an amicable and an affectionate shake by the hand of a Gentleman, for whom I have conceived the warmest regard, and with whom I have for a series of years carried on so extensive and so interesting a Correspondence . . . I should be happy — very happy to drink a Bottle of Wine with my friend Mr. Lopez My Brother Joins me in best good Wishes for your Health and that of your worthy family — and I remain with sincere Esteem — dear Sir — your very much obliged and affectionate Humble Servant Hen: Cruger Jr.[47]

Their meeting never took place, but their mutual esteem never diminished.

Lopez had learned that a merchant, to be successful, must trade in many things and many places, for the instability of eighteenth-century commerce made diversification of it an utter necessity. By 1774, his vessels were scattered over the high seas following scores of voyages. Discouraging letters were offset by good news, and through it all one thing was certain — Lopez was rich, and growing richer. Just before the Revolution he was contracting for more vessels — all of which, significantly enough, were to be large ships. In 1775, by a conservative estimate, he had part interest or owned completely over thirty vessels.[48]

[47] Newport Historical Society, Lopez Miscellaneous Papers: Henry Cruger, Jr., to Aaron Lopez, Boston, July 4, 1773.

[48] The writer has counted the Lopez vessels named in his Invoice Books, Copy Books, Sailors Book, and Shipping Book. Frequent sales and purchases make an accurate number difficult to ascertain. Between 1765 and 1770 the Lopez Ship Book in Newport Historical Society lists 39 vessels in which Lopez had an interest sometime or other during that period. In the Sailors' Book in the Newport Historical Society for the years 1767 to 1769, there are 24 vessels in which Lopez was chiefly concerned and which remained in his possession during those years. These consisted of 9 sloops, 3 schooners, 7 brigantines, and 5 ships. Shipbuilding agreements in the Newport Historical Society indicate a preference, in the seventies, for the last-named type.

Despite the optimism of 1774, the following year was by no means golden for Newport. The beginning of the town's commercial decline was at hand — the disappearance of the great merchant houses. Lopez pushed his trade and even invested a large amount of capital with Francis Rotch, of New Bedford, in foreign whaling ventures.[49] But business had come almost to a stand-still; money was "tight" in Newport, Jamaica, and London. In the spring of 1775, Lopez confessed that he had to strain every nerve to meet an emergency bill of four hundred dollars which his shipbuilders needed at once.[50] Captain Wright at Savana la Mar was in just as bad a predicament: although four of the Lopez vessels had arrived, the Old Yankee was finding it almost impossible to raise any money.

With the violence of the American Revolution, the Lopez, Rivera, and Mendes families moved out of Newport. Aaron hoped to find a spot, as he explained, "secured from sudden Allarms and the Cruel Ravages of an enraged Enemy."[51] "Such a one," he wrote to his old Philadelphia captain, Joseph Anthony, "I have . . . found in the small inland Township of Leicester in the Massachusetts Bay, where I pitch'd my Tent, erecting a proportionable one to the extent of my numerous Family on the Sumit of an high healthy Hill, where we have experienc'd the civilities and hospitality of a kind Neighbourhood . . ." While the three families were comfortably situated there, in palatial homes, Aaron was

[49] Newport Historical Society, Lopez Miscellaneous Letters: several letters to and from Rotch.

[50] Newport Historical Society, Lopez Miscellaneous Papers: Aaron Lopez to Benjamin Wright, March 3, 1775.

[51] *Commerce of Rhode Island*, II, 51, Aaron Lopez to Joseph Anthony, Philadelphia, Pennsylvania, February 3, 1779.

busily engaged in straightening out his tangled accounts and interviewing government officials about his many business problems.

He had lost at the hands of both English and Americans, for his vessels had been seized on both sides of the Atlantic, and he and his family had been forced to flee when Newport was invaded. Furthermore, he was suffering from the meanness of debtors who settled their accounts in worthless paper money. Indeed, when his old friend, Benjamin Wright, went to Leicester in December, 1777, Lopez was fighting a financial case of this kind in the courts at Boston. The Old Yankee wrote Aaron and persuaded him not "to tarry among a people who by their own confession are strongly attached to the political Laws and government of inferno." With characteristic fluency and humor he added:

I have been at your House one whole week living on the fatt of the land and my attendance fit for a Nobleman your family at present are in number only 99 and still there is a vacancy for one more and I desire you will return with all Expodition to fill it. then we shall be able to proseed to business to prevent you inattention to what I have said, permit me to hint, your Family if I mistake not inclines to Imbrace the Presbyterian Faith a Religion of all now Extant is the most fatal to Humanity and Common Honesty fraught with Superstition and oppression (whatever I may think I will not say — Rebellion) if this piece of Intelligence will not bring you home, I must Suppose you are inclined to take yourself another wife — should that prove to be the case my Friend the first ox Slead you see approaches the great Town prepare yourself to meet a man Red with in Common Rath to blast the man who oweth his greatness to paper Money.[52]

[52] Newport Historical Society, Lopez Letters, MS. Book 640: Leicester, Massachusetts, December 7, 1779, Benjamin Wright to Aaron Lopez.

The humor of "Presbyterian Wright" was needed in the Lopez household, for there the American Revolution was altogether a mournful event. Business had been abruptly stopped, and accounts were in utter chaos. To put them in order again was perhaps a superhuman task; if any one were equal to it, Lopez was. But fate ordered otherwise: journeying to Rhode Island with his wife and family on May 28, 1782, he stopped to water his horse at Scott's Pond, near Providence, and was accidently drowned.[53] The tragedy was a loss not only to his family and the State of Rhode Island, but to hundreds of admirers in the world of business. Although he and the other Jews of Newport had never been found at the social functions of the *élite* of the eighteenth century, no man in the town, at the outbreak of the Revolution, was more highly respected than he. Yet as late as 1761, this able merchant was refused citizenship by a Superior Court, the "Colony being already so full of People that many of his Majesty's good Subjects born within the same have removed and settled in Nova Scotia .... By the Charter granted to this Colony it appears that the free and quiet Enjoyment of the Christian Religion and a Desire of propogating [*sic*] the same were the principal Views with which this Colony was settled . . ."[54] A Boston merchant, however, offered his services, and through an influential relative petitioned the Governor and Chief Justice of Massachusetts in behalf of Aaron Lopez. Writing to Lopez in March 29, 1763, Henry Lloyd explained the procedure, which was easily ar-

[53] Dexter, *The Literary Diary of Ezra Stiles*, III, 25.

[54] Newport Historical Society, Lopez Miscellaneous Papers: Naturalization Papers.

ranged.[55] At Taunton, October 15, 1762, Aaron Lopez was admitted to citizenship.[56] Newport soon had good reason to be proud of the American from Massachusetts.

Probably no one in the town was better able to judge this man than Ezra Stiles, pastor of the Second Congregational Church, and later president of Yale. On the death of Aaron Lopez, he recorded in his diary:

On 28th of May died that amiable, benevolent, most hospitable and very respectable Gentleman, Mr. *Aaron Lopez* Merchant, who retiring from Newport Rhode Island in these Times resided from 1775 to his Death at Leicester in Massachusetts. He was a Jew by Nation, . . . was a Merchant of the first Eminence; for Honor and Extent of Commerce probably surpassed by no Merchant in America. He did Business with the greatest Ease and Clearness — always carried about with him a Sweetness of Behavior a calm Urbanity an agreeable and unaffected Politeness of manners. Without a single Enemy and the most universally beloved by an extensive Acquaintance of any man I ever knew. His Beneficence to his Family Connexions, to his Nation, and to all the World is almost without a Parallel.[57]

The story of the career of the Jew from Portugal is an epitome of the glory of the golden age of Newport.

[55] Newport Historical Society, Lopez Miscellaneous Papers: Henry Lloyd to Aaron Lopez, Boston, March 29, 1762.

[56] *Ibid.*, Naturalization Papers dated at Taunton, October 15, 1762.

[57] Dexter, *The Literary Diary of Ezra Stiles*, III, 24-25.

The Portuguese of Provincetown

Mary Heaton Vorse

The Portuguese of Provincetown

By Mary Heaton Vorse

With Drawings by Ariel Grant

I WAS down on T-Wharf in Boston waiting for a schooner from Provincetown whose captain I knew, for I wanted to beg a sail down if he got in this day, as his wife had told me he expected to. From the moment that my foot was on the wharf the City of Institutions was left behind and I was in a world where nothing existed but fish. Other prices may go up and down and the fish brokers of T-Wharf don't care; this week's catch of fish is the important thing. Here is a crop that one cannot foretell in advance. The only thing one knows is that if it is too rough weather there won't be any fish at all.

Down the middle of T-Wharf are the brokers' offices; on either side are two wide slips, and these are full of fishing schooners, lying side by side, as close as sardines in a box, engaged in unloading and taking in bait and baiting trawls ; and wherever you look you see fish and more fish—every sort of fish—differing, of course, according to the season ; green smelts and eels, great swordfish, and always and ever cod and more cod—cod, the great staple of the fish market, the industrious and conscientious fish that never seems to fail the fish market. Lobsters may grow scarce and flounders fight free of the net, but cod still remain constant.

The very air is full of the smell of fish; the moist planks under your feet reek with it; the oilskins of the men shine with fish scales, and even a landlubber who looks down at this array of big vessels (one-hundred-foot and fifty-foot schooners, some trim and smart as yachts and others disreputable and dirty, but all stanch and seagoing boats, most of more tons burden than those that brought our ancestors over to this country and first dropped anchor in Provincetown harbor) must realize that this business of catching fish is a serious business and one that requires men to do it ; big, strong, adequate, and enduring men is what we must have to catch the fish from out of the sea to feed us.

This is the big distributing center of the

fishing trade; it is here that the boats come from Gloucester and New Bedford and Provincetown, and it is here that the fresh fish is packed in ice and from here that it is sent hastening up into the country while one can still eat it.

I stopped an old New Englander, busy superintending the unloading of a vessel, to ask if the Josephine was in.

"She's due about now." he answered. "The Santas just went out. Tell you what," he went on, "there's a Provincetown boat by her looks; she's got a Portuguese crew. Mebbe they kin give you word of the Josephine."

For every captain, and every seaman for that matter, can recognize a vessel from his own harbor nearly as far off as he can see her.

The Portuguese boat, however, which was baiting up at the end of the wharf was a Gloucesterman. And there you have it; because she had a Portuguese crew the first supposition is that she must be a Provincetown boat, for in this town that sits sixty miles out at sea, with the bay on one side and the Atlantic Ocean on the other, the fishing business has passed during the last twenty years (the time of the great change in the fishing business from salt to fresh fish) almost entirely into the hands of the Portuguese. They own the boats; Portuguese capital owns the handsome one-hundred-foot schooners, as beautiful as any yacht; Portuguese captains command them, and Portuguese men sail them.

It is by a curious irony of fate that this historic little town where the Pilgrims first landed and that was afterwards settled by the purest of New England stock. descendants of Pilgrims, should to-day be a town that seems like a South European town. The foreign element isn't tucked away in one little quarter, as were the early Irish settlements through the New England towns. On the three-mile-long Commercial Street, that spreads along the water-front. are perpetual little crowds of beautiful dark-skinned, brilliantly colored Portuguese children; by Railroad Wharf are always knots of dark-skinned men— handsome, strong-looking fellows—waiting for their boats to go out; and as you go farther along toward the West End. "'way up along," you seem to be in a foreign community altogether. The names on the shops are Coreas, Silvas, Cabrals, Mantas; the very language of the street is foreign.

So true is this that it strikes even the children. A little Provincetown boy once landed at Ponta del Garda at St. Michael's, and he looked around at the handsome, dark-eyed children and the sailor-men loafing at the water-front, and the signs on the shops, and his comment was:

"Why, this is just like home!"

And no wonder, for it is from the Azores that the first immigrants came. Fayal, Flores, Pico, St. Michael's, began over fifty years ago sending their handsome, clean-blooded people to us, and have been doing so ever since; and during the last six years "the Lisbons" have begun to come—that is, people from Portugal itself. I say "they came;" that isn't quite true. The Portuguese immigration is unlike any other in one respect. It was we who needed the Portuguese and showed them the road to this country.

In the heyday of the whaling business, when the big fleet of whalers went out from Provincetown on voyages to the South Seas after the whale and the sea-elephant, when our coasters plied from Boston to the Indies, our skippers stopped at the Western Islands to recruit their crews, and the Portuguese men who were landed in Provincetown from our vessels found there was more money to be made in this country, and sent for their wives and children or their sweethearts.

There are not a few Portuguese families who even bear American names. A cabin-boy would be brought over by some old sea captain and raised as a son in the New England family, taking the name of the family in which he lived and forgetting his own, and yet, curiously enough, keeping his own religion.

It is one of the ironies that time plays on a country that this landing-place of the Pilgrims should to-day number more Roman Catholics than it does those of any other denomination. And not only that, but part of the service in the Catholic Church is always in an alien tongue, for the priest preaches in Portuguese for the benefit of the new arrivals, and then in English for the children of those who know English better than the tongue of their fathers. And the posters that adver-

THE PREOCCUPATION OF PROVINCETOWN IS THE SEA

tised the Thanksgiving Dance in the Town Hall said :

DANCES—AMERICAN, ST. MICHAEL'S FLORES, PICO, FAYAL

So, in this merrymaking commemorating a day so essentially American, American dances were danced upstairs; and the dances of old Portugal, the " Charmelita " and others, were danced downstairs by young people and old, some of whom were just learning English. For the life of the Portuguese and the Americans is more closely woven together in Province-town than in any other place I know of where there is a large settlement of aliens, because the interests of the Americans and the Portuguese are identical in the difficult work of getting fish out of the sea.

Of course I use Provincetown as an example, though the Portuguese are by no means confined to this one town. All down the Cape, wherever there is fishing to be done, are the same dark, able-look-ing men, the same families of beautiful children. Nantucket and Martha's Vine-yard abound with them; New Bedford and Gloucester have their Portuguese colo-nies, as have all the smaller places around " the Cape," as they call it, for the dwellers of Cape Cod have a fine dis-regard for all other capes in the world.

To understand this town and the con-ditions under which men work, one must know a little of its aspect. It is one of the few characteristic American towns. When you have seen Provincetown, you have seen Provincetown and not an example of indefinite other numbers of villages. It is on the extreme end of the Cape, and at one place only a mile and a half of sand-dunes keep it from being an island. Why the fury of the seas has not at some time swept over it and whelmed it forever one cannot under-stand.

Provincetown it is called because when the first settlers took up their home-steads the more well-to-do bought strips of land which reached across the Cape from bay to sea; and to this day many of the people own their land in this fashion— a narrow water-front, a strip of woods, then shifting sand-dunes, and then ocean front. But the early settlers kept part of their peninsula for the use of the poor, where any one might get wood or pick

berries or pasture cattle; this was called the " province land," and " province land " it is to this day. From the Government you may obtain a right to plant a cran-berry bog, or perhaps a right to erect a shooting-lodge, but you may not own your land, and the Government can turn you out at any moment if it seems best.

The very first settlement was over by the lighthouse at the other side of the long, crescent-shaped harbor, but the seas threatened to sweep the little sand-spit away, and for the purpose of keeping intact one of the finest harbors that the Atlantic coast knows, the Government bought up the settlement and took the sand-spit for its own. Then the canny New Englanders, after being paid once for their houses, asked the Government what the houses were to it.

" Nothing," answered the Government; " take them and welcome."

So one fine day was seen the spectacle of one house after another being floated across the harbor on rafts buoyed up by barrels, after the manner of raising wrecks.

" For," argued the Provincetown people, " if you can float a great wreck weighing many tons in this manner, why not a simple house ?"

And in this way was begun the little town which is some three miles long and only two streets wide—a long, gray little town it looks when seen from the water, with a great many wharves jutting out in the sea. At low tide one may see the vestiges of other wharves from which for-merly the whaling ships of the Cooks and the Nickersons and other of the town's prominent families sent forth their fleets of whalers and coasters and " bankers."

Steam killed the coasting trade and kerosene the whaling business. Well-to-do men failed, for there was no other business to turn to in Provincetown; there is no other crop there but fish. Then the same science and the new dis-coveries which had crippled the town for a time revived it, for with cold storage the trade of the fresh fisherman grew and the numbers of " bankers " diminished.

Fishing is the one preoccupation of this town—fishing on a big scale. The little sandy gardens are so small that they are not big enough to supply the needs of the town for vegetables, and the markets

SWORDFISHING

are supplied partly from Truro and partly from Boston. In the strange, low-lying back country only such things thrive as can grow in sand: scraggy little pines, blueberries and huckleberries and beach plums; and ever and ever the shifting sand-dunes encroach and slide down in a slow, glacier-like torrent on top of the occasional patches of forest trees.

So the preoccupation of Provincetown always has been, and always will be, the sea and the getting of its fish from it. This being the case, it is not too much to say that there are only a few scores of grown men in the whole town who have at one time or another not gone down to the sea in ships. Just what they consider fishing consists of I first learned from an old fellow who was driving one of the " accommodations," the five-seated barges that ply up and down the streets. He had a nautical air about him, and I asked him if he had ever been a sailor, which, by the way, was a landswoman enough question, because sailors in Provincetown eyes have to do with the United States navy.

" No," he said. " No, I never followed the sea none to speak of. Oh, when I was young I done some fishin'; I went on a few whalin' v'yages—perhaps a matter o' eighteen year in all; but I wouldn't say I'd ever done much *fishin'*."

And what is eighteen years, after all, in the life of a man drawing close to seventy, when in the old days lads of ten and twelve went fishing with their fathers and continued to fish until they were gray—or until the sea took them.

For the sea takes a mighty toll of Provincetown men. Up in the cemetery back of the town the graveyard is sprinkled with stones in memory of those who were " lost at sea," and one is always hearing stories like that of the two young Portuguese fellows who had got separated in the fog from their vessel, and who rowed in to Race Point and, half spent and cursing their luck, were picked up by the life-savers. Later they blessed their luck, for their schooner had been rammed in the fog by some passing steamer and had gone down with all hands, and they two were the only ones saved.

This big business of catching fish by the ton is naturally divided into several branches. There are the big vessels, the deep-sea men, that go out to the George's Banks; there are the seiners, that catch their fish in huge nets; there is the ever-lasting work of drawing the weirs every morning throughout ten months of the year, and on shore are the cold-storage houses where they freeze the bait in great quantities, as well as the fish for eating. There are also the " fish factories," as they call the canneries; and always and always there is the never-ending work of repairing gear of all sorts, and, above all, the work of mending and tarring nets. It is as unceasing as the work of a house-keeper ever was. For fish-nets are fragile things, and the fury of storms and the fish are continually rending their meshes; and there is no day when you walk down the street that you may not see a man netting new nets in his " store," as they call the little sheds on the water-front where the gear is kept, or that you may not encounter carts laden with nets to be spread out to dry off their accumulations of seaweed and later to be tarred, or that you may not see the nets pulled, black and dripping, from the great tar-kettles.

This work never stops, and the greater part of it is done by the Portuguese. There are, of course, American captains who own their boats; and still, especially in the cold storages, much American capital is invested; but the bulk of gear and boats is owned by Portuguese. The gasoline dories are in the hands of the Portuguese altogether, and in the winter, during the two or three months when the big vessels are hauled up, the fresh fishing is done by these gasoline dories with trawls and hand lines; and these are handled by Portuguese crews and Portuguese owners.

In the summer-time fishing inshore isn't practicable because of the dogfish. You may go and fish around the end of the Cape and dogfish may be your only reward, and there is nothing a fisherman hates more than to run into a school of these uncouth and greedy bait-snatchers. By some mysterious law of migration dogfish go out in winter and leave the waters clear for the inshore fisherman.

How all these big industries came into the hands of foreigners is a repetition of the story of the New England farms.

THE SEA TAKES A MIGHTY TOLL OF PROVINCETOWN MEN

The same causes which left our broad Connecticut Valley lands for the purchase of the Polander made it possible for the Portuguese to have such a strong hold in our fishing industries. The sons of the New England stock became ambitious and sought wider opportunities. Up and down Provincetown it is the same story; the sons of the old sea captains are in the big cities in business or in the professions. But there was still greater reason for them to go, for as the last generation grew up the bottom fell out of the whaling industry and the coasting trade. Then the Western Islanders. who, like the Polanders. had a lower scale of living than the Americans and could afford to be contented with little. put aside money and bought their homes. For it isn't alone boats and fish factories and wharves they own; they own their homes and land as well. The tax list of Provincetown shows as many Portuguese names as it does those of New Englanders.

The very system of payment on the fishing-boats made the amassing of some capital comparatively easy. for the deep-sea fishermen fish in shares. The captain and owners of a boat get a certain percentage. and the proceeds of the rest of the catch are divided equally among the crew. In a good season of ten months' fishing this may amount to a thousand dollars per man. leaving the two winter months free to make additional gains from the gasoline dories or other sorts of fishing.

The fishing of the weirs is done on another system. Here the men are paid forty or fifty dollars a month. and the work is hard. That seems a small amount on which to bring up a numerous family; but the Portuguese have the South European thrift, and on that sum men manage to save enough to own their own houses and give their children time to go through high school. It must be remembered that the scale of living is simple, and also that a great part of the food comes from the sea free of cost.

It is from the weirs that most of the bait is obtained, squid and herring being used for the purpose. And drawing the weirs is a memorable sight for a landsman. The weir is a sort of vast fish trap. and the fish swim in through the opening and cannot get out. The boats go out before dawn has broken. Three silent men dressed in oilskins man the weir boat, and there is no sound anywhere except the little chugging of the motor. And so often has the work been performed that the closing of the net gate and the pulling up of the trap. which is something like a vast gathering-string for bringing the net and its contents to the surface. is performed in almost absolute silence. Three or four laconic words and a gesture are enough. And as the bottom of the trap comes to the surface the whole air is filled with a noise like no other noise in the world—the little flap-flap of the fish on each other. There they are, pure silver and wonderful; barrels and barrels of them flapping and gasping at the bottom of their net.

And then these silent large men take huge fish-scoops like ladles and silently ladle the fish into the bottom of the boat; later, standing knee-deep among them, they pitch out great monsters—skate and gone-fish and dogfish—gasping into the sea.

The catch varies from morning to morning. Sometimes it is squid, sometimes mackerel; once in a while a baby whale is caught. And when all the traps are drawn, one chugs back again, and the fish are landed and sorted out and given over with incredible swiftness to various purposes, according to their kind. Some are taken to the cold storage, or used for smoking, or packed in ice and sent to Boston.

One feels as if one had witnessed a terrible slaughter, and as if it were impossible that the sea should continue forever to yield forth fish in such vast quantities. The catching of fish in this fashion—ladling them in by boatloads, after having treacherously snared them in a series of nets—has something wanton about it and infinitely unsportsmanlike. And yet it goes on day in and day out and the supply of fish never fails. The world is hungry and America is a broad place, and for our wholesale consumption fish must somehow be caught wholesale.

Even the trawlers put out fifteen hundred baited hooks to a man, two men to a dory, ten or twelve dories to a schooner. They must catch their fish wholesale if they are to live.

I have been asked if the Portuguese become Americanized, and if they are absorbed into our National life, or if they live apart. In speech and action certainly the children of the Portuguese parents are not to be distinguished from our children. How should they be since they live in a community so essentially New England, where the old New England ideals of honesty and thrift and scrupulous cleanliness are still undimmed? There are some slight differences in upbringing perhaps the young girls of the better class are reared in a more careful way, because South Europeans are good mothers and careful mothers. The Provincetown natives say that the young people haven't the fine manners of their fathers, who brought with them the courtesy of manner belonging to the race of the Spanish Peninsula. And this is our fault. But among all the outwanderings of the various people, although they form a tiny element in the big melting-pot of America, it seems to me that the Portuguese is one to be grateful for. There has not been a mad rush of day laborers, but a steady influx of men who come, not only to work and to make money, but to buy homes and acquire property and bring up their children as Americans. And it seems to me that they combine many of the virtues of the Italians and the Spanish; a greater beauty they have than the Spaniards, for they are a large race and strong, as men must be who follow the sea; and they have more gayety.

And since because of natural conditions our fishing-boats have passed from American hands, I think it is a thing to be glad for that they have fallen into those of such an adequate and strong and thrifty race.

TO CHESTER-ON-THE-DEE

BY JEANNETTE MARKS

Sleep, little town, thy moonlit walls
    Are hushed with long-ago!
Night, like thy river, brings to thee
    Forgetfulness of woe.

Peace, little town! Grave sleep is this
    That aches in love and tears,
With singing stream, with shining dream,
    With sense of other years.

The Coming of the Portuguese

George Rawlings Poage

THE COMING OF THE PORTUGUESE

By George Rawlings Poage
Professor of History and Social Sciences, Illinois College.

One of the most interesting passages in the history of Jacksonville is the romantic story of the settlement of the "Portuguese Exiles." Although it excited much interest at the time, outside the immediate vicinity its very existence is all but unknown. Yet it is an unique episode in the history of Portuguese immigration to the United States, and brings down into the middle of the nineteenth century conditions which we are wont to regard as belonging to the seventeenth. For these "Exiles of Madeira" were exiles for conscience's sake, and their vicissitudes show in more respects than one a striking parallel to those of the Pilgrim Fathers of Plymouth.

The story begins some eleven years before the "Portuguese Exiles" came to Illinois. In 1838, Robert Reid Kalley, a Scotchman of some twenty-nine years, started under a commission from the Free Church of Scotland, for a mission field in China. Before the voyage was well begun, his wife, who accompanied him, fell seriously ill, so that they decided to land at the first port touched by their vessel. This happened to be Funchal, on the island of Madeira.[1]

The zealous missionary appears to have accepted this occurrence as a direct manifestation of Providence. Although he had no commission to work there, and indeed his church had no mission in that field, he determined to make Madeira the scene of his labors. He was a man of considerable means, and so able, if he chose, to carry on an independent enterprise. Within a few hours of his landing he had formed his resolve and had begun to seek a practical knowledge of the Portuguese language.[2]

---

[1] Norton, *Facts Concerning the Persecutions at Madeira*, 230; Blackburn, *Exiles of Madeira*, 19; Dimmitt, *A Story of Madeira*, 16.
[2] Norton, 12-13; Blackburn, 19-20; Dimmitt, 17-19.

His wealth and preparation enabled him to organize his
first work upon what has always proved the most effective of
missionary approaches, that of the physician. He opened a
free hospital and dispensary in Funchal, thus gaining a strong
hold upon the people. The native physicians were lacking in
skill, so that Dr. Kalley's cures gained him wide reputation.
Although his enterprise was primarily one of charity, even
the well-to-do sought his services.[3]

From the very beginning, however, Dr. Kalley kept in
mind his real object, most cleverly contriving to impart his
spiritual message to those who sought him for the healing of
their bodies. He required that all who wished to consult him
should assemble at his office by nine o'clock in the morning.
Then, before proceeding to the work in hand, he would read
a chapter from the Bible, deliver a brief discourse, and offer
a prayer with special reference to the work of healing in which
he was about to be engaged. When visiting patients in their
own homes he also improved the occasion in a similar manner.[4]

He soon extended his efforts in another direction. He
found the people largely illiterate and unable to read the
Scriptures. He had very early opened a school for the teaching of English in order to facilitate his own acquisition of
Portuguese. This led to the establishment of other schools
throughout the island. His ample means enabled Dr. Kalley
to bear all the expense of teachers' salaries and textbooks, and
to offer the Madeirenses the first free education they had ever
enjoyed. Some of the sessions were held in the evening, after
the regular working hours, in order that adults might take
advantage of the opportunity. The islanders responded
eagerly. "Within a short period no less than eight hundred
adults were taught in these schools, besides the children."
In all, at one time or another, some twenty-five hundred were
enrolled. The municipal authorities of Funchal formally
voted Dr. Kalley their thanks for "his disinterested acts of
benevolence and philanthropy in the establishment of free

[3] Dimmitt, 19, 22-23.
[4] Norton, 231-232; Blackburn, 22; Dimmitt, 20.

schools, hospitals, and dispensaries in different parts of the island.'"

Thus for some time Dr. Kalley not only encountered no opposition, but enjoyed the highest popularity. Yet he was following practices which sooner or later were bound to bring him into collision with the ecclesiastical authorities. The first book which he taught the people to read in English was the Bible. Soon he began to circulate a Portuguese Bible, a supply of which he had obtained from Scotland. This was a translation made long since by a priest, Antonio Pereira, and sanctioned by the Queen and the Patriarch of Portugal. Some eighty copies had previously been sent to Madeira from Lisbon for the use of the clergy.[6]

Not content with teaching the Madeirenses to read and placing the Bible in their hands, Dr. Kalley also instructed them in its meaning. These instructions of a Scotch Calvinist naturally produced some mental difficulties among these simple folk who previously had heard only the doctorines of the Roman Catholic Church. Quite as naturally, some of them went to the priests with their difficulties, and the inevitable trouble began. It appears, however, that forcible repression was attempted only after Dr. Kalley had for some time been holding regular religious services for the islanders, and after open conversions had been made.[7]

"In 1840, the Bishop expressed a wish to see a copy of the Bible that was being put into the hands of his people. One was gladly sent to him. On the 21st of May he placed it in the hands of three canons of the cathedral of Funchal, and appointed them, as a commission, to examine it, and to report to him, as to its correctness or incorrectness. Two years and four months afterwards he published a pastoral, wherein he stated that that Commission had reported 'that there was scarcely a verse or any chapter either of the Old or New Testament which was not more or less notably adulterated;'

[5] Norton, 13-14; Blackburn, 24-25; Dimmitt, 21-23.
[6] Norton, 14; Blackburn, 20-21, 24-25; Dimmitt, 22-30.
[7] Norton, 15-16; Dimmitt, 29-30.

and he added, that he 'excommunicated *ipso facto* all who should read those Bibles.' "

Dr. Kalley at once made a verse by verse comparison of the Edinburgh and Lisbon editions of the Gospel óf St. Matthew, and found them identical. This led to a controversy between him and the Commissioners, in which he continued the comparison until upward of five thousand verses were covered, and posted certified statements of the results in the streets. Some two months after the episcopal denunciation, an order arrived from Lisbon giving these Bibles the approval of the Queen and the Archbishop; but the anathema of the Bishop was not removed.[8]

As early as 1842, regular religious services for the Madeirenses were held in various places. These were usually open-air conventicles, often on the mountain-sides. The missionary would preach, or, if he were unable to be present, one of the converts would read portions of the Scriptures. "A few hymns were sung to such good old tunes as the Portuguese Hymn and Old Hundred." "For several months there were not fewer than one thousand persons attending these meetings in the open air, every Sabbath. Often there were two or three thousand, and once they were reckoned at five thousand.'"[9]

There already existed in Funchal a little Scottish church for the worship of the British residents of the island. This church and the free exercise of their religion were guaranteed to them by treaty between those ancient allies, Great Britain and Portugal.[10] In 1843, a new minister came out from Scotland to take charge of this church. To him, "as he was about to administer the Lord's Supper on the Sabbath," came two Portuguese converts, Nicolao Tolentino Vieira and Francisco Pires Soares, requesting permission to partake of the communion. Dr. Kalley warned them of their peril, but they persisted; and, after examination by the Protestant ministers, they were admitted. Four days later they were brought before the magistrates charged with apostasy. They were

---

[8] Norton, 32-33; Blackburn, 29.
[9] Blackburn, 25-27; Dimmitt, 31-32.
[10] Norton, 19; Blackburn, 19; Dimmitt, 31.

discharged by the court, but were excommunicated on the following Sunday. An attempt was made again to arrest them; but they were hidden by their friends, and continued in hiding for six months. At that time orders arrived from Lisbon putting a stop to the persecution.[11]

The arrest of Vieira and Soares was the beginning of a persecution whose thrilling episodes do not come within the scope of this study. The ecclesiastical authorities, as might have been expected, struck first at the schools, which they attempted to suppress. The representative of the Bishop also denounced the reading of the Bibles distributed by Dr. Kalley, stigmatizing it as "a book of Hell." In spite of the loyal approval of the Bible, its readers were denounced to the priests and arrested in large numbers. They were often detained in prison for months, only to be acquitted when finally brought to trial.[12]

With the apparent collusion of the authorities, mob violence ensued, directed especially against Nicolao Vieira, who was now teaching a school at his own home. Vieira was forced to flee to the mountains, and his family and pupils were arrested. After terrible hardships, he himself escaped to Demerara, where he eventually rejoined his family when they stopped *en route* to Trinidad.[13]

One woman, Mrs. Maria Joaquina Alves, was brought to trial for denying the real presence and other tenets of the Roman Catholic Church. Although she was arrested January 31, 1843, she was brought to trial only on May 2, 1844, when she was condemned to death for blasphemy, heresy, and apostasy. The English group interested in Dr. Kalley's work petitioned the Queen of Portugal in her behalf, and an appeal was taken to the Court of Relacao at Lisbon. The decision of this court did not reach Funchal until April, 1845, Mrs. Alves meanwhile remaining in prison at her own charges. On a technicality, the sentence of death was commuted to imprisonment for three months from the date of the sentence, with a

[11] Norton, 27, 35-37, 122-124.
[12] Norton, 16-19, 20-23, 26-34.
[13] Norton, 20-24, 124-127.

fine of six dollars. After the expiration of her sentence, she was detained in prison to meet this fine and the costs of her prosecution and imprisonment, finally being released in June, 1845.[14]

At length Dr. Kalley was himself arrested under an obsolete law of the Inquisition, enacted in 1603. Despite his insistence that this law contravened both the existing constitution of Portugal and the treaty between that country and Great Britain, Dr. Kalley was convicted and imprisoned for five months.[15] The terms on which Dr. Kalley's release was secured cannot be definitely ascertained, although there are suggestions sufficient to justify conjecture. Shortly after his release, he left the island for a visit in Scotland, stopping at Lisbon *en route*. There are intimations that he was constrained by the Court of Relacao to give some kind of pledge not to engage in religious propaganda at Madeira. It appears also that some question arose subsequently as to Dr. Kalley's observance of these limitations, which he considered unjust and unwarranted. On this account it is emphatically and categorically asserted that Dr. Kalley had no connection with the ensuing phase of missionary activity at Madeira, which seems to have transpired during his absence from the island.[16]

These developments were due to the missionary zeal of William Hepburn Hewitson, acting under a commission from the Free Church of Scotland. Mr. Hewitson was a brilliant scholar who had wrecked his health by over-application to study. Resolving to devote his remaining energies to missionary enterprise, a field was sought where he might have some chance to regain his health. Southern France and Malta had been under consideration, when Madeira was suggested. The idea pleased him. On October 15, 1844, he wrote: "It is, I understand, most desirable, at present, that a minister should be sent out to Madeira to acquire the Portuguese language, with a view to preaching the gospel to the poor Portuguese in the island. During the year which would be spent

[14] Norton, 38-43; Blackburn, 41-46.
[15] Norton, 25-26; Dimmitt, 32-33.
[16] Norton, 110; Blackburn, 49, 50.

in doing nothing but acquiring the language, my health might be so far recruited, by the blessing of God on the change of air, as to enable me afterwards to labour in that part of the vineyard." On November 6 he was ordained by the Presbytery of Edinburgh, of the Free Church of Scotland, as a preliminary to his despatch to Portugal as a missionary. Accordingly, he proceeded to Lisbon, where he spent two months. There he met Dr. Kalley who was on his way back to Scotland.[17]

It is said that Dr. Kalley "was not even aware of his intended mission to the island till after Mr. Hewitson's departure from England. They first met accidentally in Lisbon . . . ." This meeting took place upon Dr. Kalley's arrival from Madeira, January 28, 1845. That very day a message also arrived from Scotland giving the consent of the Colonial Committee of the Free Church of Scotland that Mr. Hewitson should go immediately to Madeira. It is impossible not to see some connection betwen Dr. Kalley's withdrawal from the island and this action of the Colonial Committee, who apparently had been detaining the eager Hewitson at Lisbon.[18]

Mr. Hewitson at once proceeded to Madeira. As yet, no church had been organized among the converts. Indeed, only twenty-five or thirty had so-far openly renounced the church of their childhood. Mr. Hewitson lived in the house of Mr. Wood, an English clergyman, where he had a room for meetings. His labors prospered so that by May he was contemplating the organization of a church of the Madeirenses. He put his motives on record. "The time may be not far distant," he writes, "when I shall be obliged to leave Madeira by the strong arm of persecution, and it would be a great comfort to the afflicted church here, amidst their privations, to have the prospect of so soon receiving the ordinances at the hands of one of their own number."[19]

The organization of the church was actually accomplished on May 12, 1845, with Mr. Hewitson as minister and modera-

[17] Norton, 110; Blackburn, 50-60.
[18] Norton, 110; Blackburn, 61.
[19] Blackburn, 61-71.

tor of session. The first session was composed of Arsenio
Nicos da Silva, João de Freitas, João Correa, Martinho José
de Souza, João de Gouveia, and Manual J. de Andrade. The
first deacons were Antonio de Mattos, Antonio Correa, José
Marques Joaquin Vieira, Manuel Pires, and Martinho Vieira.
Of these, Arsenio Nicos da Silva and Antonio de Mattos subsequently became ministers and were respectively pastors of
the church at Trinidad and at Jacksonville. It is claimed
that this was the first Protestant church of Portuguese ever
organized; and that its direct successor today, after a series
of reorganizations, schisms and reunions, is the Northminster
Presbyterian Church of Jacksonville.[20]

The organization of the church was effected under lower-
ing skies. On the very day of its accomplishment, Mr. Hewitson wrote: "The horizon is becoming more and more cloudy.
Two or three days ago at a dinner party, the Bishop of
Madeira declared exterminating war against the Bible. He
said that he had all the authorities on his side, and he was resolved to put down all dissent from the Roman Catholic
Church.'"[21]

Mr. Hewitson found that Mr. Wood's house was too
small; so he rented another with a garden on each side where
the people might not be so closely watched by the police. The
Madeirenses, however, were quite reckless, seemingly careless
of their danger. The officials were now seeking cause for the
arrest of the missionary. The English treaty protected him
against outrageous attack, but out of prudence he discon-
tinued his meetings for a few weeks. Then he was warned by
the police to discontinue them under threat of arrest; so he
cautiously held them by night. Of one of these he writes:
"This night we are at eight o'clock to 'keep the feast' in
secret, with closed doors and windows, in our dining-room,
with this poor and persecuted little flock of Christ. The ser-

---

[20] Vasconcellos, *Brief Narrative of the Original Portuguese Church,* and *Brief
History of the Portuguese Settlement at Jacksonville.*
[21] Blackburn, 71.

vice if discovered will send his dear servant to prison, but the Lord is his keeper.'[22]

Then Mr. Hewitson fell ill. He retired to a country village for rest, but grew worse. He was brought back to Funchal in a hammock. For six weeks he was unable to attend the services of the little Scottish church. He thought it unwise to resume the public services until Dr. Kalley should return from Scotland, but he organized a class for the instruction of the converts, and then sent them out to hold meetings from house to house.[23]

For over a year persecution had been raging. Mr. Hewitson was in daily expectation of arrest. Dr. Kalley's return was signalized by Mr. Hewitson's being forbidden to preach or teach. His arrest was indeed sought, but the judge, who was the son-in-law of Arsenio Nicos da Silva, declined to issue the order on the ground that his authority did not extend over the missionary. The English merchants were forbidden to allow meeting of the Portuguese in their houses. The Bishop departed for Lisbon to seek aid, vowing, it was said, never to return until Dr. Kalley should be driven from Madeira. Affairs were clearly approaching a crisis.[24]

Under these circumstances, it seemed best that Mr. Hewitson should retire from the scene for a while. He was, however, determined to complete the course of study he had marked out for his class; and to this end he redoubled his efforts. In three weeks there were eighty-seven open conversions among the Portuguese. Then in May, 1846, a little over a year after his arrival, he left Madeira with the intention of returning in a few months. When he saw his flock again it was far away in Trinidad.[25]

The excitement caused by Dr. Kalley's return and the feverish parting labors of Mr. Hewitson was increased in June by the release of a number of the converts who had been in prison for months. It became evident that legal measures

---

[22] Blackburn, 70-72.
[23] Blackburn, 72-73.
[24] Blackburn, 74-75, 148.
[25] Blackburn, 74-75.

would not suffice for the suppression of the heresy. As early as 1843, the "Imparcial," a newspaper edited by the brother-in-law of the civil governor at that time, "openly recommended the cudgel, as the best means of convincing the country people of the truth of their religion, because they were not accustomed to arguments, but could understand the power of a stick. The gallows and the stake were also at another time recommended in it, as the only remaining cure for heresy;" and its columns were constantly filled with attacks on Dr. Kalley's followers. In 1845, these attacks had been compiled and published as a pamphlet under the title, "An Historical Review of the Anti-Catholic Proselytism carried on by Dr. Kalley in Madeira since October, 1838." This was published by subscription, and copies of it were carried to Lisbon by the Bishop. Dr. Kalley wrote a reply to this pamphlet, which was printed in Lisbon and circulated there and in Madeira in July, 1846.[26] This open controversy seems to have been the match which touched off the explosion.

The first violent outburst occurred on Sunday, August 2, 1846. Two English ladies, the Misses Rutherford, resided on the island and sympathized with Dr. Kalley's work. On the date mentioned, they allowed a group of the Madeirenses the use of a room in their house. There some thirty or forty assembled, under the leadership of Arsenio Nicos da Silva, to hold a prayer meeting and to read a letter which had come from Mr. Hewitson. News of the meeting spread and a mob gathered without. The leading spirit was one of the canons of the cathedral named Conego Telles de Menezes.

When the meeting ended, about half past twelve, da Silva and three or four others broke through the mob and escaped, though not without indignity and rough treatment. The rest, for the most part women, were compelled to remain. During the afternoon, Dr. Kalley came and went, calling professionally on one of the ladies who was an invalid. He was affronted at the gate and his groom beaten. Later, another English gentleman, Captain Tate, to whom we owe the de-

[26] Norton, 23-24.

tailed account of the riots, came to the house and remained throughout the night.

The police had been about all day without making any attempt to disperse the mob. At sunset, however, they were withdrawn. About eleven o'clock, the mob invaded the grounds and prepared to attack the house. To the remonstrances of the inmates they paid no heed, declaring that they did not care for the English consul, that there was no law for "Calvinists," and that they could appeal to the governor. After some further parley, the house was broken into. The Madeirenses had been secreted in its most remote parts. The mob was hesitant and dilatory in its search. At last, however, the victims were found, and amid blows and threats were dragged into the garden. At this stage, when the murder of the converts seemed imminent, the proceedings were interrupted by the tardy arrival of the police and soldiery. The mob was quickly dispersed and the frightened converts escorted to their homes.[27]

This, however, did not end the mob violence. Threats and demonstrations continued throughout the following week. Another outbreak should have been expected on the following Sunday, for it was the great religious festival of the island, when the fanaticism of the people would be at its height. The Misses Rutherford appealed to the British consul. He, however, did not sympathize with Dr. Kalley and his friends, and refused to interfere, referring them to the police department. The authorities demanded a promise that the ladies would permit no more meetings in their house. They refused to give such a promise in unequivocal terms, and so received no assurance of protection.[28]

Dr. Kalley, meanwhile, had been carrying on a heated correspondence with the police magistrate, the governor, and the consul both on the Misses Rutherford's account and his own. The threats continued and grew more fierce. The mob was watching Dr. Kalley's house and subjecting all who came

---

[27] Norton. 46-58.
[28] Norton. 58.

and went to insult and abuse. On August 8, Dr. Kalley received an anonymous letter exactly detailing the plans of the riot which took place on the following day. This letter, also, he despatched to the consul without apparent effect.

On the next day, August 9, 1846, the great riot occurred. The native converts as well as Dr. Kalley were subjected to attack. The Madeirenses fled to the mountains. Dr. Kalley's family first took refuge at the British consulate and later fled on board one of the British ships lying in the harbor of Funchal. After various movements and several narrow escapes, Dr. Kalley himself was finally carried on ship-board disguised as a female invalid. His house and valuable library were burned. The consulate itself was besieged and threatened with destruction. The consul chose to mingle with the crowd without official insignia. In the evening, he came down to the shore with some of the leaders of the mob and requested Dr. Kalley to show himself on the deck, in order that the fury of the mob might be appeased and order restored. This Dr. Kalley did, although he regarded the request as an insult.[29]

On the next day, the Misses Rutherford, Captain Tate, and other English residents who were identified with Dr. Kalley, in all three men and ten women, also took refuge on board the ship. The invalid Miss Rutherford died as a consequence of the excitement and exposure of the flight.[30]

It is plain that the consul and others of the English residents disapproved of the course taken by Dr. Kalley and his friends, and resented the anti-English feeling it had aroused. The British press commented with great severity on the conduct of the consul, but he appears to have received no official reprimand. Although he had gone out to his country estate in the morning, and so had not received an application which was made to place Dr. Kalley's house under the direct protection of the British flag, he returned in the midst of the riot and urged the governor to use the troops to disperse the mob which was about to destroy British property. Dr. Kalley's

[29] Norton, 56-78.
[30] Norton, 55-56.

family were sheltered in the consulate, and the consul's servant gave great assistance in Dr. Kalley's escape to the ship. All accounts of the riots are based on the narrative of Captain Tate, who was violently indignant at the consul's conduct. Even his *ex parte* testimony, however, presents these ameliorating circumstances. The consul's attitude appears to have been that Dr. Kalley and his friends had produced such strong and general feeling as only their departure from the island could allay. Since they would neither change their course, which they held perfectly legal, nor withdraw voluntarily, mob violence was inevitable; and he seems to have sought, therefore, not so much to prevent the riot, as to prevent, so far as possible, the destruction of British property and life.

The conduct of the civil authorities was indeed culpable, and in marked contrast to that of the military commandant, who earnestly sought permission to disperse the mob with his troops. The British ambassador at Lisbon at once entered a protest and the Queen of Portugal was constrained to send a royal commission of investigation to Madeira. "This commission came and made their investigations. In their view, the conduct of the government at Madeira was so unjustifiable that they requested the administration to resign. They all resigned except the administrado do concelho.

"His dismission was immediately sent from Portugal. A new governor was appointed at Madeira. In this change there was a show of disapprobation on the part of the queen against those who had encouraged and sanctioned this persecution by their silence and inaction. Whether this change was made by the queen with a conviction of wrong doing on the part of the authorities at Madeira, or whether it was effected through fear of British cannon, may be a question.

"There was also the *external* form of a trial of some of those who had been the most active and the most savage in this persecution. The result of this appearance of justice was the acquittal of all the rioters. Even those who were arrested, in the *very act of murdering* the Bible-readers, were acquitted. When the evidence of their guilt was too obvious to be denied, no penalty was inflicted. The leaders of the mob, such as the Canon Telles, were not subjected even to the form of a trial.

"The painful conclusion to which we are driven by these facts is, that the civil government and the courts of justice connived at these enormous crimes, and that the whole form of trial was a solemn mockery or a farce." [31]

From this it would appear, as it does from other incidents, that the feeling against the "Calvinists" was quite general among the populace, although Captain Tate charges that the rioters were hired from a fund raised by subscription. Later, the British government demanded and obtained full indemnity for Dr. Kalley's pecuniary losses. [32]

During the week of August 2-9, the mob also turned its fury against the native converts. The violence continued until they had no recourse but flight. "On the evening of the 5th many houses were plundered by bands of marauding ruffians, and sixty or eighty of the converts were compelled to leave their homes and pass the night in the mountains. Night after night these bands continued to repeat their desolating work; . . . till, on the Sunday, many hundreds of Portuguese subjects . . . had fled for their lives. The mob had broken open their doors, and destroyed their windows, furniture, and other property; trampling under foot the grapes and corn of those who possessed vineyards and gardens. When the work of destruction was done in the town and neighborhood, the ruthless persecutors followed the scattered flock to the mountains. . . . " [33]

The fugitives soon heard that the ship "William of Glasgow" had received Dr. Kalley and their other English friends; and there the persecuted Madeirenses also sought refuge. By the night of the 10th, several of them had reached the ship. From night to night they flocked on board the "William" until she had received all the ship could accom-

[31] Norton, 80-81. The italics appear in the original.
[32] Norton, 50-51, 95-97.
[33] Norton, 84.

modate. During the two weeks from the 9th to the 23d, two British warships lying alongside the "William of Glasgow" kept firing their guns at intervals to show the people, as the captains remarked, "that afloat, at least, the English could and would protect themselves." The sound of these guns gave great encouragement to the fugitives among the mountains, some of whom wandered for thirteen days before finding safety on the "William." [84]

Another demonstration was planned for the 16th, but the military officers sent word to the governor, whom they accused of conniving in the riots, that they would quell any further disturbance independently of the civil authorities. This was sufficient to end mob violence in Funchal. The rioters contented themselves with rowing around the "William of Glasgow" in boats, singing songs against the "Calvinistas" and otherwise insulting them and their English friends. All that day also, in spite of a consular reprimand, the warships continued at intervals to fire their guns for the encouragement of the fugitives. [85]

Dr. Kalley had originally taken refuge on the ship "Forth"; but the "William of Glasgow" had come by arrangement with the planters of Trinidad, who were greatly in need of laborers. Thus the Madeirenses were able to comply with the demand of their enemies that they should become exiles from their homes. It was necessary, however, to arrange for their passports. The authorities were by this time so anxious to allay the storm that they facilitated their emmigration by waiving the requirements of personal application and certificate of church attendance. [86]

"Some made efforts to sell their property, when they were about to leave, that they might have some means for their voyage. But no one would buy only at an immense sacrifice. One man whose property was worth $1,500 sold it for $100, &c. Those who had large and valuable property

[84] Norton, 89.
[85] Norton, 84-89: Dimmitt, 66.
[86] Norton, 89 ; Dimmitt, 70.

could not sell at all. Those who had small possessions, worth $400, or $500, could get nothing for them." [37]

When all arrangements had at length been made, on Sunday, August 23, 1846, the "William of Glasgow" loosed her sails and began her voyage to Trinidad. Dr. Kalley and the other English refugees also departed from the island. Among the two hundred and eleven passengers of the "William," was one Roman Catholic family, abjectly poor, bound also for Trinidad. This family was treated by the exiles with the greatest kindness. Soon after this, the "Lord Seaton" took about the same number to the West Indies. "Besides these 400 souls, others fled to the various vessels, and sailed for the West India Islands. About one hundred landed at Demerara, and about the same number fled to St. Vincent, and also to St. Kitts. Between 600 and 700 went to Trinidad, while others landed at other islands." When the "William" touched at Demerara, the exiles were joined by Nicolao Vieira, who went on with them to Trinidad. In all, a thousand or twelve hundred went into exile. [38]

In time, they were also joined by Arsenio Nicos da Silva. He had fled first to his estates in the interior of Madeira, where he thought he might be safe. But he became convinced that there was no safety for him on the island, so he determined to flee to Lisbon. When he returned to Funchal, he was unable to go to his own home, but lay hidden elsewhere according to arrangements made by his family, who did not agree with his religious views. His wife supplied him with money for his flight to Lisbon. He had hoped that his family, whom he had been unable to see in Funchal, might rejoin him at Lisbon; but even there he was not safe, and thought of going to Oporto. But he received letters from both the Madeirenses at Trinidad and Dr. Kalley, urging him to go and labor in that field. The missionary board of the Free Church of Scotland at the same time offering to sustain him there, he at once sailed for Trinidad. There he was ordained by the local

---

[36] Norton, 90-94, 127; Blackburn, 203.
[37] Norton, 94-95.

Presbyterian ministers and eagerly accepted as their pastor by the Portuguese exiles. This was in April, 1847, at Port of Spain.[39]

At the beginning of the year, Mr. Hewitson had sailed for Trinidad, arriving toward the end of January. At that time, there were about 450 exiles in Trinidad. Including children, there were more than 300 converts in Port of Spain and its vicinity, of whom eighty-five were members of the church. Three of the seven elders and four of the nine deacons had come from Madeira, and had regularly conducted meetings for worship. About thirty persons had applied for admission to the church.[40] Since August there had been a succession of flights from Madeira. By March, 1847, it was thought that an expected company of one hundred would be the last; but upward of 250 more arrived.

Mr. Hewitson thus describes the material condition of the exiles:

"On their arrival, a considerable number of them were engaged by planters to labor on sugar estates. Some of these were placed on an estate situated in the neighborhood of marshy ground, and, as might have been expected, were soon prostrated by an attack of fever, which, in several instances, terminated in death. A speedy removal of all who survived from the pestilential neighborhood, in which they had been so unhappily located, to the more salubrious air of the capital, was found to be necessary. The removal took place, I believe, in consequence of an order from the governor of the island— and I have great pleasure in taking this opportunity of bearing testimony to the kind exertions which his excellency, Lord Harris, was always ready to make on behalf of our refugees. Those who were employed on sugar plantations in more salubrious localities than the one above referred to, were enabled to continue their labors without experiencing so much injury of bodily health; but they, too, were occasionally disabled by an attack either of dysentery, or of intermittent

[39] Norton, 148-151; Blackburn, 161.
[40] Norton, 103, 106-107; Blackburn, 152-153.

fever;—ophthalmia likewise prevailed amongst them. I have
no hesitation in saying, that the result of the experiment,
which necessity constrained them to make, has been unfavor-
able to the hope that they will be equal to the hardships connected with cane cultivation in Trinidad, until a lengthened
residence in the island has inured them to the scorching heats
and drenching rains of its tropical climate. When I arrived,
I found only about fifty individuals (including children) who
were *supported* by the labors of cane cultivation, and of these
only about sixteen were actually, or in condition to be, *employed* in these labors. Others obtained employment on cocoa
plantations; and, as their labor is chiefly under the shade of
trees thickly planted, they are saved from the dangerous effects of protracted·exposure to the rays of a vertical sun. One
disadvantage of their situation arises from the great humidity
of the atmosphere, which, in not a few instances, has occa-
sioned intermittent fever, or ague.

"The greater proportion of the exiled brethren have
found occupation in the capital of the island, Port of Spain, or
its vicinity. Not a few of them are distributed in domestic
service among the families resident there. Some are occupied in gardening and similar labor. A few have commenced shopkeeping on a small scale, being unable to gain a
livelihood by any other means. While those of them who are
masons, carpenters, and shoemakers, are endeavoring, in their
respective departments of labor, to earn a livelihood. The
female converts, who, in Madeira, were able to support themselves by needlework, are still dependent on the same means
of support, but their earnings are comparatively small and
precarious. While some of the brethren are, by the goodness
of God, in comfortable enough circumstances, not a few have
such difficulties to struggle with as tend at once to keep them
hanging in daily dependence on the Lord, and to give
permanency to the impression—the persuasion in their minds,
that 'this is not their rest.' " [41]

Thus already it was felt that Trinidad could not be their

[41] Norton, 104-105.

permanent abiding place. Their economic situation was not encouraging and Mr. Hewitson found the spiritual atmosphere unpropitious. When Mr. Hewitson returned to Scotland, he left Mr. da Silva as pastor of the church; and it was under his leadership that plans were laid for the new migration.[42]

Reports of the persecution and exile of the Madeirenses had received wide publicity in the religious press, and came to the attention of the American Protestant Society, which had its headquarters in New York. This society already had a missionary, M. G. Gonsalves, born in Madeira, at work among the Portuguese who had settled along the New England coast to the number of five or six thousand. In the winter of 1847-48, the society sent Mr. Gonsalves to Trinidad to investigate the situation of the exiles.[43] On his return, Mr. Gonsalves brought a letter from Mr. da Silva, of which the following are the most significant passages:

"Finding myself constituted the pastor (though unworthy of so great a trust) of a church of nearly six hundred persons, it is not only my duty to feed them with spiritual aliment, but also to seek prayerfully their temporal good; endeavoring to keep them together in the faith and enjoyment of their daily bread.

"And that they may be able to hear the Word of God with profit on the days appointed, I do not see here the prospect of keeping this people in the midst of the present distress, as their labors are not paid as they should be; for in this sickly climate, when the husband and father is taken to the hospital the wife and children are left destitute, and not being able to pay the house-rent, they are turned into the streets, to beg from door to door. This state of things led me to solicit of the governor of this island (Lord Harris), a portion of land to be divided amongst the Portuguese, that they might on the same build their cabins, provided they could receive some aid in advance, to be paid by them in the

42 Norton, 105-107.
43 Norton, 111-112.

course of time. But although the governor is friendly to us, yet in his official capacity he said he could not comply with our request. I have also written on this subject to the Rev. Mr. Hewitson, of Scotland, who answered that we should find it difficult to obtain lands for families in these islands. And finally, in the midst of these efforts, the bank of West Indies failed, and sugars came down in price, and business was prostrated to the ruin of many households. Government works were stopped, and laborers can find little or nothing to do. And worse than all, our children, whose morals should be preserved at every expense, are mixed with a low, profane, wretched Roman Catholic population. I have consulted also the Rev. Messrs. Kennedy and Bodie, pastors of the English Presbyterian church, and Rev. Messrs. Banks, Kerr, Black and Berry, on a visit from the United States to this island. I said to these brethren that I believed God would in his way prepare a place for his people in some country where I might retire with the whole church, and that he would open the hearts of the faithful that they might bestow upon us the requisite aid. These gentlemen thought the United States of America offered advantages greater than any other country for a Bible-reading, spiritual, virtuous, industrious people.— . . . I have also written to the friends of Christ in Scotland, that they might still feel for this people, who must receive immediate aid, or many of them will perish with misery. I do not ask for money, but for lands. I ask what God has given to man, that he might earn his bread by the sweat of his brow. Our people are mechanics and farmers, virtuous and industrious; they will soon thrive with the blessing of God and the labor of their hands. They will soon rejoice in abundance, for they hate vice and love virtue. All these things I have made known to the Rev. Mr. Gonsalves, and he, seeing the desire of all the Portuguese to depart for the United States, for they were ready to fly, offered to take with him a small number, believing that the excellent American Protestant Society and the Christian community would assist them with all the aid in their power. But, on the whole, I thought we should wait until we should receive advice from the American Protestant Society, and the friends in Scotland, who, under God, have granted us so many blessings, and to whom we feel greatly indebted." [44]

One of the ministers at Trinidad wrote in September:

"If, in God's all-wise providence, the believing Portuguese sojourning among us, are to be removed to your country, Mr. Da Silva wishes that they should be located near each other, so that they could worship together, and have the great advantage of suitable schools for their children." [45]

In October, 1848, Mr. Da Silva wrote to the colonial committee of the Free Church of Scotland as follows:

"The sufferings in which this church is at present involved arise from the decaying state of this island. With difficulty do the people at all find labor so as to be able to support themselves and their families, and to pay the rent of their houses, which are always exceedingly high. In circumstances of extreme necessity, those of them who sicken, die as much in consequence of want as of the severity of their disease. Their little children are almost naked, and have only rags to sleep on. Such of them as are of age to be sent to school, are, as a matter of sheer necessity, put to service for food and clothing. And what is it that they learn? Everything that is opposite to the doctrine of the Gospel; and consequently the children, who should grow up to take the place of their believing parents in love to the Lord, are like seed-corn that is completely lost.

"Above forty Portuguese have already gone to the United States. I was greatly grieved on account of it, as it would have been much better not to separate them from their brethren, but to wait with Christian patience till your resolutions on the subject were ascertained. Many of these have written to their christian brethren, telling them that they had been kindly received by the Society, and that it had given them a house to live in till the arrival of the whole church

[44] Norton, 153-155.
[45] Norton, 157-158.

from Trinidad; when they might join it, and go to the place that should be fixed for their settlement.

"If you then shall approve and aid in the removal of this church to a country which offers it a hospitable welcome, we may expect that your approval of the step may not be unaccompanied with the blessing of the Lord." [46]

Meanwhile, however, the exertions and hardships of Mr. Da Silva had seriously impaired his health. His physician advised a visit to a more northern climate. Accordingly, he came to the United States, arriving at New York about the first of December, 1848. For the first two weeks his condition improved; then came a change for the worse, and he sank rapidly, dying January 10, 1849. His funeral was conducted at the Reformed Dutch Church, at the corner of Fourth Street and Lafayette Place; and he was buried in its vaults. [47]

Early in 1849, arrangements were made with the American Hemp Company for the settlement of the exiles in Illinois. The place selected was on the Meredosia and Springfield Railroad, at Island Grove, [48] about midway between Springfield and Jacksonville. "By these arrangements the American Hemp Company, which is composed of gentlemen at the west and in this city [New York], is to give both the Portuguese, who are here, and also those who are in Trinidad, immediate employment and good wages on their arrival there. They are also to furnish them with houses and every thing necessary for their comfort for one year without charge. Besides this, the company have engaged to give every family of the colony (in all one hundred and thirty-one families) ten acres of land in fee and unincumbered, on which a house can be built where they can have a permanent home. The ten acres lots are to be on the same tract of land, contiguous to each other, and, by the terms of the arrangement to be located by a committee consisting of the Hon. A. C. French, governor of Illinois; Rev. J. M. Sturtevant, president of Illinois College, at Jacksonville; and Rev. Albert Hale, of Springfield.

[46] Norton, 158-160.
[47] Norton, 160-170.
[48] *Illinois Journal*, March 27, 1849.

''Great care has also been taken that these advantages, so secured to this interesting people, should be rendered available to themselves and to their families.

''The writings have been drawn, sealed, and delivered, in which the parties are under bonds of ten thousand dollars each to fulfill their engagements.'' [48]

Word of these arrangements was sent to Trinidad, and Mr. Gonsalves began to send forward the rest of the exiles. For the execution of this plan, the society, in March and April, 1849, collected funds to defray the expense of their transportation to Illinois. Meanwhile, due publicity was given the project in that locality. In March, the ''Illinois State Journal'' published and endorsed the ''Last Appeal'' of the society in behalf of the exiles and explained the contract with the American Hemp Company. In April it devoted its editorial column to a résumé of Dr. Kalley's work in Madeira.[50]

''Every preparation was made for their departure. The buildings which the Society had rented for them in New York were rented by others, and the Portuguese were to vacate them before the 1st of May. As they were about to move it was ascertained that the American Hemp Company, who had engaged to take them, had failed to fulfill its engagements, although under a bond of ten thousand dollars to do so. This company had made no preparations to receive the Portuguese. This deranged the plans of the Society, and obliged them to rent other buildings in New-York for the Portuguese, as in such circumstances they could not send them to the West. We were daily expecting the way would be prepared for their departure to Illinois, but for weeks we were held in the most painful suspense.

''In this state no efforts could be made to obtain employment for the Portuguese. Hence they were entirely dependent upon the Society for daily bread. Their prospects for the future were dark, on account of the suspense in which they

[48] Norton, 185.
[50] Norton, 238; *Illinois Journal*, March 27, 1849, April 18, 1849.

were about their destination in Illinois, and because no other location as suitable was presented." [51]

When this news reached Illinois, however, it was not regarded as an unmixed evil. "We *never* approved of that plan," said the "Illinois Journal." "When foreigners come to our country, in our opinion, they should become Americanized as soon as possible; and this never can be done if they are located in isolated communities." [52]

"At length another door was opened. A letter was received from Rev. Dr. Sturtevant, . . . informing us of a meeting of the principal Protestant churches of Jacksonville; of the appointment of a joint committee, representing two Presbyterian churches, one Congregational, one Baptist, and one Methodist Episcopal church, and of their action respecting the Exiles. This letter proposed to have those in New-York go to Jacksonville at once, to take care of them and put them into positions to earn a comfortable living, and not leave them to themselves till they should be thus provided for.

"The letter further proposed that those in the West Indies should follow these, with the expectation of being located in Jacksonville and its immediate neighborhood, or at farthest in the three places, Jacksonville, Springfield, and Waverly, (the latter situated eight miles south of the railroad on which the two former lie, and about equi-distant from each), where 'there can be no doubt that all of them could find the means of living with comfort from the rewards of their industry.'"

"This letter was laid before the Board of Directors of the American and Foreign Christian Union, and, after careful deliberation, it was resolved to send our Portuguese brethren to Jacksonville with the least possible delay. Everything was arranged, and the day was appointed for their departure. Their passage was engaged on the Western route, over the lakes to Chicago, and thence through the canal and down the Illinois river to Jacksonville. But before the day arrived

---

[51] Norton, 238-239.
[52] *Illinois Journal,* August 7, 1849.

sickness and cholera had commenced among them. Again were we disappointed and our plans deranged.'' [53]

Indeed, the time was unpropitious for their arrival in their new home. Their friends in Illinois first sent a telegram advising that their departure be delayed, and then despatched the following letter: [54]

"Illinois College, July 10, 1849.

"Rev. Herman Norton, Cor. Sec. Christ. Union.

"Dear Sir: There are two reasons why we think the journey should not be undertaken:

"1st. There is so much pestilence all along the great thoroughfares, from the east to the west, that the journey cannot be performed by such a number of persons without much danger.

"2nd. This village is thus far unaffected by the pestilence, but there is great sensitiveness about the propagation of the disease by infection from Cholera patients.

"The Committee are of the opinion that these apprehensions are excessive, but they are real, and would be likely to stand in the way of that kindness and hospitality which would otherwise be extended to these persecuted disciples. We think, therefore, that they constitute a good reason for delaying the journey for the present. In all other respects, the facts remain the same as at the time of my other communications. We have reason to believe that neither in respect to interest in these exiles, as sufferers for the testimony of Jesus, nor in the facility of affording them employment and the means of a livelihood, will there be any disappointment.

"Judging from our experience in the prevalence of Cholera during its former visit, we entertain the hope that our thoroughfares will be safe for the journey in a few weeks from this time; still this scourge is in God's hand, and he alone knoweth the limits of ravages. We are fearful these Refugees may be greatly exposed to it in your city, and yet,

[53] Norton, 239-240.
[54] Norton, 241; *Illinois Journal,* August 9, 1849, clipping from *New York Tribune.*

with the care and skill which can be brought to their aid there, we must think they will be safer than on board canal boats and steamboats on either of the great thoroughfares. May God appear in his good time for all his persecuted ones.

"Yours in the Gospel,

J. M. STURTEVANT."

As the summer progressed, the embarrassments of the society increased. On July 19, another party of the exiles arrived at New York, bringing word that about August 1 a hundred and fifty more might be expected. No information having reached Mr. Gonsalves at Trinidad of the failure of the arrangement with the American Hemp Company, and the exiles being in great difficulties in that place, the whole company, some 450 in number, were expecting to embark for the United States as fast as arrangements could be made for their passage. The following letter appears to have been brought by this group of exiles: [55]

"Trinidad, Port of Spain, July 13, 1849.

"Rev. Herman Norton and Mortimer De Motte, Esq.

"My Dear Sirs: By the bark Henry Trowbridge, Capt. Frisby, I send to your care 74 of the exiles of Madeira. Another bark and brig will sail in a few days with 76 and 74 more exiles.—As the condition of the people is so heart-rending, they are all anxious to go to America, but not knowing how much funds you have received for the exiles, I dare not venture any more at present, though my heart aches for them. They are a devoted, pious and patient people. The people on this island are very angry because the Portuguese are going to America. They think the British government ought to have given them lands on this island and not suffer a good people to go to any other country. This poor people have sold furniture and made every sacrifice, so great is their desire to reach American soil, and unite their prayers and tears with

---

[55] *Illinois Journal,* August 4, 1849, from *New York Herald,* July 20, 1849; *ibid.,* August 9, 1849, from *New York Tribune.*

their brethren already in America's favored land. I know that in this emergency I have gone beyond my limits; no other motives but heart yearning compassion has led me to take a step for which I may be blamed; but I will suffer all things cheerfully for the sake of God's poor persecuted of the Nineteenth Century.

"Yours in the best bonds,

"M. J. GONSALVES."

This news aroused great concern in the West. "The situation of these exiles," said the "Illinois Journal" after quoting an account of the arrival of this party in New York, "calls for the sympathies of all. The failure of the plan by which they were to be colonized must be extremely embarrassing to them, and unless promptly relieved will result in great distress. . . .

"We suppose that the society at New York has means to send these emigrants to the counties of Sangamon and Morgan. Now, we take upon ourselves to say, that two good men, in two weeks' time, can find situations for these exiles, able to support themselves by labor,—as people here all have to labor—in these two counties. Hundreds of them can have situations secured in families in the towns of Jacksonville and Springfield. This may not be as pleasant to them, in the idea, as a location of their own exclusively; but in our opinion it is more plausible—it is, in fact, entirely practicable—and would result in the greatest benefit to these citizens. They would thus learn our manners, our habits (we hope our good ones only), and our way of doing business of all kinds—and become useful to themselves, and in time amalgamated with us.

* * *

"We recommend this matter to those who have seemed to have some connection with it, and especially to Rev. Albert Hale. . . . " [56]

---

[56] *Illinois Journal.* August 7, 1849.

A few days later, the "Illinois Journal" published the following letter and comment: [57]

"New York, Sept. 15, 1849.

"Mr. Erastus Wright.

"Dear Sir:—By request of the Society whose Secretary I am, I address you a few inquiries respecting the Portuguese Exiles, now under our care. We have now in this city and on Staten Island 470 of these exiles, natives of Maderia [sic], who have lost all their property and were obliged to flee from their country. . . . The majority of them are Farmers, some are Mechanics, and others were Merchants. None were so poor as to be dependent. Some were persons of great wealth. Now all are equally destitute. They are an excellent industrious class of people.

"The citizens of Jacksonville have requested us to send 100 of them there. They will take them with their families, give the Mechanics employment in the village, and the farmers, on the farms in the vicinity, so that all may assemble at Jacksonville on the Sabbath.

"It has been suggested to us that the citizens of Springfield might be willing to take a company of these exiles. My object in writing is to ascertain their desire on this subject. Your name is given to us as the proper person to address.

"Can you inform us in this matter. Can you tell us whether any and *how many* could be provided for this fall and winter in Springfield, whether they can be employed and how? Only a few of them can speak the English language.

"Will you please inform us as soon as convenient, as winter is coming on, and we are very anxious to secure them a comfortable home.

"It is their desire, if the way should be opened, to eventually settle together as a colony on the new lands. But this cannot be done immediately. Truly yours, Herman Norton, Cor. Sec'ry, etc."

"We commend the above letter to the attention of our

---

[57] *Illinois Journal*, September 26, 1849.

citizens," commented the "Illinois Journal." "The labor of these exiles is much wanted, and we now feel on this subject as we have ever done, that if pains should be taken, places for 100 or more can readily be obtained.

"They will not understand our manner of doing work, and it will take them some time to learn 'our ways.' We do not suppose they will expect wages until they can become useful. Farmers would find the men of great service. They could also be of service in town—those not mechanics—in gardens, sawing wood, and doing the thousand jobs required by families.

"Besides in assisting these people we should perform a praiseworthy act, as pleasant to those who confer, as it would be grateful to those who would receive benefit.

"We hope the Rev. Mr. Hale, Jas. L. Lamb, Erastus Wright, J. A. Barret, and Elijah Iles will consent to act as a committee to receive communications, applications, &c. on this subject from our citizens; and also correspond with the Rev. Herman Norton, of New York, on the subject."

While these exertions were being put forth in the West, the Society was striving to cope with the situation in New York. Three vessels arrived from Trinidad, bringing the total number of refugees to nearly five hundred. "They were all destitute of money and of clothing suitable for our climate. The Society were obliged to furnish them with daily bread—with medicines, and to obtain for them a large supply of clothing. . . . A brief and simple statement of the facts was spread out before the community. . . . The response to this simple appeal was so prompt and liberal that within a few weeks we were constrained to publish that the wants of the Portuguese, as regards clothing, were all supplied." [58]

As soon as the cholera abated, arrangements were made for their journey; and on October 19, 1849, the first detachment of 280 left New York on the steamer "Isaac Newton." They intended to spend their first Sabbath in Albany, the second in Buffalo, and the third in Chicago. At all these cities,

---

[58] Norton, 242-243.

and at Detroit, public meetings were held and liberal contributions made toward their expenses. Everywhere they were
received with the most cordial hospitality. From Buffalo to
Chicago, they travelled on the steamer "Key Stone," "one of
the largest and most elegant steamers on the lake." "They
will be accompanied throughout the journey by the Rev.
David Lathrop and by the Rev. Dr. Baird as far as Albany.
The Rev. Mr. Sawtell has gone before, to make the necessary
arrangements for their reception at each stopping place.

"Those of the refugees who still remain in the city [New
York], about 200 in number, will not be removed until further
intelligence is received from Mr. Sawtell, which may not be
until the lapse of two or three weeks." [59]

Meanwhile, the "Illinois Journal" was heralding their
approach. As early as November 8, it said: "The Portuguese exiles will be here today or tomorrow. Are we ready
to receive them?" And indeed, on the morrow arrived their
advance agent, the Rev. Mr. Sawtell. It was expected that
they would arrive Monday or Tuesday by the afternoon train
from Jacksonville. Again the "Journal" appealed for welcome and aid. The next evening, Friday, Mr. Sawtell gave
an address at the Second Presbyterian Church, rehearsing the
history of the exiles. On Sunday he preached at the Second
Church in the morning and at the First Church at night. [60]

On Monday, the "Journal" published a résumé of Mr.
Sawtell's address of Friday night; and reported that the
exiles had not yet reached Jacksonville by Saturday night,
and might not reach Springfield as early as expected by a day
or two. A meeting was held that day which adopted the following resolutions: [61]

"To the People of Springfield and Sangamon County.

"Resolved, that the citizens of Springfield and the citizens of Sangamon County generally, be invited to contribute
cash, furniture, clothing, food, or whatever else may be use-

[59] Norton, 244, 248; *Illinois Journal*, October 30, 1849, from *New York Journal of Commerce*.
[60] *Illinois Journal*, November 10, 1849.
[61] *Illinois Journal*, November 13, 1849.

ful to the Portuguese exiles, and to deposit the same at the shop of E. M. Hinkle, nearly opposite the Methodist church, to be distributed under the direction of the committee.

"It is expected that these Exiles will arrive in this city on Thursday afternoon, about three o'clock.

"The Committee will express the hope, and the confidence, that the generous and true-hearted citizens of this city and county, will promptly respond to this call, and donate food, clothing, and other necessaries for the destitute Portuguese now temporarily thrown upon the hospitality and generosity of this community.

"By direction of the Committee,

SIMEON FRANCIS, Chairman.

"JAMES A. BARRETT, Secretary."

Unexpectedly, however, the exiles arrived in Springfield on Tuesday, November 13, 1849. The committee hastily sent out a new appeal to meet the emergency.[62]

"To the Ladies of Springfield, and to our fellow citizens generally.

"The Exiles unexpectedly arrived in our city yesterday. Our previous advices led us to suppose that they would not reach the city until Thursday. In consequence of their unexpected arrival, we are required to make an especial appeal to you in their behalf.

"These Exiles are destitute of many things necessary for their comfort. The Committee have procured three or four houses for them, but they are without furniture of any description, except a few chairs, some three tables, three water buckets, two bedsteads and a few cups and saucers, and bedding to a limited extent—for some 130 persons. Every thing, therefore, required for housekeeping, and which will readily occur to housekeepers and others, is wanted; and if they are second hand, or considerably worn, they will not be the less acceptable. What is done in this matter we desire to be

---

Illinois Journal, November 14, 1849.

promptly done. There is scarcely a housekeeper who cannot send something for their benefit. A single chair, a tub, a bucket, and numerous other articles we have not time to name, will be gladly received.

"The Committee design to have cooking stoves put up in each house to-day;—after to-day, therefore, we think it will not be necessary to call upon the ladies of this city, to furnish cooked food for the exiles, to any considerable amount. But food will be hereafter required—Vegetables, Flour, Meal, Meat, Tea, Coffee, Sugar, &c. There are several in ill health, to whom food suitable for persons in their condition will be required.

"The Committee reiterate their invitation to the humane and christian people in the country to assist in this case. Out of their abundance, they can contribute much for the subsistence and comfort of these people, until more permanent provision can be made for them.

"The Exiles will be likely to remain together for several days. A number of families will probably continue to live in the houses provided for them during the winter. Applications for labor and for assistance, will be received by the Committee, and will be laid before these Exiles, as soon as it shall seem expedient.

"We invite the Ladies to call at the houses of these Exiles to learn their wants, and continue their kind offices for their good."

The condition of the exiles during that first winter is suggested by the following letter from Mr. Hale: [63]

"We are much occupied these days in ministering to our brethren, the Portuguese Exiles. They arrived here just in time to enter on the severe winter weather, which they now, in common with all of us, have to endure. They are not much accustomed to severe cold weather; and as our city was very full of people when they arrived, it was well nigh impossible to provide them habitations; to provide *comfortable* dwellings was out of the question, as every thing worthy of the name

---

[a] Norton, 249.

was already crowded full. But we have done what, under the circumstances, we could, and they are hoping for better times. So far as I know, they are contented and happy. Many of them find employment, at good wages and ready pay. They are highly valued as laborers, and will soon be able to take care of themselves without the aid of others. Indeed, the last thing to be looked for is that such men should long be a charge to their fellow men. If they maintain their religious principles and their habits of industry, there is but one destiny for them here, and that is plenty—independence."

Owing to the destruction of the files of the local newspapers, there appears to be no extant evidence of the measures taken in connection with the arrival of the Portuguese in Jacksonville. We are therefore thrown back upon the action at Springfield. We cannot doubt that Dr. Sturtevant and his associates were equally zealous as their friends in Springfield, and probably resorted to much the same means of arousing public interest and caring for the needs of the exiles.

Since the Portuguese had not arrived in Jacksonville by Saturday night, November 10, and the Springfield colony arrived there from Jacksonville on Tuesday, November 13, it would appear that they must have arrived in Jacksonville either Sunday, November 11, or Monday, November 12, 1849.

About two hundred of the exiles were still in New York. "On the 8th November another company of about one hundred left New-York for Illinois. They took the rail-road from Albany to Buffalo, then steamboat to Detroit, and again rail-road to Chicago. They were to remain there until future arrangements could be made for them." This left only a remnant in New York. Some had been prevented from going, by sickness or the sickness of some member of their families. To these, their detention was a great disappointment. Others preferred to remain there during the winter, having a prospect of work.[64]

Apparently this group in time joined their friends in Jacksonville and Springfield. From time to time others came

⁶⁴ Norton, 247.

from Madeira, 211 in 1851, and 273 in 1853. These later groups were led by Mr. Gonsalves. Now and then a few more came either to Jacksonville or Springfield.[65]

Antonio de Mattos was one of the original deacons of the church of the Madeirenses. "He fled to Scotland in 1846, where he became qualified for preaching the gospel. He was ordained to come to this country and take the place of Mr. Da Silva, as the pastor of the scattered flock.

"He paid a short visit to his father's family in Madeira. He saw forty of the converts in the chief city. He met them one by one, conversed and prayed with them, for it was not thought prudent to hold public meetings. . . . He remained . . . until a notice was posted on the door, that he must leave the island or suffer death.

"He then visited Trinidad on his way to this country. There he found more than four hundred exiles, many of whom had come from other shores to enjoy the protection offered them by the British government."[66] Mr. De Mattos came on to Jacksonville, and on March 15, 1850, reorganized the church of the Madeirenses, which until 1856 remained under the jurisdiction of the Free Church of Scotland. To trace further the vicissitudes of this church would transcend the limits of this study.

So the Portuguese exiles at last found a new home and freedom of conscience. Their story, however, does not end here. While not so romantic as the tale of their persecution and wanderings, their fortunes in their new home are not lacking in interest and are possibly of even greater historical significance. Unfortunately, though, they are much harder to trace in any form on which the historian can rely. Yet enough scattered bits of evidence might be brought together to afford the basis of a narrative. Perhaps at no distant date this journal will publish such an account of the later fortunes of the exiles of Madeira.

---

[65] Vasconcellos. *Brief History of the Portuguese Settlement at Jacksonville.*
[66] Blackburn, 211; Vasconcellos, *Brief Narrative of the Original Portuguese Church.*

BIBLIOGRAPHICAL NOTE

The source of greatest value for this study is the Rev. Herman Norton, *Record of facts concerning the persecutions at Madeira in 1843 and 1846: the flight of a thousand converts to the West India Islands; and also, the sufferings of those who arrived in the United States* (fifth edition, with a supplement, sketching the history to the present time, New York, 1850). Mr. Norton was Corresponding Secretary of the American Protestant Society, which was responsible for the migration from Trinidad to Illinois. The book is valuable for extracts from original documents, both correspondence elsewhere unavailable and addresses and narratives originally published in British periodicals. The book neglects Mr. Hewitson's work. It is frankly a piece of propaganda and must be used with great caution.

Second in importance is Rev. W. M. Blackburn, *The Exiles of Madeira* (Philadelphia, n. d., but copyright 1860). For the ground covered by Norton, Blackburn derives from him; but he also gives a good account of Mr. Hewitson's work derived from the *Memoirs of the Rev. W. H. Hewitson.* He also secured information from the Rev. Antonio de Mattos and others. This is the most scholarly and restrained book on the subject, and is an indispensable supplement to Norton.

Third in importance is Della Dimmitt, *A Story of Madeira* (Cincinnati, 1896). This book is of slight value, deriving from Norton primarily, but adding a few details, apparently derived from Dr. Kalley.

The file of the *Illinois Journal* for 1849 is an admirable contemporary source, though it tells much less than one would wish, or than would be found in a newspaper of the present day. The *Illinois Register*, its Democratic local contemporary, is strangely silent; I have been unable to find a single mention of the exiles in its file for 1849. The political affiliations of the two papers will suggest a highly significant explanation to anyone cognizant of the political issues and affiliations of the time.

Doubtless the files of the New York press would yield a good many references in connection with the arrival of the various companies of exiles in that city, their sojourn and departure. The *Illinois Journal* quotes extracts from the *Herald, Tribune,* and *Journal of Commerce.*

Two valuable unpublished papers by Mr. Emanuel M. Vasconcellos, *A Brief Narrative of the Original Portuguese Church,* and *A Brief History of the Portuguese Settlement at Jacksonville,* should also be mentioned. They are especially valuable on account of Mr. Vasconcellos's familiarity with the traditions of his people and for their account of the history of the church after the reorganization at Jacksonville, in part derived from the records and in part from Mr. Vasconcellos's personal knowledge.

I should also express my appreciation of the courteous assistance I have received from the Rev. W. E. Spoonts, Mr. Joshua Vasconcellos, Mr. George Day, and Mrs. J. A. Goes, of Jacksonville; Mr. E. M. Vasconcellos, of Springfield, and Miss Georgia L. Osborne, of the State Historical Library.

The Portuguese in California

Frederick G. Bohme

The Portuguese in California

By Frederick G. Bohme

In 1950, California had a population of over 7,000,000, of whom some 1,000,000 were born in foreign lands.[1] This one-seventh has been a leavening factor in the state's culture; yet, because the number is and has been steadily declining since imposition of immigration restrictions in the 1920's, the cumulative influence of the foreign born has become more and more difficult to assess.

Among foreign-born groups, the Portuguese[*2] have never been numerically significant (less than 100,000 in the entire United States at the height of foreign influx); what is significant is the fact that 35.4% of them lived in California as of 1940, the others being centered around New Bedford, Mass., and in Hawaii and Rhode Island. Moreover, of the *native-born* Portuguese in the United States, 49.1% were residents of California.[3]

The first permanent Portuguese settlers to come to North America were expelled Jews who sought refuge in Holland, then went to Brazil with the Dutch forces but fled to the Atlantic-seaboard colonies when the Dutch were pushed from Brazil by the Portuguese in 1654.[4] Some of their descendants were among those who followed the gold rush to California in 1849, where they were joined by others coming directly from Portugal or from the Azores, but their interest seems to have been more in commerce than in gold.[5] Mass migration did not begin until around 1870: whereas in the decade 1861-1870, only 2658 Portuguese landed on American shores, during the next decade (1871-80) the total was 14,082, their principal method of arrival being by fishing boats from the western Azores;[6] mainland Portuguese were not numerous until after 1910.[7]

In their California setting, the Portuguese have proved to be a peace-loving group of peasant farmers and seafaring folk. By 1950 there were

*The term "Portuguese" refers, unless otherwise specified, not only to those who came from the mainland of Portugal, but to those from the Azores, Madeira, and the Cape Verde Islands, as well. (See note 2.)

233

15,134 foreign-born Portuguese and 11,205 Azoreans in the state.[8] This is only 2.6% of the state's foreign-born population, but members of their race represent the nuclei of two important California industries, fishing and dairying.

If we go back several centuries to Prince Henry the Navigator (1394-1460), we see that the race's significance for the Pacific coast began with the sailing charts that were produced under Henry's initiative, for, based on these charts, Portuguese caravels were soon venturing at great distances from their home ports. In command of one of these vessels was Juan Rodríguez Cabrillo, or Cabrilho, to whom the discovery of Alta California is credited. Little is known of his early life; even his birth date and native city remain open to conjecture, although authoritative sources agree that he was a Portuguese, sailing under the Spanish flag.[9] On September 28 or 29, 1542, he entered San Diego Bay. Continuing up the coast, he was in the vicinity of Drake's Bay by November 16th of the same year.[10] Stormy weather forced him to turn southward, until a landing was made on present-day San Miguel Island in the Santa Barbara Channel. Here Cabrillo died in January 1543, from an illness which followed the accidental breaking of his leg some two and a half months before.[11] A granite cross in his memory has been erected on the island by the Portuguese Society of America.[12]

Cabrillo's explorations were continued by his navigator, Bartolomeo Ferrelo (Ferraio), who was a native of the Levant but frequently termed a Portuguese. After reaching a northerly point of about 42°, near the present Oregon-California border, he too turned southward.[13]

Spanish interest in Alta California lagged until 1595, when another Portuguese, Sebastian Rodríguez Cermeño, or Cermenho, sailed from Manila on the annual galleon bound for Acapulco on the west coast of Mexico. Instructed to find a suitable way-station for the galleon, he entered what is now known as Drake's Bay on November 6, 1595—he called it "La Baya de San Francisco"—and preëmpted it for the king of Spain. (Francis Drake had taken possession in the name of the queen of England in the summer of 1579.) While Cermeño was ashore, his ship foundered in a storm, and he and his party were forced to make their way south in a launch. This halted any further attempts to explore the California coast in a Manila galleon, and led to the Spanish-born navigator, Sebastian Vizcaíno's expedition of 1602, sent out expressly to explore Alta California.[14]

From this time until the 19th century, the Pacific coast was outside the bounds of official Portuguese notice, and the Spanish colonial policy discouraged the emigration of foreigners to her empire in the New World; but the ocean itself continued to be a potential source of interest, which was reinforced by Vizcaíno's report that whales abounded there.[15]

According to the U. S. census of 1850, there were 92,597 people in the state of California, includng 109 Portuguese. These figures have been officially acknowledged to be incomplete, but they serve as a starting point.[16] Prior to 1850, the student is handicapped not only by Mexican statistical laxity and Spanish anti-immigration policies, under which foreign birth would be hidden rather than revealed, but also by the frequent translation of Portuguese names into Spanish, and later into English. Portuguese names are usually distinguishable from the Spanish by their spelling; in California, on the contrary, there has been little or no effort to maintain this difference. In 1892, *A Patria*, a Portuguese language newspaper, carried an advertisement for the Lisbon House, located on Drumm Street between Jackson and Pacific in San Francisco, and owned by John Cardozo & Co. This bears sufficient resemblance to the Portuguese spelling, Cardoço, to be recognizable; but the Lusitania [ancient Latin name for present-day Portugal] Hotel, around the corner on Jackson between Drumm and Davis, was operated by Antonio S. Alamos & Co.[17] Here further evidence would be required to establish nationality. There was also "Joaquin" [not Joaquim], the "jolly Portuguese whaler," who was a friend of Robert Louis Stevenson at Monterey in 1879. When asked his "second name," the answer was, "Just Joaquin."[18]

Anglicizing was another prevalent practice. The *San Luis Obispo County History* lists two Portuguese, Barker and Clark;[19] another source lists Bennett, Perry, Marshal, Rose, Smith, Enos, Best, Martin, White, and Oliver, all said to be Portuguese.[20] *Portugalia*, a magazine published in Oakland, regularly carried the advertisements of an insurance agent by the name of Frank Pine, but noted that he was also known as Frank Pinheiro.[21] The Silveira and Carvalho families of San Leandro, some of whom changed their name to "Oakes," are discussed below.

A final difficulty is presented by multiplicity in nomenclature. One author has pointed out that where the father has three names in Portugal, the sons might take either the second or the last name, with the result that there might be ". . . the Silverias [sic] and Souzas, the Bettencourts and Josephs, the Joaquins and Roses, who are brothers. . . ."[22]

Earliest of the Portuguese to settle, Antonio José Rocha reached Alta California in 1815 on the ship *Columbia,* became a naturalized Mexican citizen, and built a home at Spring and Franklin streets in Los Angeles. Under American occupation, it became the first city hall, and the site was later occupied by the Phillips Block that housed the city's first large department store, "Hamburger's." Records indicate that Rocha, his wife, and five children, lived in Santa Barbara in 1836.[23]

Another record for 1815 is the Russian traveler Otto van Kotzebue's statement that in the latter part of that year, "John Elliot de Castro, native of Portugal, had come to Sitka on board an American ship and was there engaged by M. [Alexander] Baronof to go as supercargo with the trading ship bound for California where he was taken prisoner with the rest of the crew."[24] (Castro subsequently went to Hawaii, where he became an adviser to the king.[25])

Late in the next decade (1820-30), James Ohio Pattie wrote of hunting sea otter in the area of Monterey with an unnamed Portuguese.[26] In 1834, José María Bollon, likewise Portuguese, was said to have been in the provincial capital itself.[27] The record southward, two years later (1836), rests on census figures for the city of Los Angeles and its jurisdiction: out of a total population of 2228 there were 1675 whites; of these, 50 were foreigners, of whom 2 were born in Portugal—Jordan Pacheco, a tavern keeper; and Manuel d'Olivera, a laborer.[28]

Some two years after the American conquest of California, Solomon Nuñez Carvalho, a Portuguese Jew who had been in America for about twenty years and had gained a reputation as painter and illustrator, was asked to join John C. Frémont's exploring expedition of 1853-1854 as the official artist. He came to California in that year and painted a number of portraits, including those of Manuel Dominguez (influential in the affairs of Los Angeles during the 1830's and later as alcalde, etc.) and of Pío Pico, who had been Mexican governor of California in 1845-1846.[29] Carvalho's account, *Incidents of Travel and Adventure in the Far West* . . . , contains passages not entirely adulatory of California, and it is doubtful that he was instrumental in attracting many new immigrants. For example, there were so many murders committed in Los Angeles at that time that it "became dangerous to walk abroad after night . . ."; and not only were the miscreants in southern California two-footed, but the country was "infested with millions of ground squirrels," which destroyed vegetation and necessitated the importation of strychnine in such great quantities that it became "an important article of trade."[30]

In addition to the circumstances, already mentioned, which make difficult a true numerical analysis of the Portuguese in California over the years, there are the discrepancies between the U. S. immigration authorities' report for the period 1820-1910[31] (apparently based on custom-house records at the port of San Francisco, where, from 1848 to 1870, no distinction was made between Portuguese, Azoreans and other minor foreign groups[32]) and the figures published in San Francisco in 1946.[33]

As it is generally accepted that most of the earliest Portuguese arrivals were sailors who left their ships to mine or to trade or to farm,[34] the census reports—though incomplete owing to the scattered condition of the mining population, the loss of records during the count, etc.—give a better indication of the influx of these people to California than the immigration commission's figures for the nation. Especially is this so, because many of the immigrants continued on to this state after a stay in other parts of the country. About 1840, for example, a group of Portuguese emigrated to Louisiana to work on the sugar plantations. The men inter-married with creoles, and in 1865, after the abolition of slavery, moved to California.[35] Still others were drawn from New England,[36] and more came from Hawaii. The latter had gone to the islands between 1878 and 1899, and some 2000 of them had come to California between 1911 and 1914 due to poor working conditions and low wages in the pineapple and sugar industries.[37] Throughout the entire period, their focal point was the San Francisco Bay area, from which they spread to the Sacramento and San Joaquin valleys; a lesser number to Monterey; and another group to San Diego.[38]

From the evidence available, it appears that the first Portuguese in the far west were fishermen from the Azore Islands who had come to California through the New Bedford, Mass., shipyards, where a large whaling fleet was based and where Portuguese in considerable numbers had settled. Their vessels stopped at San Francisco, which became a way-station for the Arctic;[39] so that, aside from those who entered the mining fields either to dig or to supply the miners, the 1850 and 1860 enumerations show that a majority were, or had recently been, seamen. They were engaged in "ship whaling"—that is, the mammals were taken far from shore, and some of the processing was done on board ship. The prevalence of whales along the California coast, however, led to the opening of the "shore-whaling" technique, which, after the gold rush, became dominated by the Portuguese.

Around 1854, an American, Capt. J. P. Davenport, seems to have been the brains behind the Monterey Whaling Co., chartered that year.[40] As reported by the Sacramento *Daily Union* of March 14, 1855, "During the year a number of Portuguese whalers have established themselves at Monterey for the purpose of capturing such whales as are indigenous to the coast."[41] Between April and September 1854, they are said to have captured five California gray whales, nine humpbacks, and four killer whales, netting the men $438 each.[42] In 1855, some seventeen Portuguese organized themselves into what became known as the "Old Company," which, for the next 3 years, garnered 800 or so barrels of whale oil per year. Davenport, after having been in and out of business in that locality several times, withdrew in the early 1860's, giving way to the "New Company of Portuguese Whalers."[43] Relics of their operations are the sections of whalebone pavement preserved in Monterey.[44]

The most prominent Portuguese in the industry was Capt. Joseph Clark (né Machado), who came to California about 1852 from the Azores.[45] He was connected with a whaling ship based at San Diego in 1858, and was still there in 1860-1861.[46] At that time Clark estimated that there were some 60 whaling ships operating along the Lower California coast, a majority of the crews (although not the officers) being Portuguese.[47] After a stay at Portuguese Bend near San Pedro in 1864, Captain Clark founded, the next year, the San Simeon Co. of shore whalers of which he was sole owner. According to reports in 1878, some 25 whales were taken a year with 5 whaleboats, each 30 feet or less in length. Operations were suspended for a time in 1889, and the last recorded catches there were in 1892.[48]

At one time or another in the 1870's, there were as many as 14 stations operating at once along the coast from Crescent City to San Diego; by 1886, only 5 remained: Monterey, San Simeon, San Luis Obispo, Point Conception, and San Diego.[49] Many were abandoned due to the low price of oil in the 1880's, caused in part by the increasing competition of petroleum; but the station at Portuguese Bend (near San Pedro) was closed as early as 1875 because of the difficulty of obtaining fresh water.[50]

Whaling operations appealed to travelers and to their talent for description. Of the station at Pigeon Point, Col. Albert S. Evans had this to say: "The men are all 'Gees'—Portuguese from the Azores or the Western Islands. . . . [a] stout, hard-looking race, grossly ignorant, dirty and superstitious. They work hard, and are doing well in business."[51] The proportion of Portuguese, according to this comment, was about double that at the San Luis Obispo establishment, operating between 1869 and 1887, where about half the personnel were said to be Portuguese.[52] The station at Carmel, opened in 1862 by a group of Azoreans and Madeirans from Monterey, was described at length by Capt. Charles Melville Scammon as it appeared when he visited it in the early 1870's. As he saw it, the station was "a pleasant retreat" for the men, away from "the rough voyages experienced on board the whaling ship. The surrounding scenery is broken into majestic spurs and peaks, like their own native isles. . . ."[53] Captain Scammon estimated that over a 22-year period the returns from shore whaling had amounted to some $1,250,000 worth of oil;[54] but toward the end of the 1880's the scarcity of whales along the coast,[55] the decline in the demand for oil, coupled with the use of ocean-going vessels and more modern methods, resulted in the demise of the shore-whaling industry.

In the 1890's, a whaling fleet operated out of San Francisco, many of the ships being owned by New Bedford interests. The masters were, in general, Americans, but the lower-grade officers (boat steerers and boat headers) were nearly all colored men or Portuguese from the Cape Verde Islands.[56] Out of a total of 645 men comprising the whalers' crews in 1892, Americans formed the largest group; the Portuguese were second with 93, or only about 15%.[57] But a change was already in progress among the Portuguese, toward other activities based on the wealth of the sea. David Starr Jordan noted that in the 1880's most of the San Francisco fisheries and the chief markets were in the hands of Italians and Portuguese.[58] By 1888, the Portuguese accounted for almost 20% of the foreign-born engaged in the ocean fisheries of California.[59] The proportion varied with place. In Monterey County, for instance, although most of the white fishermen were Portuguese, they were outnumbered 2 to 1 by the Chinese; nevertheless the whites accounted for 3 times the Chinese catch. In Los Angeles County the proportion was less: of those engaged in vessel fishing, 3 out of 10 were Portuguese; and in San Francisco County, only 120 out of a total of 1782.[60]

It appears that most of the Portuguese left San Diego after the cessation of offshore whaling at that port, for the manuscript census of 1870 reveals none there whatever.[61] In 1880, there were reportedly only 1 or 2, but by 1893 several more had arrived and were fishing in 1-man boats for albacore, bonito, and yellowtail, which they pickled

for the Sandwich Island trade. Beginning with an experimental ship-
ment of 3660 pounds in 1891, this delicacy caught on readily, and in
1892 some 34,300 pounds were exported[62]—only to decline with the
advent of the canneries.

Commercial fishing in California attained its greatest growth after
the beginning of the 20th century, the Portuguese, over the years,
being sixth among the national groups so engaged, with the U. S.-born
first and the Italians second. Their importance varies: around San
Diego, the Portuguese now represent the largest foreign-born group
in the industry,[63] whereas at Los Angeles, Monterey, and San Francisco, they are minor in number compared to the Italians. The latter
first set the San Diego fishing industry in motion, but they were soon
replaced by the Portuguese, who, operating on a relatively small scale
until 1911, perfected their canning methods to such an extent that
they could tap distant markets in the sale of tuna. Prior to that time,
tuna had been thrown overboard as unfit to eat.[64]

On the bay side of Point Loma, there are now some 5000 second-
and third-generation Portuguese, principally Azoreans and Madeirans,
who own and operate a tuna fleet, which is on the high seas 3 to 4
months of the year.[65] Their lack of connection with San Diego's city
life has kept them in a peculiarly Portuguese environment, but they
have been quick to adopt modern methods. For example, their early
boats had been only 30 feet in length; contrasting with this is the
Conte Bianco, built in San Diego in 1951, which is 127 feet long,
with a cruising range of 12,000 miles. Two years before, the *Espirito
Santo* had been equipped with a helicopter for scouting purposes.[66]

Figures for the state as a whole indicate that, as of 1950, foreign-
born Portuguese represented little more than 3% of the men engaged
in fishing in California (468 out of 14,962).[67] Yet, they and their sons,
with their native skills, have played a major part in bringing an industry from small beginnings to one involving a catch of 694,977,000
pounds, valued at $71,982,774.[68]

Originating in a country with an agricultural economy, the Portuguese immigrants to California who were not fisherfolk came from
the land, and in their new environment they turned to it again. They
were by far in the majority.

In their native islands, where there were, and still are, no factories,
mines, mills, or railroads, the Azoreans had had to exist as best they
could. Many left without obtaining passports, because of the threat

of conscription; consequently there is no official record of their departure.[69] Similar conditions extended to the mainland, the bulk of the emigrants being peasants and agricultural laborers whose most pressing motive was poverty. In California they had the opportunity of remaining more fully in their own groups and occupations than in industrial areas in the eastern United States,[70] hence its attraction.

The countryside around San Leandro soon became one of their rallying points. They began arriving as early as 1854, when the district was just starting to be developed. Gradually they bought land, often paying exorbitant prices.[71] One of the investors was Antonio E. Silva, who in 1861 purchased land on the north side of San Leandro Creek, and founded a family which has been in the region ever since. In later years some of the members changed their names to "Carvalho," and others adopted the anglicized "Oakes." (It was in their honor that Oakes Boulevard in San Leandro was named.[72]) Some 20 Portuguese families were living in San Leandro by 1869, mostly engaged in diversified farming; 40 years later (1909), first and second generation Portuguese constituted two-thirds of the town's inhabitants.[73]

In that year (1909), the immigration commission made a field study of a group of these people, and found them extremely individualistic truck farmers. Of the 56 farms studied, 45 were owned and prosperous, their proprietors usually relying on hand labor for their crops and employing their own countrymen almost exclusively. They also largely married within their own group, although they associated with Americans and adopted English as a speaking language more readily than other nationalities, such as the Italians.[74] Later in the 20th century many of these truck farmers turned to dairying, and the Portuguese now produce much of the area's milk.[45]

In 1868 or 1869, certain Azoreans came from the San Francisco Bay area to work around Sacramento. They were joined by others, and took up bottom land along the Sacramento River which later became very valuable under reclamation. Almost without exception they came as young people and children, and stayed to become excellent vegetable farmers.[76] In the 1880's, Azoreans took up farming and sheep raising in Fresno County,[77] and about the same time Portuguese were found working in the vineyards of Santa Clara County.[78] Moving farther into the San Joaquin Valley, many took up leaseholds of from 120 to 600 acres in the early 1880's. Here, with larger acreages planted with field, feed, and grain crops, they operated in companies of 6 to 15 men, usually unmarried.[79]

Vegetable growing among the Portuguese in Alameda and Contra Costa counties continued through 3 or 4 generations,[80] and just south of San Francisco some began to specialize in the cultivation of artichokes.[81]

J. B. Avila, a native of the Azores, who came to California in 1883 and worked for a time in the vegetable fields near Niles and Mission San Jose, appears to have been responsible for a whole new industry. He missed one of his Azorean-diet staples, sweet potatoes, and resolved to do something about it. In 1888 he bought 20 acres of flood land near Merced at $1 an acre, whereas the going price for regular farmland in the area was $100. Here he planted some sweet potatoes from the Azores. With cultivation and irrigation, they multiplied rapidly from a small patch to 6 or 7 acres the next year. The sweet potato was soon accepted in the restaurants and hotels of San Francisco, and its cultivation spread to the Sacramento and San Joaquin valleys. From Avila's small beginning, the town of Atwater grew to be the center of the industry. Even after retiring from active farming, Avila continued to be an important potato buyer and exporter, and, as the "Father of the Sweet Potato Industry," was one of the first officers of the growers' association.[82]

After the turn of the century, Portuguese in great number were found among the fruit pickers of Sonoma County and the surrounding area, being, with the Japanese, the most numerous foreign group prior to World War I.[83] Yet by the mid-1920's the Portuguese accounted for only 2% of the total foreign workers in California labor-camps.[84]

As we have seen, the practice among Portuguese-speaking people in California was to acquire land and settle on it as rapidly as they could, with the result that, by 1920, about 15,000 first-generation Portuguese and Azoreans accounted, among themselves, for some 10% of the farms owned by foreign-born whites in California.[85]

Of great importance in recent years has been the place of the Portuguese in the dairy industry. Just before and after World War I, a group of dairy workers entered the United States and were hired as milkers in California. As their savings grew, they left their Dutch, Swiss, Danish, and other employers, and bought land and herds of their own. Today, the Portuguese constitute a major factor in the industry,[86] with representatives all over the state: in the north, around Eureka, they produce milk for the manufacture of evaporated milk, butter, cottage cheese, and ice cream; in southern California they constitute the second largest group in the industry, controlling 10 to 20% of the herds—the Dutch are first, with about 50%. About 150 Portuguese are engaged in dairying in the Los Angeles metropolitan area alone, and, of these, some 100 are first generation, many still illiterate. Nevertheless, on their 10 to 20 acres of land, they and their families own and milk herds of from 150 to 200 cows.

Portuguese activities in the San Joaquin Valley are widespread. Here they own stores and operate cattle-feed lots as well as engage in milking. In the upper valley, around manufacturing areas such as Los Banos, they maintain smaller herds of 25 to 30, but further south, around Tulare, the Portuguese are in the majority and own from 30 to 60 milch cows per farm. In ownership of their own land, they exceed even the Danish group with whom they compete. Lower in the San Joaquin Valley, from 70 to 75% of the dairy herds are said to be owned by Portuguese, their herds tending to exceed in size those of any other national group. From the fact that a quarter of the 38,-000,000 gallons of fluid milk sold each month in the state comes from this valley, and two-thirds of the 4,500,000 pounds of milk-fat, used a month in manufacturing, is also produced here, the commanding position of the Portuguese is readily apparent.[87] Several of the second generation have risen to high position in the industry. One, Dominic Veiga, has been secretary of one of the Los Angeles associations for many years; and the late Manuel Toste was for a long period manager of the Los Angeles Mutual Dairymen.

The general prosperity of the dairy industry has caused an almost complete change in the living habits of these Portuguese. On their arrival and for many years thereafter they often had been content to live at a mere subsistence level, with little interest in education or community participation. Now, with prosperity and some urging by their American-born children, comfortable and substantial homes have been built; they have encouraged the erection of churches in their midst; and their mutual benefit societies and the Roman Catholic Church (of which 98% are members) have given them social and community outlets. With the advent of greater numbers, they built their own places of worship: first at Centerville in 1888, and then in Oakland, Sacramento, East San Jose, Artesia, Point Loma, and East Oakland.[88] Also, a Portuguese Methodist Church was established in 1904 by the descendants of a group of Madeiran Protestants, who had settled in Illinois around 1850.[89]

One of their festivals, the Festa do Espirito Santo, is peculiarly Portuguese. It is celebrated annually on the Saturday preceding Whitsunday, and commemorates the prayers offered by the now-sainted 13th-century Queen Isabel of Portugal to the Holy Spirit, promising that a church would be built to His honor if the famine, from which her people were suffering, was relieved. Her prayers were answered by the arrival of ships laden with food. On this festive day a special sopa do Espirito Santo is prepared—beef soup poured over bread and mint leaves—and served to the populace.[90] Another holiday, observed by many, commemorates both the discovery of the Azores on April 3, 1432, and the death of St. Anthony on the same day 200 years earlier.[91]

Of the fraternal and mutual-benefits societies mentioned above, the first in the state was the Associaçao Portuguesa Protectora e Beneficiente, also known as the Benevolent Society of California. It was founded in 1868 in San Francisco, and was soon followed by a succession of eight others,[92] almost all of which provide disability as well as life insurance. In 1953 they represented an aggregate of 58,608 life-insurance policies to the value of $35,310,724, and assets—mostly in stocks and bonds—of $10,397,921. The Sociedade Portuguesa Rainha Santa Izabel, founded in 1898, has the largest number of policyholders —14,078—followed by the Benevolent Society with 10,022. Collectively, they are unique in that they are the only fraternal groups of any kind which were organized within the state and that are at present licensed to sell insurance. Other nationalities are represented by organizations which have their headquarters elsewhere; but, aside from the Germans who far exceed any, few measure up to the performance of the Portuguese mutual-benefit societies in California.[93]

Various other social clubs have existed. The "Clube Luso-Americano," the "Real Associaçao Benemerita Autonomica Micaelense," the "Clube Lusitania," and the "Clube Civico Portugues-Americano" (the last-named boasting over 500 members), all flourished in Oakland alone in the 1930's.[94]

While some three-fifths of the arrivals up to 1917 (when the U. S. congress passed legislation requiring a literacy test for immigrants) were unable to read or write, and have tended to remain so,[95] at least 20 newspapers have come and gone since the first, *A Voz Portugueza*, was established in San Francisco in 1880.[96] The only one which has survived thus far, aside from the bulletins of the various fraternal organizations, is the weekly *Jornal Português*, published in Oakland since 1924. These newspapers have represented the viewpoints of the Church, shades of political opinion, and the labor movements of the early 20th century, but they have also preserved close ties with the mother country. The papers whose readers were Azoreans, in particular, reported in detail the births, deaths, and social events of the various home islands in addition to vital statistics for the California community.[97]

The magazine *Portugalia*, published at irregular times from Christmas 1931 until June 1932, was devoted to club notices, advertisements, serialized histories of Portugal, a course in Portuguese for American readers, and an apparently unsuccessful subscription contest. It was merged with *O Portugal*, which continued for a short while longer.[98] Certain of the fraternal groups publish monthly newspapers or bulletins, but they deal primarily with association activities.

Portuguese-language radio programs, originating from time to time in the San Francisco Bay region through Oakland station KLX, KROW, and KTAB, have been broadcast for many years.[99] They were reported at one time from Long Beach,[100] and are still broadcast from KCOK in Tulare, the latter serving approximately 25,000 who speak this tongue in Tulare and Kings counties.[101]

The Portuguese people have found their place in the economy of California with a minimum of friction. Although many (4469 in one of the peak years of 1930) were located in the city of Oakland alone,[102] they have tended to move outward from the urban areas, and hence have had little conflict with established institutions.[103] Those who have remained in the cities have usually been domestic servants, plumbers, shopkeepers, etc., serving their own group.[104] There have been complaints, on the one hand, of their lack of enterprise compared to the Italians;[105] on the other hand, of an excess of energy: "Sometimes the small boy of the large family harnesses his smaller sister to a three-prong harrow and drives her between the rows of sugar beets and corn. . . ."[106]

With an almost continual movement toward the rural areas, it became progressively easier rather than more difficult for the Portuguese to retain their Old World way of life and family pattern, although compulsory education tends to break this down.[107] As a rule, children join their parents in family enterprises, and under this system there has been little need for the first generation to become assimilated in the American cultural and economic pattern.[108] Roughly, 50% of the first-generation Portuguese had arrived before 1910;[109] fewer after 1917 when literacy tests were applied; and only a scant number since 1930, when their quota was set at 440 per year.[110] In 1930, national figures indicate that only 19.3% of voting-age Portuguese had bothered to take out naturalization papers—or 28th among all nations in this respect.[111]

A survey in 1940 showed that nearly a third of the Portuguese (as distinct from the Azoreans) lived in rural Alameda County, and a quarter in similar sections of the San Joaquin Valley—especially in Merced, Stanislaus, San Joaquin, and King counties. There is one settlement of about 1000 foreign-born Portuguese in the Sacramento Valley, with others scattered nearby and in minor settlements in the north-coast counties.[112]

Portuguese-speaking people from the Azores are the most rural of all national groups in California. Alameda County (as of 1940) had almost twice as many as any other county; two-fifths lived in the San Joaquin Valley, and a third in Santa Clara County. Some 8% lived in the Sacramento Valley, and less than 5% in the north-coast counties.[113]

Although the numbers of Portuguese-speaking people in California have decreased due to death, returns to Portugal, and lack of fresh immigration, the statistical pattern over the years remains the same— the preponderance of rural (both farm and non-farm) over urban.[114]

The median value of a Portuguese rural, non-farm home in 1930 was $3494, which was the lowest among any group except the Spanish;[115] and they had the highest number of persons per family (3.7) next to the Spanish.[116] Small though they were, over 60% of Portuguese homes were paid for,[117] their owners in this way making themselves a permanent and stable part of the California scene. Especially since World War II, their standard of living has also kept pace with a general rise which has left behind no significant portion of the population. Thus the history of the Portuguese in California is not unique, but is rather an integral part of the larger story of the state's growth during the last century.

NOTES

1. In actual numbers: 7,211,825 and 1,021,356, respectively. *U. S. Census of Population; 1950 General Characteristics, California* ... (Washington, 1952), II, pt. 5, ch. B, Table 17, pp. 5-63. Tabulation refers to persons 21 years old and over.

2. From an anthropological viewpoint, Portuguese-speaking immigrants from the Azores were often part Flemish, with perhaps a negroid strain; those from the Portuguese mainland possesed some Moorish or Negro admixtures; and the Cape Verdeans (also known as "Bravas," from the island of Brava in the Cape Verde group, from which the majority came), being very dark in color were sometimes spoken of as "Black Portuguese." Census treatment varies over the years: Azoreans have sometimes been listed separately; in other instances, they have been included with "Western Isles," and Cape Verdeans in African (non-white) tabulations. (*See* Edlefsen, note 34 below, pp. 266-67.)

3. *The Population of California* (San Francisco, c. 1946), Table 68, p. 174.

4. Benedicta Quinino dos Santos, "Portuguese Yankees," *Américas*, V. (August 1953), 21.

5. Doris M. Wright, "The Making of Cosmopolitan California—an Analysis of Immigration, 1848-1870," *Calif. Hist. Soc. Quarterly*, XX (March 1941), 73.

6. Leo Pap, *Portuguese-American Speech* ... (New York, 1949), pp. 6-7.

7. *Ibid.*, p. 7. In 1886, J. B. Wilbor, U. S. vice-and-deputy consul general at Lisbon stated that emigration was discouraged; no official record was kept nor were departures for the U. S. noted in custom-house or police reports. U. S. Congress, 2nd sess., *House Ex. Doc.*, no. 157, (Washington, 1887), p. 323.

8. *U. S. Census*, note 1 above, Table 24, pp. 5-65; Table 5, pp. 3A-71, "Nativity and Parentage," Ser. P-E, No. 3A.

9. Henry R. Wagner, *Juan Rodríguez Cabrillo, Discoverer of the Coast of California* (San Francisco: Calif. Hist. Soc., 1941), pp. 10-14.

10. Charles E. Chapman, *A History of California: The Spanish Period* (New York, 1921), pp. 76-81, citing H. E. Bolton, *Spanish Exploration in the Southwest, 1542-1706* (New York, 1916).

11. Wagner, *op. cit.*, pp. 13-14, 20-23.

12. Federal Writers Project, *Santa Barbara, A Guide to the Channel City and Its Environs* (New York, 1940), p. 74.

13. Chapman, *op. cit.*, pp. 81-83; Robert Glass Cleland, *From Wilderness to Empire* (New York, 1944), p. 13.

14. Robert F. Heizer, *Archaeological Evidence of Sebastian Rodríguez Cermeno's California Visit in 1595* (San Francisco: Calif. Hist. Soc., 1942); Celestino Soares, *California and the Portuguese* (Lisbon, 1939), pp. 44-45; Chapman, *op. cit.*, pp. 116-23, 124ff.

15. Edwin C. Starks, "A History of California Shore Whaling," Calif. Bur. Marine Fisheries, *Fish Bulletin*, no. 6 (Sacramento, 1923), p. 6.

16. Note 3 above, p. 4.

17. *A Patria*, Oakland, Oct. 19, 1892, p. 4.

18. Anne B. Fisher, *No More a Stranger* (Stanford, 1946), p. 237.

19. *History of San Luis Obispo County* ... (Oakland, 1883), p. 387.

20. Ninth Census of the United States [1870], X, San Luis Obispo County, California (manuscript).

21. *Portugalia*, I, *passim*.

22. Emily Y. Mowry, "Portuguese Colonies in California, a Problem in Race Amalgamation," *Out West*, I (n. s.), Jan. 7, 1911, p. 116.

23. H. H. Bancroft, *History of California* (San Francisco, 1884-1890), II, 273, 393, 565; J. Gregg Layne, *Annals of Los Angeles* ... (San Francisco, 1935), p. 13.

24. Otto von Kotzebue, *A Voyage of Discovery* ..., tr. by H. E. Lloyd (London, 1821), I, 287.

25. Andrew F. Rolle, unpublished manuscript.

26. James Ohio Pattie, *The Personal Narrative of James Ohio Pattie of Kentucky* ..., in Reuben Gold Thwaites, ed., *Early Western Travels, 1748-1846* (Cleveland, 1904-1907), XVIII, 305.

27. Bancroft, *op. cit.*, II, 723.

28. J. Gregg Layne, "The First Census of the Los Angeles District," *Hist. Soc. South. Calif. Quarterly*, XVIII (Sept.-Dec. 1936), 83; "Padrón de la Ciudad de Los Angeles y su Jurisdicción, año 1836," manuscript leaves 25, 33 (photostats).

29. Solomon Nuñes Carvalho, *Incidents of Travel and Adventure in the Far West* ... (New York, 1857), pp. 246, 250; reprinted in 1954 by the Jewish Publication Society, Philadelphia. See also biographical notes on Dominguez and Pío Pico in Bancroft, *op. cit.*, II, 783, and IV, 778-79.

30. Carvalho, *op. cit.*, pp. 244, 250.

31. 61st Cong., 2nd Sess., *Sen. Ex. Doc.*, no. 756 (Washington, 1911), "Statistical Review of Immigration, 1820-1910," III, Table 9, pp. 14-44.

32. Wright, note 5 above, XIX (Dec. 1940), 343.

33. Note 3 above, p. 68. In addition to loss of records (while en route and by fire, *ibid.*, p. 4), relating to the very localities where the Portuguese were heavily concentrated, it is probable that many should have been listed as "Azoreans" instead of "Portuguese."

34. Pap, note 6 above; John B. Edlefsen, "Portuguese Americans," in Francis J .Brown and Joseph S. Roucek, eds., *One America* (New York, 1937: 3rd ed.), p. 265; Wright, *op. cit.*, XX (March 1941), 73.

35. Pap, *op. cit.*, p. 5.

36. [Joseph Berger], *In Great Waters, the Story of the Portuguese Fishermen*, by Jeremiah Digges [pseud.] (New York, 1951), p. xvii.

37. Gerald A. Estep, "Portuguese Assimilation in Hawaii and California," *Sociology and Social Research*, XXVI (Sept.-Oct., 1941), 61.

38. Pap, *op. cit.*, p. 8.

39. Berger, *op. cit.*, p. xvi.

40. Starks, note 15 above, p. 17.

41. *Loc. cit.*

42. *Loc. cit.*

43. *Ibid*, p. 18.

44. Fisher, note 18 above, p. 237.

45. *History S. Luis Obispo Co....*, *loc. cit.*

46. Benjamin Hayes, "Emigrant Notes" (manuscript, Bancroft Library).

47. Starks, *op. cit.*, pp. 11, 21.

48. *Ibid.*, pp. 26-27; *History S. Luis Obispo Co....*, *op. cit.*, p. 333; U. S. Com. Fish and Fisheries, *Report for the Year 1888* (Washington, 1888), XVI, 52.

49. Starks, *op. cit.*, p. 20; W[illiam] L. Scofield, "California Fishing Report," Calif. Bur. Marine Fisheries, *Fish Bulletin*, no. 96 (Sacramento, 1954), pp. 16-17. (Dates given are approximate.)

50. U. S. Com. Fish..., note 48 above, pp. 35, 43-44.

51. Albert S. Evans, *A la California, Sketch of the Golden State* (San Francisco, 1873), p. 44.

52. Note 50 above, pp. 52, 55.

53. Charles M. Scammon, *The Marine Mammals of the North-Western Coast of North America* (San Francisco, 1874), p. 250.

54. *Ibid.*, p. 251.

55. U. S. Com. Fish..., *Report for the Year ending June 30, 1893* (Washington, 1893), XIX, 194.

56. *Ibid.*, 1888, XVI, 76.

57. *Ibid.*, 1893, XIX, 205.

58. David Starr Jordan, "The Fisheries of California," *Overland Monthly*, XX (2nd. ser., Nov. 1892), p. 478.

59. U. S. Com. Fish..., *Report*, 1888, XVI, 21, 34.

60. *Ibid.*, 1893, XIX, 153, 195.

61. Note 20 above, VI, San Diego County, 461-531 (manuscript).

62. U. S. Com. Fish..., *Report*, 1893, XIX, 189.

63. In 1947-48, the Portuguese around San Diego numbered 318 out of a total of 2405 so employed. Calif. Bur. Marine Fisheries, "The Commercial Fish Catch of California... years 1948-1949," *Fish Bulletin*, no. 80 (Sacramento, 1951), pp. 202-203. These are, of course, first generation; a great many of the U. S.-born are of Portuguese extraction.

64. Scofield, note 49 above, p. 152.

65. Federal Writers Project, *San Diego, a California City* [San Diego, c. 1937], pp. 14, 46, 57.

66. Edward J. P. Davis, *Historical San Diego* ([San Diego], 1953), p. 103.

67. *Fish Bulletin*, note 63 above, p. 17.

68. Calif. Bur. Marine Fisheries, "The Commercial Fish Catch of California... Year 1952..." *Fish Bulletin*, no. 95 (Sacramento, 1954), p. 53.

69. 48th Cong., 2nd Sess., *House Ex. Doc.*, no. 54, pt 2 (Washington, 1885), "U. S. Consular Reports, Labor in Europe," pp. 1650-51.

70. Pap, *op. cit.*, pp. 11-14.

71. 61st Cong., 2nd sess., *Sen. Ex. Doc.*, no. 633, pt. 25 (Washington, 1911), "Immigrants in Industries . . . Agriculture," II, 489-91; Reginald R. Stuart, *San Leandro . . . a History* (San Leandro, 1951), pp. 143-44.

72. Stuart, *ibid.*, p. 163.

73. "Immigrants in Industries . . .," note 71 above, p. 489; *cf.* Pap, *op. cit.*, p. 8.

74. "Immigrants . . .," *ibid.*, pp. 293, 316-18

75. Federal Writers Project, *California, a Guide to the Golden State* (New York, 1940), p. 599.

76. "Immigrants . . .," *op. cit.*, pp. 326, 330, 341-57.

77. *Ibid.*, p. 567; Virginia E. Thickens, "Pioneer Agricultural Colonies of Fresno County," *Calif. Hist. Soc. Quarterly*, XXV (June 1946), 175.

78. William H. Bishop, *Old Mexico and Her Lost Provinces* (New York, 1889), pp. 359-60.

79. *Ibid.*, pp. 412-13.

80. Federal Writers Project, *San Francisco, the Bay and its Cities* (New York, 1940), p. 379.

81. Federal Writers Project, *Festivals in San Francisco* ([Stanford], 1939), pp. 26-27.

82. Theotonio I. Martins, "Batatas Doces," *Portugalia*, I (Jan. 15, 1932), 6.

83. Calif. Com. Immigration and Housing, "Report on Unemployment," suppl. to *First Annual Report*, December 9, 1914 (Sacramento, 1915), p. 59.

84. Calif. Com. Immigration . . ., note 83 above, *Annual Report*, Jan. 1925 (Sacramento, 1925), p. 16; *idem, Annual Report*, Jan. 1927 (Sacramento, 1927), p. 27.

85. *U. S. Fourteenth Census . . . 1920* (Washington, 1922), VI, pt. 3, "Agriculture," Table 16, p. 337. Azoreans are presumably included in this tabulation. No other figures are available for comparison. In prior censuses, the Portuguese were included with other countries, and in subsequent ones no breakdown is made by nationality.

86. Information on diary industry obtained, unless otherwise stated, from personal interview on April 22, 1955, with Mr. Ned Clinton, mgr., Protected Milk Producers Assoc., Paramount, Calif.

87. Average figures from the *Dairy Information Bulletin*, XI (Dec. 1954), *passim.* For the importance of the Portuguese, *cf.* Carey McWilliams, *California: the Great Exception* (New York, 1949), p. 114.

88. Soares, note 14 above, pp. 64-65.

89. Pap, *op. cit.*, p. 155 note. Reference to standard works has not revealed any Portuguese among the many missionaries who visited California during the provincial period.

90. Note 81 above, *loc. cit.*

91. *Portugalia*, I (Feb. 29, 1932), 4; *cf.* Easter issue, I (March 1932), 2, 3, 16.

92. Soares, *op. cit.*, p. 63.

93. Calif. Dept. of Insurance, *Eighty-sixth Annual Report ... for the Year ended December 31, 1953* ([Sacramento], n. d.), pp. 173-75, 180-81, 208 ff. Their disability insurance operations reflected a 33% loss.

94. Advertisements and notices, *Portugalia*, I (Jan. 15-Feb. 29, 1932), *passim.*

95. "Immigrants in Industries," note 71 above, p. 492; Urban T. Holmes, "Portuguese Americans," in Francis J. Brown and Joseph S. Roucek, eds., *Our Racial and National Minorities* (New York, 1937), p. 397.

96. A government survey in 1909 indicated that most Portuguese subscribed, some even to two or more newspapers. "Immigrants in Industries...," *op. cit.*, p. 355.

97. For names of Portuguese-language newspapers published in California, *see* Soares, *op. cit.*, p. 62; Common Council for American Unity, *Foreign Language Publications in the United States* (New York, 1952); W. P. A., *History of Foreign Journalism in San Francisco* [Vol. I of series entitled, "History of Journalism in San Francisco"] (San Francisco, 1939), pp. 68-69.

98. *Portugalia*, XII [I], June 1932, p. 4.

99. Holmes, note 95 above, p. 399; advertisement, *Portugalia*, I, Dec. 1931, p. 11. KTAB, operated in the 1930's by Portuguese Broadcasters [firm name], is no longer in existence.

100. Estep, note 37 above, p. 61.

101. Letter, May 1955, from J. Alan Rinehart, station manager: "We consider the Portuguese purchasing power in Tulare and Kings Counties to be far in excess of the normal per capita due to the many Portuguese dairymen and cotton-cattle ranchers."

102. *U. S. Fifteenth Census ... 1930 ...,* "California, Composition and Character of the Population" (Washington, 1933), p. 41.

103. Estep, *op. cit.*, p. 68.

104. Holmes, *op. cit.*, p. 401.

105. *Ibid.*

106. Mowry, note 22 above, p. 115.

107. Estep, *op. cit.*, p. 64.

108. Interview with Mr. Ned Clinton, April 22, 1955, note 86 above.

109. *The Population of California*, note 3 above, Table 24, p. 84.

110. Edlefsen, note 34 above, p. 266.

111. Marian Schisby, "Naturalization in the United States," in Brown and Roucek, note 95 above, p. 678. In the U. S. as a whole, only 498 Portuguese took out second papers between 1923 and 1928; 759 in 1929-36; but in 1937, alone, there were 1304 who completed this step. Holmes, *op. cit.*, p. 400.

112. *The Population of California*, *op. cit.*, p. 159.

113. *Ibid.*

114. *Fifteenth Census*, note 102 above, p. 12; and *Population of California, op. cit.*, Table 61, p. 163: as of 1940, *total urban*, 11,707; *total rural*, 17,921.

115. *Fifteenth Census* ... "Special Report on Foreign Born White Families by Country of Birth of Head ...," *op. cit.*, Table 16, p. 80.

116. *Ibid.*, Table 17, p. 95.

117. *Ibid.*, Table 14, p. 59.

118. Among the localities in California, whose names are suggestive of Portuguese activities, are: "Portuguese Bend," near San Pedro; and, in the mining area, "Portuguese Flat"; also, former "Portuguese," now "Hazel Creek." Erwin G. Gudde, *California Place Names* (Berkeley, 1949), p. 270.

The Portuguese Element in New England

Henry R. Lang

THE PORTUGUESE ELEMENT IN NEW ENGLAND.

AMONG the foreign elements of Romanic speech settled in the United States, the Portuguese is the one which so far seems to have almost entirely escaped the notice of the public. Every one knows of the existence of large numbers of Canadians in New England, of the French settlements in Louisiana, of the Spanish in Texas, New Mexico, and California, of the Italians in New Orleans and in Eastern cities like Boston and New York ; but only few seem to realize the fact that every year from fifteen hundred to two thousand Portuguese men and women are landed in Boston and New Bedford, and that there is a large colony of them in California, supporting numerous churches, besides a literary review and a weekly journal ; that there is a Portuguese settlement in Erie, Pa., also maintaining a weekly paper ; and, especially, that in New England alone we have not less than seven Portuguese colonies, numbering at present more than twenty thousand. Of those seven colonies a large one is in Providence, R. I., while the other six belong to the State of Massachusetts. Naming the latter in the order of their numerical strength and importance, they are the following : — New Bedford, Boston (including Cambridge), Taunton, Fall River, Provincetown, and Gloucester. For the most part these Portuguese colonists are natives of the Azores, chiefly from the islands of Fayal, Pico, St. George, and Flores ; only few are from Madeira, and still smaller is the number of colored Portuguese from the Cape Verde islands.

What, it is natural to ask, brought about the immigration of these islanders into New England? And when did it begin? No official records exist to answer these questions, but from the statements of some of the oldest colonists it may be inferred with sufficient certainty that the first Portuguese arrived in New England some sixty or more years ago as sailors on the whaling vessels sent out from New Bedford, then the most important whaling port of the East. Hence it is that New Bedford can boast of the oldest as well as the largest Azorian colony in the New England States. Later, it was the report of the liberties and opportunities offered in America to industrious people that induced the over-taxed and poverty-stricken islanders to try their fortunes here, and set in motion that wave of emigration to the United States which is still on the increase. The young man thus escapes the military service which means to him an exile of many years in the barracks of continental Portugal, with the gloomy prospect of at the end returning home without a penny to support him in the autumn of his life. The young maiden leaves

her native village in the expectation of better pay for her needle and
straw work, for the delicate quality of which the Azorian women
have long been famous. Most of them, no doubt, consider the absence from their native land as an exile, and intend returning as
soon as they shall have saved up their "little pile;" but, having
once enjoyed the benefits of the free institutions and the many
opportunities of this country, and become more or less imbued with
the spirit of American life, they generally conclude to make the
United States their permanent home.

The Portuguese colony in New Bedford being the oldest as well
as the largest and most prosperous in the State, it may, for the sake
of brevity, serve us for illustrating the material and intellectual
condition of the whole Portuguese element in New England. The
Azorians occupy almost the entire southern section of the city of
New Bedford, and a goodly part of the western section. The Portuguese quarter is popularly known as "Fayal." According to the
register of their church, they number now over seven thousand in
the city itself, while some two hundred live in the neighboring
country on farms partly owned by themselves. There are also Portuguese residents in the adjacent towns of Dartmouth, Acushnet, and
Fairhaven. The large majority of them, belonging chiefly to the illiterate class, are employed in our numerous cotton-mills and other
factories, in the lumber-yards, and in the service of the city street
department. The more intelligent of the young men, unwilling to
submit to the drudgery of the work in the mills, choose hairdressing
as their profession. This is done even by most of those who at
home enjoyed the advantages of a college course. Unable to speak
English, they find it almost impossible in this country to turn to
profitable account what little information of practical value they may
have acquired in a Portuguese college, mediæval as this latter still is
in its aims and methods of instruction. But comparatively low as
their present position is, they constitute the most wide-awake element of the colony. It is among the barbers that we must generally
look for the leading members of the social and other societies of our
colonies, such as the Club Social Lusitano and the Sociedade Dra-
matica of New Bedford, and the Club Social Dom Luis I. of Boston.
Many of the Portuguese settlers are engaged in fishing, as especially the colonies of Provincetown and Gloucester. The women earn
their living either in the mills or as servant-girls and seamstresses.
All, both men and women, are looked upon by the community as a
valuable accession to the laboring population. They are industrious, thrifty, honest, and as a rule far more refined in their senti-
ments and manners than the Canadians. Some of the older residents
among them have acquired considerable wealth and own handsome

houses. The New Bedford colony supports a substantial church in which the Roman Catholic service is conducted in Portuguese by three priests, one of whom is also in charge of the colony at Fall River. They have a charitable society which a few years ago erected a spacious building called "The Monte Pio Hall." It is in this building that the social life of the colony centres, where the celebrations of national holidays, balls, dramatic performances, and other entertainments take place. On such occasions, one cannot but admire the decorum and courteous demeanor observed by these people. Several of the other colonies, such as Boston and Taunton, have their own churches and social clubs, but it is New Bedford that has always given the initiative for any demonstration of national spirit. It is here that the Club Social Lusitano, on the 1st of December of every year, celebrates by a sumptuous banquet and a ball the liberation of Portugal from Spanish rule in 1640, a celebration to which delegates from the other New England colonies and the Portuguese consul in Boston are invited. It is in New Bedford, again, that some ten years ago a Portuguese weekly, called "O Luso-Americano," was published, which unfortunately, enjoyed only a very short existence. A similar enterprise was started a year ago, with the title, "O Novo Mundo" (The New World), and continues to be published.

But if the maintenance of a Portuguese church, the existence of clubs devoted to the observance of national festivals, and the cultivation of dramatic art may be considered as so many laudable signs of the loyalty of our colonists to their native land, it is none the less evident that they are undergoing a rapid process of assimilation to their new surroundings. The inexorable struggle for existence, to which they are subjected almost immediately upon their arrival here, the novelty of their occupations and their every-day life, the more or less intimate contact into which they are thrown with the far more numerous English-speaking population, with its practical, sober way of looking at things, — all these manifold influences unite in producing a marked change in their habits of speaking and thinking. Their new experiences suggest to them ideas which they had not been called upon to express in their mother-tongue, and they are forced to resort to the medium of the English language, by which alone they may hope to make themselves intelligible to all ; their new surroundings fail to recall to their minds many of the traditions which had ever been associated with their former homes and haunts, and the freshness of these traditions gradually fades away. With them must needs disappear much of the native vocabulary which was embodied in them. In order, however, to appreciate Azorian speech and folk-lore, such as it survives in our midst, it will be necessary to inquire briefly into what it is and has been in its original home.

Whether the Azores were discovered in 1350 or a century later, and by whom, does not concern us here; suffice it to say that their occupation and colonization by the Portuguese began in 1436 and was practically accomplished in 1457. The speech of the Azorians, which divides itself into two main groups, one represented by St. Michael, the other by Fayal, reflects on the whole the middle and northern Portuguese of the fourteenth and fifteenth centuries, and has suffered no perceptible influence either from the strong influx of the Flemish at the end of the fifteenth century or from other foreign, notably Moorish, elements. As all colonial speech, the Azorian is markedly archaic in its nature. And as the Azorians, in their isolated position, have preserved to us an older stage of the Portuguese language, so are their folk-songs the most ancient in the whole domain of Portuguese tradition, their origin dating back to that epoch of Portuguese history previous to the fifteenth century when poetic creation was still free from literary influences. These folk-songs naturally divide themselves into two main classes, one purely traditional, the other still in constant elaboration. The first class comprises the traditional, historical songs such as the ballad or romance, which, though portraying events and conditions which have long ago ceased to exist, are still piously repeated by the people. To illustrate: in one of these ballads, collected by Theophilo Braga on the island of St. Michael, we find the following passage: —

> Hei — de atar o meu cabello,
> E virá — lo para traz,
> Com uma fitinha vermelha
> Que me deu o meu rapaz.

Roughly translated, this is: "I shall tie my hair, I shall gather it in a coil with a scarlet ribbon which my lover gave me." Here we have an allusion, frequent in these songs, to an ancient Portuguese law, according to which a single woman had to leave her hair flowing, a married woman was to wear it gathered in a knot in token of her conjugal submission, and a widow had to wear it covered under a cap.

It is highly significant for the venerable age of insular tradition, that on the Azores the historical songs are popularly called *Aravias*, a designation derived from *Arabe*, and still bearing witness to the fact that at the beginning of Portuguese nationality and when these ballads were in process of creation, the Arabic was the common vernacular of the Christian as well as of the Moor; the modern term *romance* marking the ascendency of the neo-Latin idioms over their predecessor. To this may be added that in Fayal a kind of rhyme sung by the children is called *Aravenga*, a name which also testifies to the indebtedness of the ancient Portuguese to the Moor.

While many of these historical songs are still remembered by our Luso-Americans, they have ceased to be repeated by them, and are rapidly passing into oblivion.

In connection with this traditional, historical poetry must be mentioned a form of popular drama which has survived on the Azores. It is called *Mouriscada*, a term derived from *Mouro*, Moor. The representation consists in a dialogue and a sham battle between a Christian and a Moor, thus commemorating the reconquest of the Spanish peninsula from the Arabs. It is therefore a parallel to the Italian *teatro dei marionetti*, the well-known *opra* of the Sicilians, of the character of which there is so welcome an illustration in the *Teatro italiano* on North Street in Boston. It is greatly to be regretted that the *Mouriscada*, the popular theatre of the Azorians, should have been abandoned by our Azorian colonists, who, perhaps owing to the influence of their clergy, substitute for it on their excellently conducted stage in New Bedford, representations of a decidedly ecclesiastical and literary character.

The second class of popular poetry comprises those songs which, though in a large part also traditional, are still a living growth, echoing the actual life of the people by whom they are sung and embodying their loves and hates. It is the lyric poetry of the Portuguese people. As these love-songs belong to the few elements of insular tradition which, to a limited extent at least, still form a vital part in the social life of our American colonies, it may be well to give here a brief characterization of their nature.

The *cantiga d'amor*, or love-song, is an octosyllabic quatrain, the second and fourth lines of which rhyme. These quatrains have two distinct, antithetical parts, the first two lines containing as a rule a general idea, mostly drawn from nature or natural objects, whereas the last two lines express a particular idea, which stands in a certain antithesis to the first and applies to a given case. To illustrate : —

Já lá vae o sol abaixo,	There already the sun goes down,
Já não nasce onde nascia :	The light of day has passed away :
Já não dou as minhas fallas	Already I have ceased to speak
A quem as dava algum dia.	To whom I used to speak one day.

It will be noticed that the sentiment of this quatrain is as direct as it is simple. The antithesis or comparison between the two parts is clear. As the sun has gone down and is no longer seen, so has my love for you disappeared. The same is the case in the following instance : —

Candeia que não dá luz,	Candle which gives no light,
Não se espeta na parede :	Never is hung from the wall :
O amor que não é firme,	Love which is not strong,
Não se faz mais caso d'elle.	Never is noticed at all.

Often the comparison between the two parts is so perfect as to result in the complete absorption of the two terms in one, in an image. Such is the case in the following quatrain, in which the beloved, but inaccessible, woman is identified with the rose: —

Oh ! que linda rosa branca	Amor perfeito plantado
Aquella roseira tem !	Em qualquer parte, enverdece ;
De baixo ninguem lhe chega,	Só em peito d'homem vil
Lá cima não vae ninguem.	Amor perfeito fenece.

Here the two terms of comparison, the woman and the flower, blend in the word *rosa*, " rose," which is also a proper name. Quatrains like this one, wherein the comparison results in a sort of play on words, are numerous in the lyric poetry of the Spanish peninsula.

Even in quatrains in which the comparison is not perfectly clear, or where it has become quite obscured, the people invariably make a pause after the second line, showing that they are conscious of this formal distinction.

Satirical epigrams are also clothed in the metrical form of these love-songs. Only one instance of this kind may here be quoted, as illustrating very strikingly the conception in which the social position of woman is held by the people : —

Tambem o mar é casado,	Even the sea is married,
Tambem o mar tem mulher ;	Even the sea has a wife,
É casado com a areia,	He is married to the seashore,
Bate n'ella quando quer !	He beats it whene'er he likes.[1]

These songs are invariably accompanied by the *viola* or the *rabeca*, the favorite musical instruments of the islander, and are sung to the *Chama-Rita*, the most popular dance of the Azorians, which is still continued in our American colonies.

Equally rich as in folk-songs is the Azorian in folk-tales, many of which are yet to be collected, in nursery-rhymes, riddles, and superstitions. Here also the insular tradition has preserved much that is no longer remembered in Portugal. Of the popular tales, especially the so-called *contos da carouchinha*, and of nursery-rhymes, a goodly number may still be heard in the homes of our Azorian colonists, by the cradle or the fireside. Many of them, however, while they are still remembered for a time, are no longer repeated or observed. This is especially true of the superstitions, the number and intensity of which corresponds to the social as well as the intellectual condition of man. The greater the number of accidents to which men are exposed, the greater the dependence of their physical and moral welfare on agents which they cannot control, the greater, therefore, their fear of the unknown, the more intense will be their supersti-

[1] Cf. J. Leite de Vasconcellos, *Revista lusitana*, i. pp. 145, 176.

tious beliefs. Now, such is precisely the state of mind which plagues, famines, earthquakes, and similar causes have produced in the inhabitants of the Spanish peninsula and of the Azores. Hence the intensity and tenacity of superstition there, hence also its comparatively rapid disappearance here, where fear-inspiring natural phenomena are far less numerous, and where the social medium gives a much freer scope to the independent action of the individual. Still, it must not be supposed that superstitious belief and practice entirely cease to exist in our Portuguese colonies. They do not show themselves as openly as in their former home, but they may continue to play, in many a case, the determining part in the choice of a course of action. As a clue to the mental characteristics of our colonists, the superstitions surviving among them are entitled to a careful study.

Here follow a few specimens of Azorian folk-lore, collected among our Luso-Americans, in addition to the popular folk-songs which have been spoken of before.

There is a Portuguese proverb which says : " A fé é que nos salva, e não o pao da barca ;" in English : "It is faith that saves us, not the wood of the ship." This adage is the remainder of a popular story still current in the northern part of Italy, but unknown in Portugal. Two versions of it exist in Azorian traditions, of which the one from St. Michael, being the more perfect, will be given here : A maiden who was very ill and had lost all faith in the physicians, asked her lover, who was going to Jerusalem, to bring her from the holy city a piece of wood from the Saviour's cross, which she wished to take in wine, to see if it might cure her. The young man, having forgotten the request of his betrothed, cut a piece of wood from the ship in which he was returning home, to deceive the girl. Finding, after some time, that she had really taken it and was entirely cured, he exclaimed: "It is faith that cures us, not the wood from the ship."

The following game, unknown in Portugal, is quite popular among Azorian children, especially in Fayal. The words are almost all unintelligible, a fact which shows that they must be very old.

> Minzin Minzol,
> Cazim Cazol,
> Por mor de ti,
> José Manzol.
> Cascaranhas.
> Malaguetas.
> Tringue lá fóra.

The game is played as follows : A girl holds out her apron with one hand and all her companions take hold of the edge of the apron with two fingers of each hand. The girl thereupon recites the rhymes, one line for each hand, moving her finger from right to left.

The hand which is touched at the last line — *Tringue lá fóra* — must be withdrawn.

The Azorians are fond of lending zest and humor to their familiar conversation by jocular sayings in which their language is very rich. Thus to the question : What time is it ? (*Que horas são?*) the playful reply is : *Horas de comer pão ;* that is, Time to eat bread. To the favorite exclamation, *Paciencia !* they answer: *Morreu o pae a Vicencia.* A narration interrupted by *então,* "then," is jocularly continued by the rhyme : *Sardinhas com pão,* "Sardines with bread," very much as in English a person saying, "Well, well !" is playfully asked : "How many wells make a river ? "

To mention, finally, a characteristic gesture, the Azorian woman is accustomed to express her high appreciation of the value of an object, a present for instance, by taking the flap of her right ear between the forefinger and the thumb and exclaiming : *Está d'aqui !* that is to say : It is from here ! This gesture plainly points back to the presence of the Moors in Portugal, whose women wore their most precious ornaments on their ears.

Having examined some of the aspects of Azorian folk-lore, such as it survives among us, it now remains for us briefly to consider the changes which the native speech of the Luso-American is undergoing. The influence of the new condition of things shows itself in the vocabulary, in the accent, and finally in the total loss of the ability of speaking Portuguese. The vocabulary shows a constantly increasing mixture with English elements, of which only a few instances can be mentioned here: *bordar,* "to board," for *hospedar ; bordo,* " boarder," for *hospede ; bins,* "beans," for *feijões ; carpete,* "carpet," for *tapete ; o bebe tá chulipe,* "the baby is asleep;" *estima,* "steamer," for *vapor ; gairete,* "garret," for *airiques ; notas,* " notice," for *noticia ; offas,* "office," for *escritorio ; salreis,* " celery," for *aipo.* Often it is the signification of a Portuguese word which is affected by the influence of the English. Thus our Luso-American speaks of *ter um frio,* "to have a cold," the proper Portuguese expression being : *estar constipado.* Or again he says : *Esta gravata olha bem,* "this cravat *looks* well," where *olhar,* "to behold," is a direct translation of the English "to look," meaning "to appear" as well as "to behold." Interesting is the word *"espalha-grace,"* wherein one may recognize a popular attempt to interpret the English term " sparrow-grass," which in its turn is a popular etymology for "asparagus." There are cases in which the Portuguese idiom influences the English. Thus an English-speaking Azorian may be heard to say : " I had cabbages for dinner," the form *cabbages* being due to the plural form of the corresponding Portuguese term, *couves.*

But not only the speech, nay the very names of our Azorian colonists are Anglicized, though it is the proper name which as a rule longest resists the destructive influence of foreign elements. This custom of Anglicizing their names dates back to the earliest times of these colonies when the Portuguese sailors commonly adopted the names of their American captains. To quote a few instances: the family name *Luiz* is disguised in the English *Lewis*, *Mauricio* in *Morris*, *Pereira* in *Perry*, *Rodriguez* in *Rodgers*. Still more. The Portuguese Christian name *Joaquim*, quite common among the Azorians, is by the practical English mind interpreted as representing the two English names Joe King, an appellation readily adopted by our Portuguese colonists. That these latter should be so willing to abandon their real names will appear less strange when we consider that in their old as well as in their new home they were wont to be called by nicknames in preference to their first or family names. A few years ago an old man was living down on Hanover Street in Boston, whom every one knew by his nickname, "*Bate-canellas*," "Old Knock-knee," but hardly any one by his family name, *Carvalho.*

The most potent factor in Americanizing our Azorian colonists is the American school. The Azorians are keenly sensible of their want of education and seize with eagerness every opportunity to learn. Whereas the Canadians everywhere maintain their parochial schools, the Azorians, fervent Roman Catholics as they are, send their children to the American public school. In consequence of the education they here receive, they become estranged from their inherited traditions and their native speech, which most of them cease to speak; but much as this loss may be regretted, we must rejoice in the consideration that it is more than outweighed by what they gain in return. To the many sterling qualities, such as kindness of heart and delicacy of sentiment, which they already possess, our Luso-Americans now add a mind stored with useful information and better trained to cope with the many difficult problems of American life. Formerly obliged to earn their living by hard and confining manual labor, they now enter into a wider sphere of activity and usefulness and rise in the social scale. From whatever point of view we may consider our Portuguese colonists, they bid fair to become a highly respectable element of our population, more and more able to contribute to, and hence worthy to participate in the benefits of the material and intellectual progress of our commonwealth.

APPENDIX.

As the preceding article was only intended to be read as a short lecture, not to be published, it is not clothed in that rigid form which a treatise appearing in a scientific journal should invariably have. The author may therefore be pardoned for making here a few additions and corrections.

1. The lines beginning *Hei de atar o meu cabello* are a lyric quatrain and should be mentioned in the section treating of lyric poetry.

2. For the remarks on the quatrain, cf. J. Leite de Vasconcellos' article on *cantigas populares* in the *Revista lusitana*, i. pp. 143–6 and 176.

Of two quatrains, no translation is given in the above paper. Here it is : —

O how white and sweet the rose
That blooms on yonder briar :
From below it can't be reached,
Nor attained by climbing higher.

Perfect love, whene'er you plant it,
Sweetly blooms in every part :
Perfect love will fade away
Only in the villain's heart.

In the second quatrain there is a play of words on the expression *amor perfcito*, " perfect love," which is used both in its ordinary literal sense and as a popular name of the flower which we call " pansy."

It need hardly be said that the English renderings given were solely meant to convey to the audience some idea of the form and feeling of these quatrains, but claim no other merit whatsoever.

3. In conclusion, we may here mention the following publications as bearing on the Folk-Lore of the Azores : —

THEOPHILO BRAGA : Cantos populares do Archipelago açoriano. Porto, 1869. — O Povo portuguez nos seus costumes, crenças e tradições. Lisboa, 1885. 2 vols. — O Conde de Luz-bella. Fórmas populares do theatro portuguez. In : Revista lusitana, i. pp. 20–30. — Ampliações do Romanceiro das ilhas dos Açores. Revista lusitana, i. pp. 99–116. — Cancioneiro popular das ilhas dos Açores. Revista lusitana, ii. pp. 1–14.

F. ADOLPHO COELHO : Revista d'Ethnologia e de Glottologia. Lisboa, 1880–1881. 4 fasciculos.

FRANCISCO D'ARRUDA FURTADO : Materiaes para o estudo anthropologico dos povos açorianos. Ponta Delgada, 1884.

HENRY R. LANG : Notas de philologia portuguesa. In : Zeitschrift für romanische Philologie, xiii. pp. 213–216. — Tradições populares açorianas. In : Zeitschrift für rom. Philol. xiii. pp. 217–224 and 416–430. — Tradições populares açorianas. In : Revista lusitana, ii. pp. 46–52. Respigas do vocabulario açoriano. Ibid. pp. 52–55.

Henry R. Lang.

Traditional Ballads Among the Portuguese in California

Joanne B. Purcell

Traditional Ballads Among the Portuguese in California: Part I

THERE HAS BEEN a continual immigration of the Portuguese people to California since the 1780's. Between 1780 and 1880 Portuguese were attracted to California by the whaling industry and in 1848 by the Gold Rush. Since then they have turned to cattle ranching and dairy-farming in the San Joaquin Valley, to salmon fishing along the Sacramento River, to mining and lumbering in Mendocino and Fort Bragg, and to tuna and albacore fishing in Southern California. Oakland is the "unofficial Portuguese capital in California,"[1] and "colonias" are established especially in Newark, San Leandro, Hayward, San Diego, San Jose, and Santa Clara.

This is the first of a two-part article.

My field-work among the Portuguese in California has been greatly facilitated by the support and cooperation of Alberto Lemos, publisher and editor of the *Jornal Português* of Oakland, and George M. De Medeiros, general manager of the Dairyman's Cooperative Creamery Association of Tulare. The initial contacts which they obtained for me were of inestimable value in laying the groundwork of my collecting project. Such directors of Portuguese radio programs as Joaquim Esteves of San Jose, Joaquim Correa of Tulare, and Agnelo Clementino of San Rafael offered additional contacts. I received valuable support from Rev. Lourenco Avila of San Diego, Father Carlos Macedo of the Five Wounds Church in San Jose, and Sister Lourdes Marie of the Five Wounds Convent in San Jose. Our informants and singers have been very generous with their time and hospitality and have made an effort to answer many questions, to understand the nature of the project, and to contribute to the collection.

I am very grateful to Dr. D. K. Wilgus, chairman of the Folklore and Mythology Group at UCLA, who granted the use of tapes and equipment necessary for my field-work; to my husband, R. C. Purcell, of the Dept. of Music at California Institute of the Arts in Los Angeles for transcribing and annotating the music; to Dr. A. Machado da Rosa of the Dept. of Spanish and Portuguese at UCLA for his interest and advice, and to his colleague, E. Mayone Dias, for spending many hours poring over the transcriptions with me and answering innumerable questions; to Dr. Wayland D. Hand, director of the Center for the Study of Comparative Folklore and Mythology at UCLA, who has given me assistance in editing this article and who expressed great interest in the project; and to Dr. S. G. Armistead, now at the University of Pennsylvania, who gave me invaluable direction in analyzing the ballads collected and in determining their correlation to the Pan-Hispanic and Pan-European ballad traditions.

[1] A. M. Vaz, *The Portuguese in California* (Oakland, 1965), p. 63.

[1]

The original immigrants brought many traditions of the "old country" with them and have kept them alive through participation in family reunions, religious festivals, banquets, folk-dances, and other functions, through fraternal societies, brotherhoods, and churches, and through Portuguese newspapers and radio programs which have kept them informed of activities here and abroad.

The informants who have contributed to my collection of Portuguese traditional ballads from California immigrated primarily from Madeira Island, e.g., Mrs. Maria I. Santos and Mrs. Dolores Pequeno, Faial (Azores), São Jorge (Azores), and Pico (Azores), e.g., the Goulart family; others are from Portugal and other areas, e.g., Mrs. Maria Santos (born in Cascais, near Lisbon, and raised in Oliveira do Hospital, District of Coimbra, Portugal) and Sister Yvonne Barros (born and raised in Pangim, Goa, India).

My informants represent two generations which have immigrated in two separate periods. The elder generation, in their sixties and over, immigrated to California mainly in the early 1920's, e.g., Mrs. Maria Santos (from Portugal, 72 years old), Mr. Enos, and Manuel Goulart. The younger generation, in their thirties and forties, have immigrated within the past ten to twelve years, e.g., Mrs. Pequeno, Sister Yvonne, José Goulart Jr., and Mrs. Maria I. Santos (from Madeira).

The father of the family, in each case, seems to have had considerable influence in the oral transmission of ballads among my informants. Sister Yvonne recalls chiefly her father's singing of these songs. Mr. Enos remembers learning the "Nau Catrineta" from his father. Dolores Pequeno learned ballads (especially the "Conde d'Alemanha") from her father and grandfather. Manuel and José Goulart were taught ballads by both their parents, "Rico Franco" by their father and the "Noiva Arraiana" by their mother.

There appears to have been a considerable influence of written texts upon the oral transmission of some of the ballads. For instance, Manuel and José Goulart and the latter's son, José Jr., learned many variants from their neighbor in Pico (Azores), a woman named Bárbara. Bárbara recited the ballads from memory to them, but had learned them from her sister Rita, who had read them to her. Some ballads have been transmitted through the schools both in oral and written forms. According to most of my informants from the Islands, the "Nau Catrineta" was taught both in the primary and secondary schools. Sister Yvonne recalls "A Condessa" being sung both at school and at family reunions. Mrs. Santos (from Portugal) remembers learning "Frei João," "Jesus Peregrino," and other songs from a fourth-grade reader, popularly known as the *Livro do Cruzado*, used in her village, Oliveira do Hospital. Mrs. Santos says that the songs learned in the school books were sung in the streets, in any season of the year, in public festivities, and at family reunions.

Our ballad singers in California sing both with and without accompaniment. At times the music is an asset and encourages a singer to remember the songs. But on other occasions, it discourages the singer from continuing. The men, not the women, play the stringed instruments; they learned how when they were small children in the Islands. On some of my field trips, the men enjoyed exchanging the instruments so that each player had a chance to play all the different instruments present at a gathering. Instruments used are primarily the Spanish guitar, known as the "violão," and the "guitarra," a Portuguese guitar which has six double strings and is plucked like a mandolin (see FIGURES 1 and 2). The "violão" is also called the "viola" by some informants from Faial (Azores). Judging from Portuguese ballads collected in California, it doesn't seem that ballad music has been influenced by commercialized singing styles. However, some of these ballads, such as the "*Nau Catrineta*" and "Frei João," are sung in a Fado style. Mrs. Santos (from Portugal) still sings in wide intervals and in archaic Dorian and Mixo-lydian modes.

In addition to instrumental accompaniment, some of the ballads are sung in connection with games and dances. José Goulart mentions that the "*Nau Catrineta*" is danced to in Pico, one of the Azores Islands. The people would dance, then stop to sing a few lines, then resume the dance; this pattern would continue until the ballad ended. It has also been danced to in Brazil.[2] "A Condessa" is accompanied by a children's game which is related to the Anglo-American children's play-ballad "Nuts in May." My discussion below of the game is based on my informants' descriptions of how it was played years ago in Madeira Island and in Goa. The dances and games that accompany the ballads seem to be disappearing along with the ballad-singing tradition.

A few ballads together with other songs and traditions have been taught through children's youth groups in California. For example,

---

[2] Cf. Felícitas, *Danças do Brasil* (Rio de Janeiro, 1958), pp. 132–164.

FIGURE 1. Manuel Goulart
holding a *violão* (Ocean Beach;
June, 1967).

FIGURE 2. Two guitars owned by the Goulart family, a *guitarra* (left) and a *violão*.

Mrs. Maria Santos (from Portugal) taught songs including a few ballads to a youth group that she organized in Oakland. In spite of such occasional exposure to ballads, the younger generation raised in California has not retained or perpetuated them. Instead they tend to imitate the dance, lyric, and Fado songs diffused on phonograph records.

On the other hand. the response I obtained (with some persistence) from the elder generation of immigrants is amazing. In the five-month period from March 20 to September 1, 1967, I collected approximately 70 variants of 27 different ballad themes. This article includes 12 texts of seven ballads:"*Nau Catrineta*," "A Condessa," "Frei João," "O Casamento da filha do galo." "Dom Varão." "A noiva arraiana," and "Jesus Peregrino." The "*Nau Catrineta*" is still quite popular and is often remembered when no other ballads are. Both the "*Nau Catrineta*" and "Dom Varão" are usually recited rather than sung. The story of "Dom Varão" is often remembered and the verses forgotten; when the verses are recited in "Dom Varão," prose narrative is frequently brought in especially at points where the rhyme scheme changes. "Frei João" is often recognized but exists only in small fragments. "A Condessa" is still enjoying a wide distribution. I have variants coming from São Jorge and Faial (Azores), Madeira Island, Lisbon (Portugal), Goa (India), and from Rio Grande do Sul (Brazil). Informants recognize the religious ballad "Jesus Peregrino" but do not remember the verses. The single variants of "O Casamento da filha do galo" and of "A noiva arraiana" are the only versions obtained from informants in California.

The ballads are discussed here in terms of narrative stages. Letters corresponding with the narrative stages referred to have been placed to the right of the verses. Narrative stages are not indicated in the variants of "Frei João," since in this case only fragments of the ballad have been collected. The texts are edited according to the way each informant orally rendered his version. For this reason some phonetic indications are provided. What is most striking in this respect is the pronunciation of Terceirans who run their consonants together within a word and from one word to another. eliminating the vowel-sounds in between. An example of this is in the Terceiran version of "*Nau Catrineta*."

"*NAU CATRINETA*"

1 A

From: Pico Island, Azores

	Lá vem a *Nau Catrineta* que tem munto qu'contar.	A_1
	Já não tinham que comer, já não tinham que manjar.	D
	Deitaram sola de molh' p'ra n'outro dia jantar	E
	mas a sola era tão dura que não a puderam rilhar.	F
5	Deitaram sortes a bordo p'ra ver qual s'havia matar.	G
	Qual foi cair a sorte no capitão general.	H
	—Sob', sobe meu gageiro acima ó tope real.	I
	Vê se vês terras d'Espanha ou areia'd'Portugal.	J
	—Eu não vej' terras d'Espanha nem areias d'Portugal.	K_1
10	Vej' set' espadas nuas todas set'pa't'matar.	L
	—Sob', sob' marujinho acima ó mastro real.	I
	Vê se vês terras d'Espanha e areias d'Portugal.	J
	—Eu já vej' terras d'Espanha areia'd'Portugal.	K_2
	e também vej' três meninas debaixo d'um laranjal.	M
15	—Todas três são minhas filhas todas três t'e'voi de dar.	N
	Uma para t'vestir e outra p't'calçar,	O_1
	e a mai'nova delas todas para contig'casar.	P_1
	—Não quero as tuas filhas que te custaram a criar.	Q
	—Tu q'quer'mê gagei', qu'alvíssaras t'e'voi de dar?	R
20	Só s'o meu cavalo branc' sempr'pronto a galopar.	S
	—Eu não quero o teu cavalo que t'custou a ensinar.	T_1
	—Dar-te-ei tanto dinheiro que não no possos contuar.	U
	—Não quero o teu dinheiro que te custou a ganhar.	V
	—Mas então q'quer'meu gajeiro, qu'alvissaras	
	t'e'voi de dar?	R
25	Quero a tua alma para comigo lovar.	X_1
	—Renego de ti, Demónio p'ra que m'andas a tentar?	Y
	A minha alma é para Deus e o meu corpo dou ao mar.	Z
	E veio um anjo e não o deixou afogar.[3]	AA

1 B

From: Terceira Island, Azores

	Havia ūa *Nou Catrineta* por mar a passear.	A_2
	Já nã havia q'comuê nem tão pouc'que manjar.	D
	B'taram sola de molho para guisar p'ó jantar.	E
	Mes a sola era muito dura, já ninguém na podia rilhar.	F
5	B'taram sort's por tod's par'ver cal ia a matar.	G
	Três vez's coub'p'sorte ao capitão general.	H

---

[3]V. 1*b munto* 'muito'; vv. 10*a*, 13*a*, *Vej* 'Vejo'; vv. 15*b*, 19*b*, 24*b t'e'voi de dar* 't'eù hei de dar' and 'te vou dar'; v. 22*b cuntuar* 'contar'; v. 25*b lovar* 'levar.'
Recited by José Goulart (San Diego; May 20, 1967).

—Acima, acima, gageiro,   torna-te bem a afirmar.   I
Vê s' vês terras d' França   e ao Rei d' Portugal.   J
—Eu não vej' terra' d' França   nem reinos d' Port'gal. K_1
10   Vej' três 'spadas nuas,   todas três p'a t' matar.   L
—Acima, acima, gagê,   torna-t' bem a afirmar.   I
Vê s' vês terras d' França   e o Rei d' Portugal.   J
Disse el':
—Já vej' terra d' França   e reinos d' Portugal. K_2
Tambén vej' três donzelas   debaixo d'um laranjal.   M
15   —E a mais bonitinha d'ela   é para com vôs casar. P_1
—Eu não quero as vossas filhas,   que vôs c'stou a ganhar.   Q
Diz o patrão:
—Mas eu vou-t' dar tanto dinheiro,   que tu não
    sabas contar.   U
—Eu não quero o vosso dinheiro   que vos c'stou a ganhar.   V
Diz:
—Mas vou-t' dar o meu cavalo   p' em terra passear.   S
Diz el':
20   —Não, eu não quer' o voss' cavalo   que eu em
    terra sei andar. T_2
Ê quer' ũa *Nau Catrineta*   p'ra no mar passear X_2
Porque quem desta escapou,   também d'oitr' há d' 'scapá.[4]

1 C

From: Oliveira do Hospital, Portugal

Lá vem a *Nau Catrineta*   que tem munto que contare. A_1
Ouvide agora, senhores,   uma historia de pasmare: B
Passava mais d'ano e dia   que iam na volta do mare.   C
Já não tinham que comer,   já não tinham que manjare.   D
5   Deitaram sortes à ventura,   qual s'havia de matare.   G
Logo foi cair a sorte   no capitão generale: H
—Sobe, sob' marujinho,   a esse mastro reale.   I
Vê se vês terras de Espanha   ou praias de Portugale.   J
—Não vejo terras de Espanha,   nem praias de Portugale. K_1
10   Só enxergo três meninas   debaixo d'um laranjale.   M
Uma assentada a coser,   outra na roca a fiar, O_2
a mais bonita de todas,   contigo a yei-de casare. P_1
Todas três são minhas filhas,   ai, quem mas
    dera abraçare.   N
Podes ter tu por certeza   qu' uma d'elas vai casare. P_2
15   —Não quero as tuas filhas   que te custaram a criare.   Q

---

[4]V. 1a *ũa* 'uma,' *Nau* = [Nó]; v. 2a *comué* 'comer,' *Já* = [ja]; v. 2b *manjar* = [mižaı
v. 4a *Mes* 'Mais'; v. 5b *cal* 'qual'; v. 6a *coub'* = [tkub]; v. 10a *'spadas* 'espadas'; v. 11a *gagê*
'gageiro'; v. 16b *c'stou* 'custou'; v. 21a *Ê* 'Eu'; v. 22b *'scapá* 'escapar'; vv. 10a,13a, 14a *Vej'*
'Vejo.'
Recited by Manuel M. Enos (Tulare; March 20, 1967).

—Darei-te tanto dinheiro   que não o possas contare.   U

Darei-t' o meu cavalo branco   que nunca houve

outro iguale.   S

—Não quero o teu cavalo branco   que te custou a ensinare.   T₁

—Não tenho mais que te dare,   nem tu mais que me pedire.   W

20 —Capitão, quero a tua yalma   para comigo a lovare.   X₁

—Renego de ti, Demónio,   que me estavas a tentare.   Y

Pegou num anio nos braços,   não o deixou naufragare.[5]   AA

Lá vem a Nau Cat-ri — ne — ta que tem mun-to que con—

ta- re. Ou- vi-de a-go—ra, sen-ho— res, um—a his-to—ri—a de pas—

ma—re: Pas-sa—va mais d'a—no e di— a que i-am na vol-ta do

ma—re. Já não tin—ham que co—me—r, já não tin —

ham que man—ja — re.

1C. Sung in a Mixo-lydian mode. This transcription is a bare outline
due to the fluent vocal sliding (portamenti) throughout and the
vocalizing of enlarged intervals, especially the third.

This ballad in stages A to D relates how the ship *Catrineta* has
been at sea for such a long time that there is nothing left on board

[5]V. 6 was repeated in singing; v. 12b *yei-de* 'hei-de'; v. 20a *yalma* 'alma'; v. 20b *lovare* 'levare.'
Sung by Mrs. Maria Vicente Santos (Oakland; March 22, 1967).

to eat or drink. Shoe leather was too tough to be eaten (E–F). Lots were cast to see who would have to be killed (G). The lot fell to the Captain (H). The Captain in his desperation calls upon a mate to climb the mainmast in hopes that land may be seen (I–J). In these versions the mate does not fall into the sea from the mast as in some other published texts. He does not see land (K$_1$) but does see three naked swords with which to kill the Captain (L). Shores are at last discovered in stage K$_2$, and the mate perceives three damsels beneath an orange tree (M). In stage N the Captain declares that the three damsels are his daughters. One of the damsels is sewing in stage O$_2$ of text 1C. The Captain then begins to make a series of offers which marks the beginning of the traditional contamination of "La tentación del marinero" in "*Nau Catrineta.*"[6] In stage O$_1$ of variant 1A, he offers one daughter to dress the mate and another to put his shoes on, and in stage P$_1$ he offers the youngest to the mate to marry.[7] He offers a daughter in marriage in all three of versions. He also offers his white horse (S) and his money (U). The mate refuses these offers (Q,T,V) and demands the Captain's soul (X$_1$) in texts 1A and 1C. The Captain denies the Devil (disguised as the mate) his soul (Y), as it will go to heaven and his body will be cast into the sea (Z). At this crucial point an angel intervenes in stage AA and keeps the Captain from drowning or from shipwreck. Instead of demanding the Captain's soul in version 1B, the mate refuses the Captain's offers and demands to have the ship (X$_2$).

The characteristic casting of lots in the "*Nau Catrineta*" occurs in all the variants that I have collected (as in verses 5–6 of renditions 1A, 1B, and 1C) and also in nearly all the published versions of the "*Nau Catrineta.*"[8] The casting of lots is also a characteristic of the French versions entitled "La Courte Paille"[9] and of the ballad "La Muerte de Don Beltrán."[10]

The contamination of the Pan-Hispanic ballad "La tentación del marinero" in the "*Nau Catrineta*" occurs in stages N to Z of the ver-

---

[6] Cf. Braga, *Romanceiro*, III, 317–324; Vasconcellos, II, nos. 604–615; Catalán no. 24; and Gil García, p. 30. Full bibliographical information for works cited in my notes is listed at the end of this article.

[7] This offer appears in the Spanish Vuelta del marido (é) and the Judeo-Spanish "Arbolero" (í).

[8] Cf. Vasconcellos, II, nos. 598–603, 1015–1016; Braga, *Romanceiro*, I, 1–32, and *Cantos*, pp. 285–297; Pires de Lima, *A mulher*, pp. 45–49; Thomás, pp. 43–46; and Romero, I, 102–108.

[9] Cf. Barbeau, pp. 435–436; Barbeau and Sapir, pp. 125–132; and Rolland, I, 301–303.

[10] As in Wolf and Hofmann, II, nos. 185–185a; Vasconcellos, I, nos. 17–33, and II, no. 984; and Braga, *Romanceiro*, I, 207–211.

sions above. And although it does not appear either in the above mentioned French texts or in the published examples of the "*Nau Catrineta*" in Romero's variants and in Braga's *Cantos Populares*, the temptation is part of the "*Nau Catrineta*" in the Vasconcellos, Pires, Thomás, and Braga collections. In "La tentación del marinero" gold and silver will be offered, whereas money is offered in the "*Nau Catrineta*" (U-V). In "La tentación del marinero" the ship will be offered, whereas the Devil demands to have it in stage X_2 of variant 1 B of "*Nau Catrineta*." In both ballads the Devil is denied the soul as in stage Y of the above texts, and the body is to be cast into the sea (cf. stage Z). However, there is an elaboration in "La tentación del marinero" which relates what parts of the body will go where and for what specific purposes. This elaboration does not occur in those texts of the "*Nau Catrineta*" referred to above. The Captain being saved by an angel in stage AA seems to be a rare element in the other published versions. One variant resembling this stage has been published by Pires.[11]

The contamination from "La tentación del marinero" creates a strange twist in the circumstances which characterize the "*Nau Catrineta*" ballad. In the beginning the Captain expects that his life may be saved should land be spotted. Land is spotted, but his life is still in jeopardy. When he tries to save himself by offering all his worldly possessions, the cannibalistic mate is unexpectedly transformed into the Devil in pursuit of a Christian soul. The Captain no longer is concerned about saving his life and prefers to cast himself into the sea to save his soul.[12]

"A Condessa"

2 A

From: Goa

—Aqui mora a Viscondessa,   somos filhas de francesa.   A
—Aqui lhas vimos pedir   para com elas casar.   B
—Não dou as minhas filhas,   nem por oiro nem por prata,   C
   nem por sangue de dragão,   que bonitas que elas são.
5 —Não quer' esta por ser rosa,   nem quer' esta por ser cravo,   F
   nem esta por ser jàsmim,   quero esta para mim.[13]

---

[11]P. 49.
[12]Bibliography:
Portuguese—Braga, *Romanceiro*, I, 1–32, 207–211, and III, 313–328; Braga, *Cantos*, pp. 285–297; Pires de Lima, *Romanceiro*, pp. 45–49; Romero, I, 102–108; Thomás, pp. 43–46; Vasconcellos, I, nos. 17–33, and II, nos. 598–615, 984, 1015–1016.
Castilian—Gil García, II, 30; Catalán, no. 24; Wolf and Hofman, II, nos. 185–185a.
French—Barbeau, pp. 435–436; Barbeau and Sapir, pp. 125–132; Rolland, I, 301–303.

A—qui mo — ra Vis-con-des-sa, so-—mos fil — has

de fran-ce—sa.   A—qui lhas vi—mos pe —dir

pa-ra com e — las ca — sar.

2A. Sung in a major mode. The rhythm suggests a dance in a 6/8 meter.

2 B

From: Madeira

—Ás minhas filhas não dou   nem por ouro nem por prata,   C
nem por sangue de lagarta   que me custou a criar.
—Volta atrás condessinha;   por seres homem de bem,   E
eu te darei minha filha,   se tu estimares bem.
5 —Estimo estimarei,   sentada numa almofada   G
enfiando continhas d'oiro,   volta atrás minha esposada.[14]

As   min has fil-has não do — u   nem por ou—ro nem por pra-ta   nem

por san-que de la— gar-ta   que me cus-tou a   cri — a — ar

2B. The singer was accompanied with guitars and mandolins. The melodic structure is sequential. The beginning sequence starts with a dominant anacrusis suggesting a major key. However, the tonal finalis is minor.

---

[13]V. 5a *quer*''quero.
Sung by Sister Maria Yvonne Barros (Five Wounds Convent, San Jose; March 25, 1967). Sister Yvonne recalls learning this song in 1925 when she heard it sung at school and at family reunions. She has not heard it sung since 1947.
[14]Vv. 3, 4, *bem* = [bãĩ]
Sung by Mrs. Maria Santos (San Diego; May 6, 1967).

2 C

From: Madeira

—Condensia, oh Condensinha,   Condensia do Aragão,   A
  quero pedir as suas filhas   destas tudas que aqui 'stão.   B
—E as minhas filhas não du   nem per ouro nem pu prata   C
  nem po' sangue d'aragata   que me questou a criar.
5 —Tão alegre c' aqui vinha,   agora não vou achar.   D
  Pedi a filh' à Condensia,   Condensia não ques me dar.
—Volta p'a trás cavalheiro   por ser's um homem de bem.   E
  Met' a mão niste mistério,   escolhe qual a convém.
—Esta quero, esta não quero,   esta yá que me convém.   F
  Est' é como_pão da cista,   vem cá comigo, meu bem.[15]

Con—den — sia, oh Con-den—sin — ha,   Con-den-sia do A—ra-

gã — o,   que— ro   ped-ir   as   su—as   fil — has   des—

tas   tu — das   que a-qui   'stã — o.

2C. This version is identical to variant 2B except for the opening interval which is a fifth instead of a sixth as in text 2B and which thereby initiates a minor mode at the beginning. At the end of every sequence except the last the singer returns to the original anacrusis.

This song accompanies a children's game. According to my informants—Sister Maria Yvonne Barros, Mrs. Maria Santos, and Mrs. Dolores Pequeno—the children form a ring known as a "roda." Sister Yvonne and Mrs. Pequeno say that the Countess was placed in the middle of the circle, whereas Mrs. Santos says that no one played the part of the Countess. The suitor or suitors negotiate

[15]Vv. 1, 6 Condensia, Condensinha 'Condessa'; v. 2 tudas 'todas'; v. 4a aragata 'lagarta' (according to another informant who is from the same village as the singer and who was present during her rendition of this version); v. 4b questou 'custou,' criar = [criaį]; v. 5b achar = [ašaį]; v. 6b ques 'quis,' dar = [daį]; vv. 7-10 bem = [bãį], convem = [čovãį]; v. 9b yá 'é a.'
Sung by Mrs. Dolores Pequeno from Madeira (San Diego; May 20, 1967).

with an intermediary, the mother of the girl being wooed, in the game accompanying texts 2A and 2C, as they also do in the Anglo-American versions in Newell's *Games and Songs of American Children.* However, according to Mrs. Santos there is no intermediary, even though the verses indicate that the Countess (rather than the daughters) refuses the suitors.

In all three versions a girl is selected by one boy who represents all the boys. The game is repeated until all of the girls have been selected, as is the case in the Anglo-American tradition. According to Mrs. Santos, the girl selected enters the center of the circle and is joined later by each additionally selected girl as the game is repeated. By contrast, however, Dolores Pequeno says that the couples leave the circle and that the game is repeated until there are no more girls left in the original ring.

The texts transcribed above incorporate narrative stages from A through G. In stage A the nationality of the Countess and her daughters is indicated. In stage B the boys come to marry the girls. The rejection of the suitor occurs in stage C: the Countess refuses to sell her daughters for gold or silver. In stage D, not mentioned in versions 2A and 2B, the suitor leaves dejectedly. In stage E, present in both the Madeiran renditions, the Countess calls the suitor to come back and select a daughter. Stage F, omitted in variant 2B, represents a selecting process. And in stage G, occurring in 2B only, the Countess is assured that her daughter will be well cared for, esteemed, and adorned.

In stage A of rendition 2A the girls are represented as daughters of a French Countess. In some of the texts given by Théo Brandão in his article "A Condessa," the Countess is known as the Filha de França (Cananeian, Paraensean, and Cariocan versions).[16] Rodney Gallop offers a variant from S. Miguel Island in his *Cantares do Povo Portugês* where the Countess is referred to as the "Senhora Condessa do Porto Real Franés."[17] In version 2C she is from Aragão, a place which appears in some of Brandão's texts from Brazil and Northern Portugal.[18] According to variants from Castilian speaking areas, it is the "caballero" who is coming from France.[19] In the Anglo-American game the suitor is a Spanish knight.

[16]Brandão, nos. xvii–xix.
[17]P. 145.
[18]Brandão, nos. ix, xxi, xxii, xxv, l, anexo.
[19]Brandão, nos. xxvi, xxvii, xxx, li, lii, liv, lvii, lx; Gil. I, 93, no. 18; Menéndez Pidal, "Los romances," p. 39, no. 16, and "Catálogo," no. 130.

Sister Yvonne's rendition of stage B parallels an example given by A. F. Coelho in his *Jogos e Rimas Infantis*.[20] Both indicate that the boys have come to marry the girls. In the Madeiran version 2C it is only one boy who makes the request. My informant from Goa says that the girls often took both parts: the suitors as well as the daughters and Countess. This may partly explain why the women recall this song and not the men.

The Countess, in stage C of my Madeiran texts, refuses to sell her daughters for gold or silver, since it was a task to raise them. Stage C in the Goan version closely coincides with Gallop's text from S. Miguel. In both these variants the Countess refuses to sell her daughters for gold or silver, since they are so beautiful. However, the version from S. Miguel adds that she refuses to sell them even for cotton thread, which seems to be on a par in purchasing value with gold and silver. Instead of refusing to sell them for thread, the Countess in the Goan rendition adds that she refuses to sell them even for the blood of a dragon: "Nem por sangue de dragão." This refusal occurs in a variant from Madeira Island cited by Théo Brandão.[21] My Madeiran text 2B reads "Nem por sangue de lagarta" and in 2C "Nem por sangue d'aragata." Similar variations appear in a number of Brazilian versions, as exemplified in Théo Brandão's article, where the Countess refuses to sell her daughters even for the blood of Aragon, of a lizard, etc., as in the following: "Nem por sangue de Aragão," or "de lagarta," "de aratá," or "de alicata." The refusal embodied in this section seems to be the most indispensable part of the ballad. Other sections may be omitted, yet in most fragments the refusal remains. The Castilian variants lack the refusal to sell the daughter for gold and silver that the Portuguese and Brazilian ones have ("Nem por ouro, nem por prata"), nor do they have anything like "fio de algodão," i.e., "hilo de algodón," in the refusal. Instead, to the statement, "Qué lindas hijas tenéis," the Countess in the Castilian versions replies at first in a non-committal fashion about whether she had daughters or not, but then affirms that she is quite capable of supporting them, indicating that she has no need to marry them off. In a French version published by Van Gennep[22] the daughters are in a Convent and to the question, "Avez-vous des filles a marier?" the mother first enumerates how many she has, then refuses to sell them for money,

---

[20] P. 66.
[21] No. xlvii.
[22] Cited in Brandão, no. xlv.

silver, or gold. This refusal shows a closer parallel to the Portuguese than to the Spanish.

In a number of the Hispanic variants the gentleman turns away either angry or disappointed, as in stage D of text 2C. The Countess calls him back to select the most beautiful daughter, as in stage E of both of the Madeiran texts 2B and 2C. The turning away and calling back does not occur in the Goan rendition 2A. Instead the Goan text moves directly from the Countess' refusal to the selection of a girl, which takes place in stage F of texts 2A and 2C.

Variants that compare the girl to a carnation, rose, or jasmine, as in stage F of the Goan text, seem to be characteristic of the Castilian versions.[23] This comparison appears in a Portuguese text from S. Miguel Island,[24] and in an unpublished variant that I have recently received from Lisbon. In the Castilian variants the girl is chosen because she is similar to a rose or a carnation, whereas in the versions from Goa, S. Miguel, and Lisbon those girls that resemble a rose, jasmine, or a carnation are rejected, while one girl is accepted.

Both examples 2A and 2C end after the selection has been made. However, according to the singers of these two renditions, there are many more verses. The Madeiran example 2B omits stage F and goes directly from stage E to stage G, where the gentleman says that he will esteem and adorn the Countess' daughter. The adoration of the daughter is a characteristic motif of other Hispanic variants of this ballad.[25]

"Frei João" (Fragment)

3 A

From: Oliveira do Hospital, Portugal

—Ó Feliz, abre-me a porta,   qu' eu 'stou c'os pés na geada;
2   Se me não abres a porta,   não és Feliz nem és nada.[26]

---

[23]Brandão, nos. xxix-xxxii, xxxiv, xxxvii-xliii, li, lii, liv, lv; Gil; Menédez Pidal, "Los romances," p. 39, no. 16.

[24]Cf. Gallop.

[25]Bibliography.

Portuguese—Brandão; Coelho, pp. 66-70; Gallop, *Cantares do Povo Portugues*, p. 145; Vasconcellos, II, nos. 682-683.

Spanish—Gil, I, 93, no. 18; Menéndez Pidal, "Los romances," p. 39, no. 16, and "Catálogo," no. 130.

Anglo-American—Newell, pp. 39-45.

[26]Both vv. 1 and 2 are repeated; v. 2b, variant in repetition: "nem es F."

Sung by Mrs. Maria Vicente Santos (Oakland; March 22, 1967).

3A. Sung in an archaic melodic structure suggesting a Dorian mode in
the first two lines. The last two lines suggest a return to a major mode.
The wide intervals that this singer sings are not tempered. If this vocal
line were measured on an oscilloscope, it would be interesting to see
how close the informant is to just-intonation.

3 B (Fragment)

From: Pico, Azores ·

Frei João s'al'vantou   numa manhã de geada.
Toma limão verde,   doce limoná.
Foi bater à portareia   da Morena malfadada.
Toma limão verde,   doce limonada.

---

[27]V. 3a Ande 'Onde.' The refrain seems to be unrelated to the rest of the ballad. Its eleven
syllable line is in marked contrast with the fifteen syllabled verses pertaining to the ballad.
    Vv. 1 and 2 were sung by José Goulart and vv. 3 and 4 by his brother Manuel (San Diego;
May 20, 1967).

—Ande vens à mulher minha   que vi est' uma raiada?
Toma limão verde,   doce limonada.
4 —Venho d'ouvir missa nova   que disso venho consolada.
Toma limão verde,   doce limonada.[27]

3B. A simple folktune in a major mode. The scale-like contour makes
the melody easy to remember.

Both fragmentary variants are representative of the Pan-Hispanic
"La Adúltera" assonated in *a-a* as catalogued in Menéndez Pidal.[28]
In the Portuguese tradition it is usually referred to as "Frei João,"
"A Mulher Falsa," "Nas Malhas," and "A Morena."[29]

Lines 1 and 2 of rendition 3B usually introduce the ballad and
precede the first two lines given in variant 3A. The first two lines
of 3B where Friar John rises early one frosty morning and goes to
knock on the door of his beloved mistress parallel stage 1 of "La
Adúltera" in *á-a* as discussed by S. G. Armistead and J. H. Silverman in *The Judeo-Spanish Ballad Chapbooks of Yakob Abraham Yoná*.
Stage 1 also includes a serenade by the lover. In my variant there is
no mention of the Friar coming to serenade his mistress. Verse 1*a* of
rendition 3A, where Friar John begs Feliz to open the door, and
verse 1*b*, where he complains of the cold, correspond to stages 2 and
3 of "La Adúltera" (*à-a*) according to Armistead's and Silverman's
classification.

Friar John's threat to Feliz (verse 2 of variant 3A)—that if she
doesn't open the door she won't be "Feliz" or anything—plays on
the word "Feliz," which means "happy" or "fortunate." The pun

[28]"Catálogo," no. 80.
[29]As in Thomás, pp. 50–52; Vasconcellos, I, nos. 417–427, and II, nos. 732–734, 1011;
Carré Alvarellos, nos. 117–120; and Braga, *Romanceiro*, II, 78–110.

implies that mistress Fortunate will be neither fortunate nor Miss Fortunate anymore nor anything at all if she doesn't open the door. This threat by the lover heightens his complaint of being left out in the cold in stage 3 (verse 1*b*).

Verse 2 of text 3B closely resembles one in Vasconcellos.[30] There are texts with phrasing similar to lines 1 and 2 of version 3A in Braga, Thomás, and Vasconcellos.[31] Verse 1 of rendition 3A most frequently begins in these published texts as: "Abre-me a porta, Morena ——." The "Ó Feliz" of variant 3A may stem from "Infeliza" ("the unfortunate one") which occurs in Vasconcellos' version no. 424:

> "Infeliza, abre-me a porta   qu' estou co'os pés na geada.
> Se me não abrir's a porta,   nem és firme nem és nada."

The phrase structure of these two lines parallels that of text 3A. Vasconcellos' variant does not have the pun on the name Feliz. Instead Infeliza is declared unfaithful if she doesn't open the door.

Verses 3 and 4 of rendition 3B are lines that are sung after the husband's unexpected return in the collections referred to above. Line 4b is usually rendered: "D'isso venho regalada" or "que Frei João cantava." In my text the adulterous wife covers up the reason for her absence from home by declaring that she is returning consoled from hearing mass. With the ballad terminating at this point, the wife avoids the punishment and death that occur in other printed variants of "Frei João." Different from when the adulterous wife is chastized, the concluding tone here seems to be that of the wife mocking the husband.

Rendition 3A seems to be an independent couplet and is considered complete within itself by other informants who recall having heard the text. Some informants have rendered thse two lines as a Fado. When fragments of "Frei João" from Vasconcellos' *Romanceiro* were read to these and to other informants, they identified these excerpts as pertaining to a song different from the "Ó Feliz" rendition.[32]

---

[30]I, no. 417.

[31]Braga, *Romanceiro*, II, 97 and 108; Thomás, p. 50; Vasconcellos, I, nos. 417-419, and II, no. 1011.

[32]Bibliography:

Portuguese—Braga, *Romanceiro*, II, 78-110; Thomás, pp. 50-52; Vasconcellos, I, nos. 417-427, and II, nos. 732-734, 1011.

Galician—Carré Alvarellos, nos. 117-120.

Judeo-Spanish—Menéndez Pidal, "Catálogo," no. 80; Armistead and Silverman.

BIBLIOGRAPHY

Armistead, S. G., and J. H. Silverman. *The Judeo-Spanish Ballad Chapbooks of Yakob Abraham Yoná*. Forthcoming.

Barbeau, M. *Le Rossignol y Chante, Première partie da Répertoire de la Chanson Folklorique Française au Canada*. Ottawa, 1962.

Barbeau, M. and E. Sapir. *Folk Songs of French Canada*. New Haven, 1925.

Braga, T. *Romanceiro Geral Portuguez*. 2nd. ed.; 3 vols.; Lisbon, 1906.

————. *Cantos Populares do Archipelago Açoriano*. Porto, 1869.

Bendito, R. *Canciones Folklóricas Españoles*. Madrid, 1962.

Brandão, T. "La Condessa," *Revista de Dialectología y Tradiciones Populares*, X(1954), 591–643.

Carré Alvarellos, L. "Romanceiro Popular Gallego," *Douro-Litoral*, VIII (1958), 757–803, 889–910; IX (1959), 77–137, 285–350, 585–711.

Catalán, D. "La recolección romancística en Canarias," prologue to M. Morales and M. J. López de Vergara, *Romancerillo Canario* (La Laguna, 1955).

Catalán, D. and A. Galmés. "El tema de la boda estorbada: Proceso de la tradicionalización de un romance juglaresco," *Vox Romanica*, XIII (1953), 66–98.

Coelho, A. F. *Jogos e Rimas Infantis*. 2nd. ed.; Porto, 1919.

Córdova y Oña, S. *Cancionero Popular de la Provincia de Santander*. Santander, 1947.

Cortés, N. A. *Romances Populares de Castilla*. Valladolid. 1906.

Doncieux, G. *Le Romancéro Populaire de la France*. Paris, 1904.

Gil García, B. *Cancionero Popular de Extremadura*. 2nd. ed.; 2 vols.; Badajoz, 1961.

Larrea Palacín, A. de. *Romances de Tetuán*. 2 vols.; Madrid, 1952.

Lomax, J. A., and Alan. *American Ballads and Folk Songs*. New York, 1960.

Mendoza, V. T. *El romance español y el corrido Mexicano*. Mexico, 1939.

Menéndez Pidal, R. "Catálogo del romancero judío-español," *Los Romances de América y otros estudios* (6th ed.; Madrid, 1958), pp. 114–179.

————. "Los romances tradicionales en America," *Los Romances de América y otros estudios* (6th ed.; Madrid, 1958), pp. 13–51.

————. *Flor Nueva de Romances Viejos*. 13th ed.; Buenos Aires, 1962.

Milá y Fontanals, M. *Romancerillo catalán*. Barcelona, 1882.

Newell, W. W. *Games and Songs of American Children*. New York, 1963.

Nigra, C. *Canti Populari del Piamonte*. Turin, 1957.

Pires de Lima, F. C. *A mulher vestida de homem*. Coimbra, 1958.

Pires de Lima, J. A. and F. C. *Romanceiro minhoto*. Porto, 1943.

Rolland, E. *Recueil de chansons populaires*. 5 vols.; Paris, 1883–1890.

Romero, S. *Folclore brasileiro*, Vol. I: *Cantos populares do Brasil*. Rio de Janeiro, 1954.

Sampedro y Folgar, C. *Cancionero musical de Galicia*. 2 vols.; Galicia, 1942.

Thomás, P. F. *Velhas canções e romances populares portuguêses*. Coimbra, 1913.

Vasconcellos, J. Leite de. *Romanceiro Português*. 2 vols.; Coimbra, 1958.

Wolf, F. J. and D. C. Hofmann. *Romances Viejos Castellanos (Primavera y flor de romances)*. Ed. M. Menéndez y Pelayo. Santander, 1945.

Traditional Ballads Among the Portuguese in California: Part II

JOANNE B. PURCELL

"CASAMENTO DA FILHA DO GALO"

4

From: Madeira

    Respond' o galo   para a galinha: **A**
    —Vamos casare   a nossa filhinha.
    Noivo já temos;   falta o padrinho.   **B**
    Falta o padrinho;   da onde virao?
5   Respond' o rato   do seu buraquinho,
    que já estava pronte   p'a ser o padrinho.
    —Padrinho jás temos,   falta a madrinha.   **C**
    Falta a madrinha;   da onde virá?
    Respond' a cabra,   qu' estava na vinha,
10   que já estava pronte   p'a ser a madrinha.
    —Madrinha já temos;   falta os convidados.   **D**
    Falta os convidados;   da onde virao?
    Respond' a borboleta,   qu' estava no are,
    que já estava pronte   para acumpanhare.
15   —Convidados já temos;   falta o almoço.   **E**
    Falta o almoço;   da onde virao?
    Respond' a rã,   do fondo do poço,
    que já estava pronte   p'a dar o almoço.
    —Almoço já temos;   falta o jantare.   **F**
20   Falta o jantare;   da onde virao?
    Respond' o peixe,   do fondo do mare,
    que já estava pronte   p'a dar o jantare.
    —Jantar já temos,   falta ia ceia.   **G**
    Falta ao ceia;   da onde virao?
25   Respond' a frumilga,   que estava na arreia,
    que já estava pronte   para dar a ceia.
    —Ceia já temos;   falta a carne.   **H**
    Falta a carne;   da onde virao?
    Respond' o porco,   que estava no chiqueiro,

30   que já estava pronte   p'a ir ao picadeiro.
        —Carne já temos;   falta a batata.   I
        Falta a batata,   da onde virao?
        Respond' a batata   dobaixo da terra,
        que já estava pronti   p'a ir a panela.[33]

4. Singer was unaccompanied. The simple tune is in a major mode; one wonders why the flat third appears toward the end. With the flat third, the final chord may be major or minor. The flat third is in a definite verbal stress position and is consistent. The overall form is abbreviated for the purposes of textual repetition. This variant ends on a dominant tone, giving the impression of an antecedent phrase with no consequent phrase. The song was sung by the same singer on two occasions and was recorded both May 20 and June 17, 1967. In both recordings the melodic structure is identical.

This song is a cumulative children's ballad also known as "El Casamiento del Piojo y la Pulga" in the Pan-Hispanic tradition and as the "Frog's Courtship" in Anglo-American balladry. In the Pan-Hispanic tradition the louse and the flea ("el piojo y la pulga") wish to marry but lack the essentials for a wedding. A frog, rat, wolf, pig, mosquito, and various other creatures answer to the bride and groom's needs by offering their services as best man, bridesmaid, musician, dancer, and so forth.

According to Dolores Pequeno's rendition, the parents instigate

---

[33] vv. 6a,10a,14a,18a,22a,26a,30a,34a *pronte, pronti* 'pronto'; v. 7a *jás* 'já'; v. 23b *falta ia ceia* = [łáłtajɔséjɔ]; v. 25a *frumilga* 'formiga'; v. 33b *dobaixo* 'debaixo'.

The above example varies between 9 and 11 syllable verses which correspond with the 10-12 meter typical of other Castilian and Galician versions. The Madeiran rendition does not follow the consistent couplet pattern characteristic of both the Hispanic and Anglo-American variants. Instead, each couplet is followed with two lines in anticipation of the succeeding couplet, thereby forming a more complex rhyme scheme.

Sung by Mrs. Dolores Pequeno (San Diego; June 17, 1967).

the wedding arrangements for their daughter, stage A. The parents also mediate in versions from Carré Alvarellos' collection, *Romanceiro Popular Gallego*. The marrying couple in Castilian variants, as well as in another Galician variant, initiate their own wedding festivities, without parental mediation (cf. Bendito, Córdova y Oña, Mendoza, and Sampedro).

Once the best man in stage B, bridesmaid (C), and guests (D) are furnished for the wedding, the rest of the ballad in the Madeiran text is concerned only with the preparation for the wedding feasts, including lunch in stage E, dinner (F), and supper (G). The need for the potato in stage I to accompany the meat (H) with the meal is stressed, rather than the characteristic bread or wheat of the above cited references. Dancers and music included in the festivities of the Pan-Hispanic and Anglo-American texts do not form a part of the festive preparation of Mrs. Pequeno's version.

The cat, in the Castilian and Galician variants, who enters after the wedding preparations have been made and disrupts the wedding by eating up the best man, a rat, does not appear in our Madeiran version, nor in Carré Alvarellos' collection (nos. 138, 140, 142, 143, 145, 146). Mrs. Pequeno's rendition ends in a lightly humorous manner with the potato answering from underground (v.33) that it was ready for the cooking pot (v.34). It concludes with a gay and festive tone, rather than with the Galician and Castilian texts' ironical note.[34]

"DOM VARÃO"

5

From: Pico Island, Azores

—Já s' acabaram as guerras   em baix' e em Maranhão.   A
   Três filhas que Deus me deu,   sem ter um filho varão.
   Respond' a filha mai' moça   por ter maior discrição: B
—Oh meu pai, oh minha mãe,   serei o filho varão.
5 —Mas com' podes ser isso?   Filha -------.   C
   Tinds as mãos muito alvas,   filha, vos conhecerão.
—Venham lu'as para elas,   d'elas não s' tirarão.   D

[34]Bibliography:
   Castilian—Bendito, *Canciones Folklóricas*, p. 2; Córdova y Oña, *Cancionero Popular*, pp. 39, No. 23; Mendoza, *Romance y Corrido*, pp. 743–748.
   Galician—Carré Alvarellos, *Romanceiro Popular Gallego*, nos. 137–146; Sampedro y Folgar, *Cancionero Musical de Galicia*, I, 131, II, 43.
   Anglo-American—Lomax, *American Ballads*, pp. 310–313.

—Tends os peitos mui' grandes,   filha, vu conhecerão.   E
—Venha cá um alfaiat'   talhar u' justo gibão.   F
10 —Tends o cabelo comprido,   filha, vos conhecerão.   G
—Venham tesouras para el',   c'o cabelo vai p'r' o chao.   H
A rapariga cam' nhou mas quando chegou a casa do outro rei e   I
quand' conheceu o príncipe e o rei e o príncipe ficou descon-
fiado e p'ro falar com ela e p'ros olhos dela virava-s' p'ro pai e
para a mãe e dizia:
    —Oh meu pai, oh minha mãe,   por amores eu diria   J
    qu' os olhos de Dom Varão   são d' mulher, d'homem não.
E o pai diss'· le:
    —Pois convidai-o, vós, meu filho,   p'ra ir à caça contigo   K
15   qu' se ela for mulher   não vai saber atirar.
    Dom Varão com' discret',   sua arma carr'gara,   L
    logo o primér tir'   duas pederniz matara.
    —Oh meu pai, oh mia mãe,   por amores e' diria   J
    qu' os olhos de Dom Varão   são d' mulher, d'homem não.
20 —Pois convidai-o vós meu filho,   para ela vir dormir contigo.   M
    Si ela for mulher   não se vai q'rer ditar.
    Dom Varão, com' discret',   sua bota descalçou   N
    e na cama se deitou,   p'ra el' não se virou.
    —Oh meu pai, oh mia mãe,   por amores e' diria   J
25   qu' os olhos de Dom Varão   são d' mulher, d'homem não.
    —P's convidai-o vós meu filho,   para vir jantar contigo.   O
    Se ela for mulher. . . . .
    —Oh meu pai, oh mia mãe,   por amores e' diria   J
    qu' os olhos de Dom Varão   são d' mulher, d'homem não.
30 —Pois convidai-o vó', meu filho,   para ir ao banh' contigo.   P
    Se ela for mulher   não vai saber nadar.
    Dom Varão, com' discret',   sua bota descalçara.   Q
    Sentara. . . . .   saltara de prantear.
    —Que tind's vós, Dom Varão,   que estás tanto a chorar?   R
35 —Notícia' me vieram ter   T
    que meu pai que era morto,   minha mãe enterrar.
    —Pois se é assim, Dom Varão,   trata já d' cam'nhar.
Fui o que ela quis ouir porque ela não se queria despir para ir   U
tomar banho·com el'. Quando ela chegou a casa, uma carta
escreveu:
    —Três meses que eu andei   na companhia do filho do rei;   V
    e eu com el' é comia,   e com el' é que dormia,
40   e com el' é qu' ia á caça . . . .
    Se donzela vim, donzela vou.   Se me quer's alg'ma coisa   W
    Bat' à porta do meu pai.
Quando o príncipe chegou a casa e encontrou aquela nota,   X
saltou no se' cavalo e foi buscá-la a casa do pai.[35]

---

[35]Vv.6a, 32a *tind's* 'tendes'; v.7a, *lu'as* 'luvas'; vv.8a, 10a, *tend's* 'tendes'; 8a *mui* 'muito' =
[muĩ]; v.8b, *vu,* 'vos'; v.11b, *c'o* 'que o'; *chao* 'chão'; vv.14b, 20b, 26b, 30b, contigo = [kõntíji]

This ballad begins with the father complaining that he has no son to take his place and serve in the war, stage A. In the Italian tale of *Fanta-Ghirò* (cf. Pires de Lima, *A mulher vestida de homem*, pp. 116–121), the king who has three daughters has received an ultimatum from a neighboring king. The war in our text (v. lb) is taking place in Baixo de Maranhão.[36] Maranhão is also mentioned in a variant from Elvas (cf. Pires, *A mulher*, p.223). In Gil's text the war takes place in Leon, but in most other versions it occurs between France and Aragon.[37]

In our text (v.2a) as well as in variants from Leiria, Monchique, De Ponte de Sor, Villa Nova de Gaia, Areias, and S. Jorge Island, the father has three daughters.[38] There are more frequently seven daughters in other published versions. In some of the Portuguese and Brazilian variants, it is the oldest daughter who offers to serve. In our text as well as in other Portuguese, Brazilian, Castilian, Catalonian, Judeo-Spanish, and French variants, it is the youngest who makes the offer (cf. stage B). All three daughters attempt to serve according to the Italian *Fanta-Ghirò*. The two eldest daughters fail as their identity is discovered, whereas the youngest daughter serves successfully, and her identity is not discovered until the battles have been won.

The father protests that the daughter would be discovered by the whiteness of her hands (C), her bustline (E), and her long hair (G) in our variant. These feminine features recur frequently in the above mentioned references. Other features that the father is certain will reveal his daughter's identity—such as the legs, feet, shoulders, face, and eyes—occur less frequently in the other printed texts and do not appear at all in our version. The determined daughter replies with such solutions as wearing gloves on her hands (D), wearing a tight jacket (F), and cutting the hair (H) in our variant. The latter two solutions appear frequently in the Portuguese, Galician, and Brazilian texts consulted. In Larrea's variants from Tetuan (pp. 93, 97), the jacket will conceal the chest; the hair is not cut but hidden under a hat which even-

---

or [kõntígu]; v.16b, *carr'gara* 'carregara'; v.17a, *a primér* 'ao primeiro'; v.17b, *pederniz* (sic) = perdiz + codorniz; vv.18a, 24a, *mia* 'minha'; v.20a, *mea* 'meu'; v.21b, *ditar* 'deitar'; v.26a, *P's* 'Pois'; v.30b, *banh* ''banho'; v.36a, *mãe enterrar* 'mãe a enterrar'; v.37b, *cam'nhar* 'caminhar'; prose after vv.37, *Fui* 'Foi'; *ouir* 'ouvir'; v.41b, *alg'ma* 'alguma'; v.42a, *Bat* ''Bate'.

Recited by José Goulart, Jr. (Ocean Beach; May 20, 1967).

[36]Our informant made special note during the recitation that the shoals of Maranhão was a place known for its many shipwrecks.

[37]Cf. Sampedro y Folgar; Menéndez Pidal, *Flor Nueva*, p. 181; Braga, I, 95, 98, 108, 120, 127, 131, 136; Vasconcellos, nos. 192–193.

[38]Cf. Vasconcellos, nos. 195, 200, 1002; Braga, pp. 105, 136, 140; Pires, *A mulher*, p. 187.

tually falls off and reveals the long hair. The gloves in Nigra's Italian variant appear later in the ballad as a part of the tests.[39]

The daughter leaves home and serves under the prince's command according to stage I of our version. Fanta-Ghirò, in the Italian tale, takes command of her father's troops and is invited to the enemy prince's palace to discuss the problem before initiating the battle. The prince tells the queen that he is disturbed by the beauty of Fanta-Ghirò. He already suspects that Fanta-Ghirò is a woman disguised as a man. In our text as well as in most other Portuguese versions and in some Castilian and Catalonian variants, the prince complains to his parents that, out of love, he is certain that D. Varão's eyes are not those of a man but of a woman (cf. stage J). In our text as in the Portuguese, Spanish, Catalonian, and Italian versions mentioned above, the mother suggests ways of testing D. Varão (K–P) to reveal her identity as a man or a woman. The tests are based on the differences between a man's and a woman's behavior in specific situations.

Two tests, an invitation to dine (O) and an invitation to bathe (P) with the prince, appear in our rendition and are the most frequently recurring tests in the Thomas, Braga, and Vasconcellos' collections and in Pires de Lima's *A mulher*. These two tests also occur in Gil's text from Extremadura, Mila's Catalonian variant, and in the Italian tale *Fanta-Ghirò*. D. Varão is invited to dine but is not invited to swim in the variant published by Pires de Lima in his *Romanceiro Minhoto*. She is invited to swim but not to dine in Nigra's Italian version and in the Castilian texts from Menéndez Pidal's *Flor Nueva*, and Cortés (pp.18,19,21).

In addition to the bath and dinner in our variant, D. Varão is also required to bed with the prince on night (M). D. Varão discreetly insists on sleeping in uniform according to some of the Portuguese versions. In stage N of our text, D. Varão takes off her boots, but no mention is made whether she slept in uniform or not. Instead, it is made clear that she does not turn towards him.

D. Varão is taken hunting as another form of a test in stage K of our variant. The hunt does not appear in any of the cited Portuguese

---

[39]For additional texts where the gloves are worn to conceal the hands see: Pires, *A mulher*, p. 185 from Viana do Castelo, p. 223 from Elvas; Braga, I, 102 from Foz do Douro; p. 112 from Loulé, p. 121 from Porto da Cruz; p. 128 from Madeira; p. 133 from Terceira; p. 137 and 141 from S. Jorge Isl., Azores; Vasconcellos, nos. 195 from Leiria, and 200 from Monchique; and Sampedro y Folgar, p. 115 from Galicia; Menéndez Pidal, *Flor Nueva*, p. 181; Cortés, p. 17 from Burgos; Larrea, pp. 93, 97.

and Spanish variants—except in Braga's version (I,117) where D. Varão is quite ready to hunt—and thereby, does not reveal any of the feminine shyness towards the idea of hunting. Except for the mention of a hunt as a test, there is no further correlation between Braga's text and ours. Milá mentions that in the Catalonian prose form the heroine is invited to hunt. In our version it is stated that a woman wouldn't know how to shoot, but D. Varão discreetly carried her firearms and at the first shot killed two birds. The Italian tale relates that Fanta-Ghirò brandishes the weapons and shoots with them.

The other texts cited above frequently include taking D. Varão on a stroll down the street or to the store where it is expected that she will admire the jewelry. However, she admires the swords or daggers. There may be some relationship between going on a "hunt" as in our text and going to the "store," and between D. Varão's ability to use weapons as in our variant and her admiring them in the store.

Our version does not include the test where D. Varão is taken to the orchard or garden which appears frequently in other texts.

The last test in nearly all of the variants referred to is the bath or swim as in stage P. Up to this point, D. Varão has not avoided any of the tests, but she does avoid the bath. In stage Q of our variant, in other Portuguese texts, and in Gil's Extremadurian version (no.57), she is found weeping.[40] The prince asks for the reason (R), and she invents the sad news that according to a letter that she has just received her parents are ill or dying as in stage T.

The sequence of the father's protests and D. Varão's tests vary considerably from one variant to another. A sequence paralleling our text was not found among the other versions consulted.

The concluding scene (U–X) also varies. In our text D. Varão returns home (U) and explains in a letter (V) that she was in the prince's company for three months (v.38), ate, slept, and hunted with him (vv.39–40), yet remained a maiden (W). She invites him to knock at her father's door should he care for her, stage W. Her declaration that she is still a maiden recurs frequently in the formerly cited Portuguese versions as well as in *Fanta-Ghirò* and in the Castilian text from Menéndez Pidal's *Flor Nueva*. In some versions D. Varão will declare that she has served for seven years without anyone suspecting that she was a woman except for the prince or

---

[40]Other Portuguese texts in which she is found weeping in this scene: Braga, I, 135, from Terceira Island; 147, from Goa, III, 371 from Asturias; Vasconcellos, nos. 196, 197, 200, 1002, 1003; Pires, *A mulher,* pp. 187, 191, 272, 278, 281.

captain, who has suspected it by her eyes. In some of Braga's and Vasconcellos' variants, she will declare this at her father's door or as she departs on her horse heading for home. In other texts she calls to the prince to follow her home and knock on her father's door. However, in none except the Italian story *Fanta-Ghirò* does she state it in a letter to the prince as in our variant. In our text she writes the letter after arriving at her father's house, whereas in *Fanta-Ghirò* it is explained in prose that the prince came to marry her after having received the letter. Other Portuguese versions that mention in prose, in conclusion, that the young man marries her are found in Pires, *A mulher* (p.197), and Vasconcellos (Nos.185,190–193). A wedding is mentioned in verse in a variant from Montalegre (cf. Pires, *A mulher*, p. 203).

"NOIVA ARRAIANA"

6

From: Pico, Azores

	—'Eu esteja com minhas tias, sentadinhas a fiar.	A
	—'Eu venha com meu sobrinho, se é qu' me vem visitar.	B
	—Cá da minha rica esposa qu' eu aqui deixei f'car?	C
	—A vossa rica esposa comigo não quis 'star.	D
5	Hoje se faz a boda, amanhã vae a casar.	E
	—Diga-m', a tia, ond' é qu' eu le qu'ria falar.	F
	—Menin', não ides lá, que vos podem matar.	G
	Eu chiguei ao portão ond' estavam a jantar.	H
	—Arrojem-s' ali cadeiras p'ro senhor s'assentar.	I
10	—Arrojem as cadeiras p'ra lá, não m' quero assentar.	J
	Peço licença é ao noiv' p'ra com a noisa falar.	K
	Aqui d'El Rei, quem m'acode! Justiça deste lugar!	L
	O' meus primeiros amor's, eu não 's posso deixar.	M
	Como vim, torno a voltar.[41]	N

This fragment of *El Navegante* known as *A Noiva Arraiana* in Portuguese has preserved in concise form one of several Pan-Hispanic ballad narratives concerning the disrupted wedding in which the long absent husband (or wife) reclaims his (or her) spouse at the very moment when he (or she) is about to marry another.[42]

---

[41]Vv.1a,2a *'Eu* 'Deus'; v.3b *f'car* 'ficar'; 4b *'star* 'estar'; 11b *noisa* 'noiva'.
Recited by Manuel Goulart (Ocean Beach; May 20, 1967).

[42]For further discussion of the disrupted wedding theme in balladry, see Armistead-Silverman *Yakob Yoná*, no. 23 (*La vuelta del hijo maldecido*).

The nephew's encounter with his aunts in stages A–C of our variant closely parallels Vasconcellos' text (no.102). Braga's variant from S. Miguel Island (Azores; I, 85–86) has initial verses which coincide with our version. In the synthetic text of the *Navegante* published by Catalán-Galmés in their article "El tema de la boda estorbada" (pp.76–77), the nephew encounters an aunt, but the aunt asks for signs or proofs by which she may recognize him. The asking for proofs or signs, which also occurs in Vasconcellos' nos. 92–96 and 994, does not appear in our version nor in Vasconcellos' nos. 97–102. Instead, in Vasconcellos' nos.97–102 and in Braga's texts (except for pp. 86–87), the nephew immediately asks about his parents (who have died), his white horse, boats, sword, gold ring, and lastly about his wife. In our variant there are no questions about parents, horse, etc.; the nephew immediately asks about his wife (C) as in Vasconcellos' nos. 97 and 99.

Our variant jumps directly from the encounter with the aunt, her news about the wedding (D–E), and her warning to her nephew (G), to the scene of the disrupted wedding and the recognition of the husband (H–N). The aunt's warning that the nephew would be killed should he interrupt the wedding also appears in nearly all of Vasconcellos and Braga's texts, as well as in the *Conde Antores* studied by Catalán-Galmés (p.78), where he shows that this scene comes from the *Navegante*.

The nephew's arrival at the door of the wedding banquet in stage H, the pulling out of chairs (I), his refusal to sit down (J), and his request to be permitted to speak with the bride (K) in our text coincide closely with Braga's version from S. Jorge (I, 77–79). The arrival at the door and the pulling out of chairs is mentioned in prose in Braga's version from S. Miguel (I, 85–86). The subsequent verses in the text from S. Miguel are also similar to our variant and to Braga's S. Jorge text. These stages (H–J) do not appear in Braga's other variants, though the nephew's demand to speak with the bride does occur. The arrival at the door of the banquet hall appears in Vasconcellos' text no.994 only, but the pulling out of chairs is not present in any of his texts.

According to Catalán-Galmés, the disruption of the wedding and the recognition of the nephew occurs in variants from Orense, Zamora, and Tras os Montes (p.78). The synthetic text proceeds immediately from the aunt's warning (G) to the arrival at the wedding banquet (H) and the consequent disruption (I–M), as in our version and Vasconcellos' and Braga's texts. The last two lines of the synthetic text (p.79) coincide with stages L and M of our version in which the nephew demands justice and claims that he can not forget or leave his first love. This scene also appears in *Antores* and in *Conde Sol* as presented by Catalán-Galmés (p.87), but it is preceded by the threat either to kill the Count (as in *Antores*) or to arrest the *romera* (as in the *Conde Sol*).[43]

The demand for justice in stage L combined with the nephew's reclaiming his first love (M), as in the synthetic *Navegante* cited above and in our version, also appears in Vasconcellos' nos.98 and 101 and in Braga's versions from S. Miguel, S. Jorge, Algarve, and Almeida's text. In the last hemistich of our rendition and in the last line of Braga's variant from S. Jorge (p.79) the nephew departs from the wedding scene (N).[44]

"JESUS PEREGRINO"

7

From: Oliveira do Hospital, Portugal

Vind' o lavrador d' airada,		A
mas ai oh meu Jesus,		
incontrou um pobrezinho.		
O pobrezinho lhe disse:		B
mas ai oh meu Jesus,		
—Levai-me no seu carrinho.		
O lavrador o levou,		D
mas ai oh meu Jesus,		
p'ra melhor casa que tinha.		
E mandou fazer a cama,		I
mas ai oh meu Jesus,		
da melhor roupa qu' havia.		
5 Depois da ceia na mesa,		F
mas ai oh meu Jesus,		
pobrezinho não comia.		
Levantou-se o lavrador,		L
mas ai oh meu Jesus,		
foi-lhe prèguntar que tinha.		
Ele mandou-o ir p'ra cama,	(Substitution for I–K)	
mas ai oh meu Jesus,		
e pobrezinho não dormia.		

[43]Catalán-Galmés note that this scene in *Conde Sol* derives from *Antores* which, in turn, has been contaminated by *El navegante* (p. 87).

[44]Bibliography:

Castilian—Catalán-Galmés, "El tema", pp. 66–98.

Portuguese—Braga, I, 71–87; Vasconcellos, I, nos. 92–102, II, no. 994.

Judeo-Spanish—Armistead-Silverman, *Yakob Yoná*, no. 23.

Levantou-se o lavrador,
   mas ai oh meu Jesus,
foi-lhe prèguntar que tinha.
O achou crucificado,
   mas ai oh meu Jesus,
   numa cruz de prata fina.
10 —Se eu soubera quem tu eras,
   mas ai oh meu Jesus,
   na minha casa t' eu tinha.[45]

Vind'o la - vra—dor d'ai — ra — da, mas ai oh meu Je—sus,

in — con—trou um po— bre — zin — ho.

7. This song has the characteristics of a Mixo-lydian mode. The final
tone indicating this mode is repeated six times in the melodic structure.
The vocal range is no more than a perfect fourth—except for the opening note. Again Mrs. Santos slides into her tones and vocalizes
enlarged intervals.

Mrs. Santos states that she learned this ballad from her school
book about sixty-two years ago. This ballad now appears in a third-
grade reader (authorized by the Ministry of National Education)
that is used throughout the Portuguese communities and probably
influenced oral tradition.[46] Mrs. Santos' rendition coincides closely
with the phrase structure of the text in the reader. In the following

[45]V. 1a *airada* 'arada'; v. 1b *incontrou* 'encontrou'; v. 3b Singer first sang "p'ra sua casa"
then correct, "p'ra melhor casa que tinha."
  Sung by Mrs. Maria Vincente Santos (Oakland; March 22, 1967).
  The six-syllable refrain in our variant seems to have little correlation with the other printed
texts. Braga's version from Minho e Beira Baixa (pp. 566-568) has a three-syllable refrain
"Ai Jesus." A refrain "Ai, meu Jesus" appears in a variant from Coimbra, which is close to
Oliveira do Hospital, where our informant learned her version (cf. Braga, II, 568). Vasconcellos offers two versions with a refrain: "Ai meu Jesus" (no. 839 from Vila Nova de Fozcoa),
and "Valha-me Deus e mais a Virgem Maria!" (no. 843 from Cadaval).
[46]Cf. Ministério da Educação Nacional *Livro de Leitura da Terceira Classe* (Lisbon, 1958),
pp. 138–140.

analysis, each letter stage corresponds with a single verse of the school text and is accompanied with a brief description of the narrative elements it represents: (A) the farmer finds a poor man; (B) the poor man requests to be taken in a cart; (C) the poor man is helped into the cart; (D) he is taken to the farmer's home; (E) supper composed of the best food in the house is ordered; (F) the poor man does not eat; (G) the poor man weeps; (H) the poor man sighs; (I) the bed is ordered to be made up with the best of linen; (J) describes the types of luxurious linen used; (K) the poor man sighs in the middle of the night; (L) the farmer gets up to see what is the matter; (M) the farmer's heart jumps, out of fear; (N) he finds the poor man crucified on a silver cross; (O) the farmer explains that, if he had only known who the poor man was, (P) he would have found even better room and board for his guest than the best that he possessed; (Q) the farmer is told to be quiet; (R, consisting of two verses) the farmer is told that he and his wife will be rewarded in paradise.

Mrs. Santos includes stages A,B,D,F,L,N,O, and a substitution for I-K. Her version does not include stages C,E,G,H,J,M, and P-R of the school text cited above. These verses seem to be unnecessary to the dramatic import of the ballad in our variant as well as in other published texts collected from the oral tradition.

For other printed versions that omit stage C of the school's text in which the poor man is helped into the cart, see Pires de Lima; Vasconcellos, nos.815–816,818,819,822,828,835,837–838; and Gil.

Stage E, in which supper is ordered, is preserved in all variants consulted excepting Vasconcellos' nos.831 and 836. The phrasing of stages E and I is identical and can lend itself toward the substitution of the request to make the bed (I) for the request to prepare dinner (E), as our singer did in v.4 of her rendition. Instead of the bed's being prepared after supper as in the school's text and other printed versions, it is prepared before supper in our variant. In order not to reiterate the making of the bed again after supper, our version substitutes with the farmer ordering the poor man to go to bed, and instead of the poor man sighing in the middle of the night as in stage K of the reader's text, our variant substitutes with the poor man not sleeping. These substitutions for stages I-K do not occur in any of the other references.

Stages G-H, which describe the tears and sighs of the poor man while at the table, do not appear in our version nor in any of the other printed variants except in Vasconcellos' no.843 from Cadaval.

In Vasconcellos' text, only the tears of the poor man (G) and not the sighs (H) appear. These two stages do not occur even in those variants that are otherwise almost identical to the text of the third-grade reader (cf. Thomas' version from Minho; Braga, II, 566–568, from Beira Baixa).

Our informant's version does not describe the types of sheets used (J) that appear in the majority of the other texts except Vasconcellos' nos.824,827–829, Braga's variant from Alemtejo, pp.569–570, and Gil's version from Extremadura.

The farmer's fear expressed by his heart jumping or thumping as in stage M does not occur in our variant, Gil, Pires, Vasconcellos, nos.815–843, 845–846, or in Braga, pp.566–517; Only Thomas' variant and Vasconcellos' no.844 include this stage.

In our text the farmer gets up twice to see what is the matter with the poor man (L). He gets up once right after supper because the poor man would not eat (v.6) and a second time after putting the poor man to bed (v.8). This verse (repeated in our version) occurs only after the poor man has gone to bed according to the school text and other cited references.

Mrs. Santos' version terminates with stage O just prior to where the farmer exclaims that he would have found even better room and board for his guest, stage P. The conclusion (Q–R), where reward is promised to the farmer and his wife, varies more than the former stages. Two variants that most closely coincide with the school text are Thomas' version and Braga's variant from Minho e Beira Baixa (cf.II, 566–568).

Doncieux in *Le Romancérco Populaire de la France* (p.374n.) states that some mediocre songs have been collected entitled *Le Miracle du Crucifix* in which the poor man disappears and in his place is found a crucifix. This parallels stage N of our version and of the third-grade reader in which the farmer finds the poor man crucified on a silver cross. It also appears in the Castilian tradition (cf. Gil) and in the majority of the cited printed texts of the Portuguese tradition. It does not occur in the variant presented by Doncieux as representative of the French tradition. Doncieux links this ending with the legend of Saint Elizabeth of Hungary who gives the conjugal bed to a leper. Her infuriated husband lifts the sheet to find the image of the cross in place of the leper.

In the French tradition (cf. Doncieux) the song is known as *Mauvais Riche (The Bad Rich Man)*, as compared to *El labrador y el pobre (The Farmer and the Poor Man)* in the Castilian text (cf. Gil), and as *Jesus Peregrino (Jesus the Pilgrim)*, *Jesus Mendigo (Jesus the Beggar)*, or *O lavrador da arada (The Farmer)* in the Portuguese tradition. In our text as well as in all other cited Portuguese, French, and Spanish versions, Jesus is disguised as the poor man.

The rich man refuses to give crumbs from the table or alms to the poor man in the French variant, but the farmer offers the best he has in the Castilian and Portuguese versions. In the French text, the wife offers the poor man soup for supper and a bed. Her actions parallel the farmer's charity in the Castilian and Portuguese versions. In Doncieux's text the charitable wife is rewarded, and the miserly husband is forbidden entry to paradise, whereas, both the charitable husband and wife are rewarded in the Portuguese and Castilian variants.[47]

[47]Bibliography:

Portuguese—Braga, II, 566–571, III, 600–605; Pires de Lima, *Romanceiro Minhoto*, pp. 69–70; Thomás, pp. 53–55; Vasconcellos, II, nos. 815–846; *Livro de Leitura de Terceira Classe*, pp. 138–140.

Castilian—Gil, II, p. 44, no. 72.

French—Doncieux, pp. 366–375.

[Editorial Note: For fuller references to the books cited in the notes, see WF, XXVIII:1 (January 1969), p. 19.]

Spanish Immigration to the United States

R.A. Gomez

SPANISH IMMIGRATION TO THE UNITED STATES *

IN our preoccupation with the Spaniards of earlier centuries and their subsequent impact on the history of the United States, we have tended to overlook the Spanish immigrants of modern decades. The presence of large numbers of Spanish family names in the United States, particularly in New York City and in western states, has obscured the fact that very few Spaniards have come to the United States directly from Spain.[1] It is the purpose of this paper to investigate the data on modern movements of Spaniards to the Americas in general, with special emphasis on the United States, and to consider the pattern of Spanish settlement in the United States that resulted from these movements.

The emigration of great numbers of Spaniards from Spain during the last decades of the nineteenth century and the first decades of the twentieth century was significant enough to place Spain among the most active migratory peoples of Europe, ranking behind the United Kingdom and Italy and ranking closely with Austria-Hungary and Germany.[2] So great was the exodus that much Spanish literature has been concerned with the subject: official reports, university studies, generally distributed books, and occasional treatment in regional novels.[3] The tenor of some of this writing is sufficiently soul-searching in its nature to place it in the general category of the introspective writing of the " generation of 98." By the turn of the twentieth century enough attention had been focused on the problem that legislation was soon passed attempting to prevent unnecessary emigration and to lessen some of the evils of it.

---

* The author is indebted to the American Philosophical Society for a travel grant which greatly facilitated research in the United States and Spain. This paper is intended as a framework for a book on the subject.

[1] The terms " Spaniard " and " Spanish," when used hereafter in this paper, refer to Spaniards who have come directly from Spain or who have come after only reasonable transitory movement through other countries.

[2] League of Nations, International Labor Office, *Migration In Its Various Forms* (Geneva, 1926), pp. 7-9. Prepared for the International Economic Conference, 1927.

[3] Some representative titles: Vicente Borregón Ribes, *La emigración española a América* (Vigo, 1952); Ramon Bullón Fernández, *El problema de la emigración. Los crímenes de ella* (Barcelona, 1914); José Casais y Santaló, *Emigración española y particularmente gallega a Ultramar* (Madrid, 1915); Domingo Villar Grangel, *La emigración gallega* (Santiago, 1901); Eduardo Vincenti, *Estudio sobre emigración* (Madrid, 1908); and special publications of the Consejo Superior de Emigración such as *La emigración española transoceánica, 1911-1915.*

Even today there exists official machinery for emigration since Spaniards still leave, although in far lesser numbers than forty years ago. Under the Ministry of Labor is found the Spanish Institute of Emigration provided with provincial offices throughout the country where information and assistance are made available for prospective emigrants. Spain has long demonstrated an interest in the broader problems of European migrations and has been an active member of the Intergovernmental Committee for European Migrations.[4] The Church has often expressed its concern for the many spiritual and moral problems connected with emigration to foreign places; in Spain, where the Church is an exceptionally active institution, this has meant close coordination between the Church and official agencies.

STATISTICS ON SPANISH EMIGRATION

It is impossible to be precise as to the number of Spaniards who left Spain or as to the number arriving in any particular country.[5] Official Spanish figures are not precise for reasons Spanish officials themselves have pointed out: the difficulty represented by large numbers who left the country illegally; the practice of keeping records on only third-class passengers leaving Spanish ports (in accordance with the legal definition of " emigrant "); the lack of distinction, for some years, between Spaniards and aliens who emigrated from Spain; occasional confusion as to whether figures include emigrants to Africa and European countries; and, finally, the problem of tallying immigrants coming back into Spain. Also, the figures of receiving countries in the Americas offer many complications.

From 1882 to 1947 it is reasonably adequate to place the total number of Spanish emigrants at approximately 5 million.[6] However, during this

---

[4] The most recent meeting was held in Madrid in September, 1961. See *ABC*, Madrid, for September 19, 23, and 30, 1961.

[5] The problem is difficult for any migratory movement. In 1922 the International Labor Office tried to assist with *Methods of Compiling Emigration and Immigration Statistics.*

[6] The figures on Spanish migration presented in this and following paragraphs represent a comparison of those found in the following sources: (1) Spanish official figures from *Estadística de la emigración e inmigración de España* from 1891 through 1923 (but covering from the year 1882), published in nine volumes by the official Spanish statistical agency known from 1891 to 1919 as Dirección General del Instituto Geográfico y Estadístico; also, *Anuario estadístico de España, 1960.* (2) U. S. figures taken from the *Annual Report of the Secretary of Labor* for 1923 and 1924. (3) Argentine figures from Dirección General de Inmigración, *Resumé estadístico del movimiento migratorio en la República Argentina, 1857-1924.* (4) Cuban figures from U. S. Bureau of the Census, *Cuba. Population, History, Resources, 1907* and Republic of Cuba, *Censo de 1943.*

period, approximately 3.8 million returned to Spain. A useable figure for net emigration, then, might be 1.2 million. The great bulk of this emigration took place in the quarter-century from 1900 to 1924; roughly two-thirds of all Spanish emigration from 1882 to 1947 (approximately 700,000 net) took place during that short period.

A certain pattern of movements to and from Spain from 1882 to 1947 is observable as follows:

1882-1898:   Heavy net emigration to Argentina and Cuba
1899-1900:   Decline (Spanish-American War)
1901-1913:   Heavy net emigration; beginning of substantial movement to the U. S.
1914-1918:   Net immigration (World War I)
1919-1930:   Heavy net emigration but virtual disappearance of emigration to the U. S. after 1921
1931-1947:   Decline; net immigration 1931-1934 (depression); followed by Civil War, World War II

SPANISH MOVEMENT TO LATIN AMERICA

Quite naturally, Spaniards flocked to Latin America in exceptionally great numbers, especially to Argentina and Cuba. Cuba was, of course, a Spanish colony until the end of the Spanish-American War and it served, therefore, as an outlet for Spaniards wishing to go to familiar surroundings in the western hemisphere. Furthermore, inducements were being extended to agricultural workers.[7] Argentina was a much greater attraction, having made a determined bid for immigrants.[8] Argentina, indeed, in the records of international migration, ranks second only to the United States in terms of immigration, both gross and net.[9] To a much lesser extent stood Brazil, Mexico, and Uruguay as attractions for Spaniards wishing to emigrate to Latin America.

Argentina has accounted for as much Spanish emigration as all other countries combined (and more, if the entire movement from the 1850's is considered). A comparison of Spanish and Argentine reports indicates that approximately half of the entire number of Spaniards emigrating from 1882 to 1947 is clearly attributable to Argentina's powerful attraction—about 600,000 net, with the possibility of a higher figure approach-

---

[7] On the attractions of Cuba, see Consejo Superior de Emigración (Spain), *Emigración transoceánica, 1911-1915*, pp. 135-136. Also, J. M. Alvárez Acevedo, *La colonia española en la economía cubana* (Habana, 1936), *passim.*

[9] In *Anuario Estadístico Interamericano*, 1942, immigration totals from 1820 to 1924 are given as follows: U. S. A.—33,188,000; Argentina—5,486,000; Canada—4,520,000; Brazil—3,855,000. All of these are gross figures, not accounting for departures.

[8] Indeed, the preamble of Argentina's Constitution of 1852-1853 extended equality of treatment for aliens.

ing 60 per cent.[10] Another 25 per cent or so went to Cuba, probably about 300,000 net. The remaining emigrants from Spain to the Americas (perhaps 15 per cent) would be distributed among Brazil, Mexico, the United States, Uruguay, and others.

Three great geographical areas of Spain have furnished all but a small percentage of emigrants: the Cantabrian and Atlantic coasts from the Basque provinces near France to Galicia near Portugal, with special emphasis on Galicia; the Mediterranean coast of Valencia and Murcia; and Andalusía in the southwestern corner. Some attention must also be given to the Canary Islands as well. The great central tableland contributed comparatively few emigrants; Catalonia, with its center of population in Barcelona, has not been as great a contributor as its importance suggests. Taking the years 1910-1915 as a representative period, the twenty most active provinces were as follows (the figures representing the gross number of transoceanic emigrants):

1.	Coruña	61,560	11.	Barcelona	15,682
2.	Pontevedra	53,106	12.	Valencia	12,230
3.	Orense	52,745	13.	Santander	11,837
4.	Lugo	51,883	14.	Alicante	10,911
5.	Oviedo	47,652	15.	Granada	10,770
6.	Almería	36,722	16.	Málaga	8,676
7.	Canarias	30,270	17.	Burgos	8,512
8.	Leon	29,415	18.	Murcia	7,978
9.	Salamanca	20,969	19.	Logroño	7,735
10.	Zamora	19,087	20.	Vizcaya	7,709

Total for all 49 provinces: 602,081 [11]

Speaking in the largest possible terms of Spanish geography, two great currents of migratory movement are represented: a northerly-to-westerly flow from Cantabrian and Atlantic provinces, adding northern Leon and the northern part of Old Castile (Burgos, Logroño, Santander); and a southerly-to-westerly flow out of Andalusía, the Levantine coast, and the Canary Islands. Employing the traditional regional terms, the order would be as follows:

1. Galicia (Coruña, Lugo, Orense, Pontevedra)	219,294	36.4%
2. Leon (Leon, Salamanca, Zamora)	69,471	11.5
3. Andalusía (Almería, Granada, Málaga)	56,168	9.3
4. Asturias (Oviedo)	47,652	7.9
5. Levant (Valencia, Alicante, Murcia)	31,119	5.2

[10] Estimates for the longer period from 1857 place the number at about one million, as does *Anuario estadístico de España, 1960*, p. 48.

[11] Consejo Superior de Emigración (Spain), *Emigración transoceánica, 1911-1915*, passim.

6. Canary Islands	30,270	5.0
7. Old Castile (Santander, Burgos, Logroño)	28,084	4.7
8. Catalonia (Barcelona)	15,682	2.6

(Vizcaya omitted from this grouping)

It is to be noted that Galicia stands clearly in front as the most substantial contributor to Spanish emigration. If we speak of the regional groups in larger terms, nearly two-thirds (63.1 per cent) are northern provinces (Galicia, Leon, Asturias, Old Castile, and Catalonia representing the regional groupings of these); of these, the northeastern regions dominate (55.8 per cent) in the picture (Galicia, Leon, Asturias); and Galicia, by itself, accounts for 36.4 per cent. These patterns may be safely employed as representative of the Spanish emigratory experience in general.

Special attention, then, should be paid to the massive movement of Spaniards from Galicia to American countries. This movement was so spectacular that much of the Spanish literature on emigration is focused on it. Most of the *Gallegos* went to Argentina and settled in Buenos Aires and vicinity. In 1953 one estimate stated that there were over 700,000 *Gallegos* in Buenos Aires, thus making it quite easily the largest Galician city of the world.[12] In addition to Buenos Aires, large groups of *Gallegos* are to be found in Caracas, Havana, and Montevideo. The *Centro Gallego* is a widely known mutual benefit organization in Latin American cities.

The *Gallegos* came from all vocational groups with especially large numbers of agricultural laborers, sailors, fishermen, waiters, and small shopkeepers. In many cities of Latin America they became middle-class merchants and their children have moved into professional classifications. Galicians, among the Spanish stereotypes, have long been known for their shrewdness and have been said to possess more of the qualities necessary for successful businessmen than most other Spanards.[13]

The Motivations for Emigration

The reasons for Spanish emigration offer no new source for the contemplation of international migrations. Largely, the motivations

---

[12] *Faro de Vigo. Número especial conmemorativo del centenario, 1853-1953.* Two contributors to this issue write about Galicia in Argentina: Antonio Lozano, pp. 92-93; Salvador Lorenzana, pp. 172-173.

[13] General Franco, Spain's Chief of State, is a Galician. It is sometimes said that his native shrewdness has provided him with the necessary qualities to achieve success militarily and politically. Recently, in *ABC* (Madrid), in the special twenty-fifth anniversary issue honoring Franco's accession to power, October 1, 1961, José Maria Pemán of the Spanish Royal Academy, referred to this *prudencia gallega.*

appear to be centered on economic pressures or desires. Some doubt exists as to whether or not so much emigration was justified by the existing economic conditions. An old popular song dating from before the turn of the century speaks for one point of view:

> A las Indias van los hombres,
> a las Indias por ganar:
> las Indias aquí las tienen
> si quisieran trabajar.[14]

Certainly Spaniards were " west-minded " and naturally so. Long before the Germans, Russians, Austrians, Poles, and even the Italians formed very widely distributed desires for a westward movement, the Spaniards had already established a sort of national highway to it. And even though the independence movement in Latin America largely erased the colonial system, Spaniards were likely to look to the Americas quite as naturally as the frontiersmen of early North America considered the western lands beyond the mountains.

The situation in agricultural areas represented an almost constant pressure for emigration. In the first place, the seasonal character of agricultural employment aroused desires to seek employment elsewhere for part of the year. Thus arose the fantastic *golondrina* movement by means of which thousands of Spaniards annually attempted to gain the advantages of working in two growing seasons: one in the spring-summer of Spain and another in the spring-summer of South America, mainly Argentina, where the warm season extended from November to April.[15] The *golondrinas* were not, properly speaking, emigrants, but they were so recorded in the official records of embarkation. The Italians engaged in this swallow-like movement between Italy and Argentina to an even greater degree than the Spaniards. A lesser but still significant temporary emigration to the Americas was also to be found in other than annual agricultural movements. Many were the Spaniards who emigrated to Argentina, Cuba, or the United States only long enough to gain sufficient savings at general skilled labor or mercantile activity, after which one lived in Spain at a rather higher level than before the venture. Indeed, there were Spaniards who " commuted " between Spain and somewhere in the Americas over a long period of years, usually maintaining a principal household in Spain.

Another pressure to emigrate, with an agricultural base, resulted

---

[14] Quoted by J. M. de Pereda in " A Las Indias," a short story in the volume entitled *Escenas montañesas*.

[15] See Mark Jefferson, *Peopling the Argentine Pampa* (New York, 1926), pp. 182 ff.

from population pressure on the land. In southern Spain, in the sugar-cane and fruit regions of Andalusía and the Levantine coast, population pressure was that of an excessive supply of labor on large plantations. In Galicia, in the north, the pressure was largely of another kind: the *minifundio*, or excessively divided land into plots too small for subsistence.[16] So scrupulously were lands divided among children that there were parcels of land no larger than the few square feet necessary to surround a tree. In the cases where, as sometimes in the interior of Galicia, lands were kept larger by primogeniture, the result would be the same—the other sons would have to move on, either to lands available through their wives or out of the area entirely. Since Galician families tend to run very large, the problem of pressure on the land was often acute.

Not always primarily economic in nature, but very strong in effect, was the attraction provided by the letters from relatives and friends already in residence in the Americas. Once a settlement of Spaniards was established there was a natural follow-up of relatives and friends from the old country. It might be pointed out that most Spaniards were literate and thus encountered no difficulty in communicating with their friends. In Cuba, for example, in 1907, it was reported that as many as 74 per cent of the "foreign whites" were literate; nearly all of these were Spaniards.[17] In addition to appeals from abroad, the Spaniards who returned to their cities and villages after some years' absence, perhaps with savings sufficient to mark them as among the more affluent of their communities, were appealing advertisements for the Americas.

It appears that the military draft laws were to some undeterminable extent influential in causing emigration. Since emigration statistics show that males in the age group from 15 to 55 constituted the bulk of emigrants (outnumbering females by about three to one),[18] it is obvious that thousands of prospective draftees were among them. Indeed, reports of port inspectors cited the desire to avoid military service as a common inducement to emigrate.[19]

It is said that many Spaniards emigrated solely out of the desire for adventure, although it is likely that this number is not significant. Gali-

[16] Vicente Borregón Ribes, *La emigración española a América* (Vigo, 1952), pp. 155-156.

[17] U. S. Bureau of the Census, *Cuba*, p. 206.

[18] United Nations. Department of Social Affairs. Population Division, *Sex and Age of International Migrants: Statistics for 1918-1947* (New York, 1953), pp. 261 ff.

[19] Dirección General del Instituto Geográfico y Estadístico, *Estadística de la emigración de España, 1891-1895*.

cians are apparently constrained to cite this motivation by pointing out that they have occupied one of the *finisterres* of the world and that, as mariners, taking to the sea is natural to them.[20] It may well be that the number so motivated may be outnumbered in Spanish experience by " reluctant emigrants " who were compelled to emigrate with husband, father, or elder brother.[21]

A most significant force in encouraging emigration might be described as external to Spain, family, or friends: the inducements extended by American republics, by agricultural interest groups, and even by steamship companies. Argentina, Brazil, and Cuba extended inducements involving land and/or employment; sugar planters in Cuba and Hawaii [22] and the Panama Canal enterprise were active recruiters. Agents were frequently sent to Spain to recruit such workers and perhaps to contract for their services before embarkation.

Special attention should perhaps be given to steamship companies and their activities in stimulating emigration. The literature of emigration and immigration is filled with usually condemnatory descriptions of their roles.[23] Some steamship companies apparently drummed up business without any particular concern for the welfare of the prospective passengers, even perhaps deceiving them as to their destination in some cases. Or, at the very least, this charge may be laid to the agents employed by such companies. There were, of course, perfectly legitimate and honorable enterprises of this kind, performing an adequate service without any skullduggery involved. Unscrupulous agents there were in good number, however, who cheated many emigrants; some, it was charged, were closely allied with local political chieftains.[24] Whatever the extent of these practices, it is a recognizable economic advantage for a steamship company, otherwise facing the possibility of returning with empty holds, to return with human cargo under third-class steerage arrangements—the best kind of cargo, since it frequently required no handling whatever. It was even possible to have the passengers carry on the cots and other furnishings necessary to their passages.[25]

With respect to economic motivations, there has existed for some time a debate on the true economic effects of massive emigration: one

---

[20] Salvador Lorenzana in *Faro de Vigo. Número Especial*, pp. 172-173.

[21] The author's father always maintained that he was reluctant to leave Spain and that he was tricked into leaving by his older brother.

[22] See later paragraphs on the Andalusian migration to Hawaii.

[23] Ramon Bullón Fernández, *El problema de la emigración* (Barcelona, 1914), pp. 32 ff.

[24] J. Casais y Santaló, *Emigración española*, p. 9.

[25] J. M. de Pereda, " A Las Indias," *Escenas montañesas*, has a description of this.

school of thought holds that emigration results in a loss of skilled or potentially skilled manpower which is necessary to a nation's economic health and growth; the other line of thought holds that massive emigration carries away an economic liability in the form of unemployable population and, in addition, may be the means for the introduction of new income from external sources. In the case of Spain, there is impressive evidence that new income in the form of savings earned abroad, and then introduced into the Spanish economy, by means of money orders sent back for the most part, has been a significant factor.[26]

EMIGRATION PROCEDURES

Spain has been admirably supplied with sea ports for the transportation of emigrants. Indeed, such ready outlet to the sea may itself have been a very important spur to emigration. A glance at the map of Spain will confirm that there are major sea ports located very conveniently to all parts of the country—almost as if spaced by design for easy outlet. Beginning in the north and moving around the coast of Spain in a counter-clockwise direction, we find Bilbao, Santander, Gijón, Coruña, Vigo, Cádiz, Málaga, Almería, Alicante, Valencia, and Barcelona.

The Galician ports of Coruña and Vigo have been the busiest embarkation centers, carrying half or more of all the passengers involved.[27] These ports have serviced, in addition to Galicia, neighboring Leon and Asturias. The second busiest group of ports are in Andalusía—Almería, Cádiz, and Málaga, which have served southern Spain. Barcelona has been important as the embarkation point for passengers from Catalonia, Aragón, Navarre, and the Balearic Islands. Two other groups are worthy of mention: the Cantabrian ports of Bilbao, Gijón, and Santander (serving that area and some neighboring areas to the south) and the ports of Palma and Tenerife on the Canary Islands.

Until 1907 there was no substantial legislation on emigration procedure. There existed a scattered series of laws, royal decrees, and ministerial rules that pertained to the subject.[28] Central to all these was the established principle of free emigration to which Spanish policy had adhered for many decades. Probably the basic law was best expressed by the Royal Order of 1888 which placed the responsibility on the

---

[26] Vicente Borregón Ribes, *Emigración española*, discusses this.

[27] All official Spanish reports give details on ports of embarkation; see especially Consejo Superior de Emigración, *Nuestra emigración por los puertos españoles en 1917*.

[28] Eduardo Vincenti, *Estudio sobre emigración* (Madrid, 1908), pp. 26 ff. gives a good survey of law applicable until 1907.

governors of the maritime provinces and port inspectors. A prospective emigrant would have to contact the officialdom of the maritime province through which he proposed to leave. The law provided a delay of fifteen days to follow a request for clearance. These requirements, plus the ordinary hurdles in contacting governmental officials, worked most to the advantage of residents of maritime provinces. If one were to seek departure from a foreign port, the law required going through the governor of one's own province of residence and also the Spanish consul in the foreign port—a procedure that sometimes proved as convenient as leaving from a Spanish port. Emigration, therefore, if it were to be legally accomplished, had to be well planned and might involve considerable travel in Spain itself. In addition, all this had to be geared to the possibility of securing passage on a steamship. Also there existed the problem, in many cases, of either securing clearance from, or buying one's way out of, military service. The law provided for buying up one's service in the military at the rate of 2,000 pesetas.

For a large number of prospective emigrants, the aforementioned complications meant acting through agents of emigration who not only could handle the official complications but also could establish contact with steamship lines. Usually, in fact, the agents were actively engaged in the interest of a certain steamship company.

Clandestine emigration was very common.[29] One form of this centered on departure from a foreign port. Gibraltar and Bordeaux, convenient to the south and north respectively, were very extensively used for that purpose. Agents were very important to this procedure since one had to make passage connections through a distant port in a foreign country. The emigrant, choosing this route, simply left Spain as a temporary visitor and boarded ship under the general direction of the agent, and without bothering to clear through any officialdom. This was occasionally begun as a contract arrangement, the agents in these negotiations often being paid so much per head. Agricultural workers by the thousands took this route to the Americas. By this method of emigration one could avoid complications at home or succeed where the legal route had failed him; and, in addition, he might have employment promised him.

In using the clandestine channels, the emigrant might be taking a great risk, especially when involved with an unscrupulous agent. He might find himself stranded in a foreign port, either the victim of a

---

[29] Consejo Superior, *Emigración, 1911-1915*, is quite candid about the subject.

deception or the victim of having a longer time to await passage than his financial position allowed. Even today the offices of the Spanish Institute of Emigration display colored posters warning against placing one's self in the hands of agents who conduct clandestine emigration procedure.

The precise number of clandestine emigrants can never be determined. A comparison of figures published by Spain and receiving countries for the same years indicates, however, that clandestine emigration in some years may have approached 40 per cent of all departures; Spanish figures for 1911-1915 indicate at least 25 per cent.[30]

Whether legal or clandestine, the emigration procedure frequently brought about distress. At many points along the way hardships might be encountered. It might start at home with the difficulty of raising the money necessary to make all the arrangements; this might require submitting to usurious rates for loans, perhaps as high as 30 per cent,[31] or otherwise suffering financially. Frequently an unnecessarily high commission would be paid for the services of various people involved—perhaps even an occasional public official. Later, in the port, awaiting transportation, there were the preying sharpsters of all kinds. Upon embarking the emigrant might find the third-class passage overcrowded, unsanitary, and poorly fed. The journey might take weeks (as for example the Andalusians who went to Hawaii) with fatalities along the way. Upon arrival there might be unemployment and for many the loneliness of separation from one's home and friends.

The Church has long been distressed by not only the possibilities of the miseries aforementioned but also by the fact that religious devotion appears to decline among the newly-arrived in foreign places. Therefore the Church has tried to prevent as much unjustified emigration as possible and also to hold foreign communities of Spaniards more closely to their old religious habits. A very prominent effort for a time was the organization of the Association of San Rafael, several chapters of which were in evidence by 1913.[32] Through this organization attempts were made to remedy the adverse religious, moral, and economic effects of emigration, particularly in some of the ports.

With the passage of a comprehensive emigration law in 1907, new administrative machinery was provided: a Superior Council of Emigration, local juntas, and machinery for tighter inspection in the ports

---

[30] *Ibid.*, p. 227.

[31] Consejo Superior, *Nuestra emigración*, p. 468.

[32] *Enciclopedia universal ilustrada* (Barcelona), XIX, 985.

of embarkation, including medical care.[33] Clandestine emigration was attacked not only by the tighter machinery but also by the attempt to offer more accessible assistance in all the provinces. Clandestine emigration was not halted by these approaches, however.

MODERN SPANISH IMMIGRATION IN THE UNITED STATES

If it were not for the presence of very large numbers of Spanish-speaking people of Mexican and Puerto Rican origin, Spanish family names in the United States would be as scarce as Turkish names and would be much scarcer than Finnish names.[34] Although Spain is numbered among the most migratory nations, only a comparatively small number of Spaniards came directly to the United States.

In the nineteenth century the number of Spaniards who came to the United States was quite insignificant, only approximately 42,000 reported by official U. S. figures from 1820 to 1900, an average of about 500 per year.[35] This was negligible when compared to the considerable numbers of other Europeans coming during the same period. In much of the reporting of that time, Spain usually appeared in the " all others " category. The census of 1900 shows only 7,050 Spaniards among the foreign-born out of a total of 10.3 million foreign-born of all origins.[36] They were largely resident in four maritime states: New York, Louisiana, California, and Florida (in that order of significance).

The overwhelming majority of the Spaniards who came to the United States did so in the quarter-century from 1900 through 1924, particularly beginning in 1903 and with especially large numbers in 1917, 1920, and 1921.[37] Indeed, 30 per cent of them arrived in the last three years mentioned. Thus, Spanish immigration actually concentrates, and then falls to negligible numbers, in the short space of five years before the passage of the first quota legislation in 1921. Somewhat over 174,000 Spanish immigrants came in the years 1900 through 1924; over 52,000 of these came in the years 1917, 1920, and 1921; in 1922, as a result of the Quota Law of 1921, the number dropped to 665.

---

[33] Biblioteca Iegislativa de la Gaceta de Madrid, *Ley y reglamento provisional para la aplicación de la ley de emigración de 1907* (Madrid, 1908).

[34] Mexicans and Puerto Ricans are not subject to quotas.

[35] *Annual Report of the Secretary of Labor*, 1923, appends a detailed chart for the years 1820-1923.

[36] See table on " Foreign-born Population by Country of Birth " in *Historical Statistics of the U. S.*, p. 66.

[37] *Annual Report of the Secretary of Labor*, 1923 and 1924.

The figures so far mentioned are those representing gross immigration. Account has to be taken of the numbers of Spaniards who returned to Spain after their arrival in the United States. Official U. S. figures indicate that from 1908 through 1940, approximately 72,000 Spaniards returned to Spain from the United States.[38] Not all of these are actually chargeable to the period from 1900 through 1924, of course, but it is only realistic to view the returnees in terms of the full flow since a high percentage of them, certainly, are chargeable to the period. This experience of emigration of Spaniards from the United States is a significant 41 per cent, if taken as a ratio of 72,000 to the gross number 174,000; and, even if considered as the emigratory effect over a longer period, the percentage would be very high. Many returned during World War I or in the slump years immediately following that conflict; an extremely large number returned after the first impact of the great depression of the 1930's.

The net immigration of Spaniards to the United States, then, from 1900 through 1924 (but using the 1908-1940 figures for the returnees) would approximate 102,000. Certainly 110,000 would be a reasonably safe figure to employ, allowing for various contributions to the uncertainty of the official records. This small number of Spaniards formed the foundation of the impact of modern Spanish formed the foundation of the impact of modern Spanish immigration to the United States.

The Immigration Acts of 1921 and 1924 cut off Spanish immigration almost to the vanishing point.[39] The Quota Law of 1921, which geared the number of immigrants from European countries to a ratio of three per cent of the number of each country in the United States as of 1910, provided a Spanish quota of 912. The Act of 1924, however, which was aimed at reducing severely the influx of southern and eastern Europeans, based on two per cent of 1890 numbers, brought the Spanish quota down sharply to only 131 per year. This quota was revised upward to 252 in 1929.

A few thousand Spaniards have come to the United States since 1924 in addition to the small quotas provided. Some came as non-quota immigrants in accordance with provisions allowing relatives to join residents in the United States. A very small number have been admitted through private bills passed in the Congress.

---

[38] No figures available before 1908.

[39] Charles Gordon and Harry N. Rosenfeld, *Immigration Law and Procedure* (Albany, 1959) gives a good brief survey of U. S. immigration legislation, pp. 5 ff.

Spaniards for a few years benefited through special legislation. Acts passed in 1954, 1955, and 1956 provided for the admission into the United States of a total of 1,135 sheepherders, a labor specialty in critically short supply at the time.[40] Although the Acts did not single out Spaniards specifically, the effect was to admit Spanish and French Basques for the most part. The numbers admitted, however, were chargeable to national quotas and the result was to mortgage the Spanish quotas entirely through 1960 and partially for a few years thereafter. This special legislation was not renewed in 1957 due to the recommendation of the Committee of the Judiciary of the House of Representatives in a report delivered in February, 1957.[41] The report charged that the provisions of the three bills had been subject to abuses. It was charged that some sheepherders brought over were actually engaged in other kinds of work; some were not filing alien address cards; some were violating the provisions of the Selective Service Act; and some, it was charged, were brought over in the first place who were not sheepherders at all. Since those admitted under the special bills were considered permanent residents, and not temporary workers, some outrage had been expressed at the abuses.

The following table will serve to show the general pattern of settlement and migration of Spaniards in the United States:

States in Order of Number of U. S. Residents Indicating Spain as Country of Origin 1860-1950

1860	1870	1880	1890	1900	1910	1920	1930	1940	1950
La.	La.	N.Y.	N.Y.	N.Y.	Cal.	N.Y.	N.Y.	N.Y.	N.Y.
N.Y.	N.Y.	La.	La.	Haw.	Fla.	Cal.	Cal.	Cal.	Cal.
Cal.	Cal.	Cal.	Cal.	Fla.	N.Y.	Fla.	N.J.	Fla.	N.J.
			Fla.	Cal.	Haw.	Pa.	Fla.	N.J.	Fla.
				La.	Ida.	N.J.	Pa.	Pa.	Pa.
					Tex.	Haw.	Haw.	Haw.	Ohio
					Ariz.	W. Va.	Ohio	Ohio	Ida.
						Ida.	W. Va.	W. Va.	Mich.
						Ohio	Mich.	Ida.	Conn.
						La.	Nev.	Mich.	Nev.
						Conn.	Ida.	Nev.	W. Va.
						Nev.	Ill.	Ill.	Ill.
						Tex.	Conn.	Conn.	Mass.
						Ariz.	Tex.	Tex.	Tex.[42]

Since only states have been included that show any significant number of Spaniards at the time of each census, the first service the table per-

---

[40] 85th Congress, 1st Session, House Report 67 (1957).

[41] *Ibid.*

[42] Compiled from U. S. Bureau of the Census. *Census of 1950.*

forms is to show the light distribution geographically until the census of 1920. In addition, the following observations, in chronological order, appear significant:

1. Until 1890 the Spaniards in the United States were largely centered in two natural settings: New York City, the major port of entry for most shipping lines, and the centers of the old Spanish colonial influence in California and Louisiana.

2. With the census of 1890 we find recorded the first modern settlement of Spaniards in Florida, a center of concentration that is still important tody. To some extent Florida had been a Spanish interest from colonial days but had not furnished an attraction similar to that New Orleans provided for Louisiana.

3. The census of 1900 brings into the picture the beginning of one of the most spectacular movements of Spaniards into the United States—Andalusian sugar workers who went to Hawaii in very large numbers. Hawaii appears significantly in the censuses of 1890 through 1940, although a movement to California began shortly after their arrival and continued until most had gone to the mainland by 1920. The California flow was so strong that California out-ranked New York as a " Spanish state ' in the census of 1910.

4. In the years from 1900 to 1910, a new pattern is introduced in the mountain West and Southwest. Spaniards began turning up in the great grazing lands, particularly in Idaho.

5. Finally, the censuses of 1920 and 1930, and continued with little change in 1940 and 1950, show a movement greatly influenced by the expansion of heavy industry following World War I. The New York contingent expands out into New Jersey and Connecticut; appreciable numbers are discovered in such industrial states as Illinois, Michigan, Ohio, and Pennsylvania; in West Virginia are found Asturian coal miners and metalworkers.

The census of 1950 sets forth the following states with appreciable numbers of residents who claimed Spain as country of origin.

New York	14,705	Michigan	890
California	10,890	Connecticut	886
New Jersey	3,382	Nevada	815
Florida	3,183	West Virginia	712
Pennsylvania	1,790	Illinois	714
Ohio	1,141	Massachusetts	659
Idaho	985	Texas	604

Total: all states 45,565 [43]

---

[43] *Ibid.*

New York City Area. Close to half (41 per cent) of all those Spaniards who claimed Spain as country of origin in 1950 lived in the area of New York City—that is, in New York City itself and nearby Connecticut and New Jersey communities. This urban settlement is characteristic of the later waves of immigration in general. The 1950 census shows Spaniards still largely urban with only California, Idaho, and Nevada indicating any appreciable rural settlement.

Spaniards in New York gathered at first in a number of tenement districts, especially in Brooklyn. These clusters were fairly compact in their Spanish identity with close associations socially and with wide subscription to mutual benefit societies.[44] Laborers, restaurant workers, cigar salesmen, seamen, and small shopkeepers they were for the most part, with very large representation from Galicia. The next generation moved out into the general flow of American life and most of the settlements had lost their compactness by the late 1920's and early 1930's.

Today Spaniards are to be found scattered in all parts of the greater New York area with some special concentrations in northern New Jersey and Greenwich Village. On any fine day one can find groups of them in the vicinity of Columbus Circle. New York furnishes a very widely distributed Spanish language newspaper, *La Prensa*, which is especially evident today due to the greater circulation brought about by the arrival of a very considerable community of Puerto Ricans. In New York City may be found offices of the Casa Galicia and the Centro Vasco Americano, among other more broadly defined organizations.

California. Ranking next to New York is a large concentration of Spaniards in California—about 24 per cent of the 1950 total. These are found largely in the Los Angeles and San Francisco areas although appreciable numbers are settled in the rich agricultural valleys.

The San Francisco area has a sizeable group from all parts of Spain. There is a special quality of Spanish representation, however, in that there are many Andalusians, most of whom came from Hawaii (see following section). San Francisco also has a distinctive Basque touch; in the area of Broadway and Columbus Avenue are a number of Basque restaurants and hotels. The Unión Española de California, the Unión Española Benéfica, a Basque club, and others, provide social and mutual benefit programs. Spanish picnics are held fairly frequently under the sponsorship of one or more of such organizations.

---

[44] See Prudencio de Pereda's novel, *Windmills in Brooklyn* (New York, 1960) for a delightful description of a fictional Spanish group based on the author's youth in Brooklyn.

In the Los Angeles area the emphasis is more on northern Spaniards who have been attracted to the heavy industry such as those in Fontana, the location of a Kaiser steel mill. The Sociedad de Beneficencia Mutua is prominent in the area with an office in Los Angeles. An organization of great significance to Spanish cultural interests is also located in Los Angeles: the Del Amo Foundation. The Foundation, founded by Dr. Gregorio Del Amo, is engaged in maintaining cultural exchange programs between Spain and southern California; its secretary is Eugenio Cabrero who came to the United States from the province of Santander.[45]

The Andalusía-Hawaii-California Migration. One of the most numerous groups of Spaniards in the United States came from the sugar and fruit plantations of Andalusía to work in Hawaii.[46] Although a number had arrived earlier, most came in six shiploads in the years 1907, 1911, 1912, and 1913. This migration is one of the more spectacular clandestine emigrations from Spain, for Spanish records carry no official enumeration of it. The ships sailed from Gibraltar after contacts were made through agents for the Hawaiian Sugar Planters Association. For the most part, the recruiting took place in the provinces of Almería, Cádiz, Granada, and Málaga in Andalusía although some were contacted in Murcia. All together in the six shiploads involved were transported 7,735 workers. The long journeys took their toll in lives and sickness.[47] The inducements were however, great: free transportation, free housing, and guaranteed employment at a wage stipulated in advance.

Shortly after the first movements to Hawaii, the sugar workers became interested in moving on to the mainland, to the city of San Francisco and vicinity. Many went to work as laborers in the task of cleaning up the city after the earthquake and fire of 1906. World War I attracted more of them and by 1920 most of the original workers had made the move, settling in the city or in other Bay cities such as Leandro, Hayward, and Crockett. Many settled in nearby agricultural communities such as Mountain View and Sunnyvale where they owned, or worked on, fruit acreage.

---

[45] Mr. Cabrero contributed the section on Spain in F. J. Brown and J. S. Roucek, *Our Racial and National Minorities* (New York, 1937), pp. 388-394.

[46] See George F. Schnack, *Subjective Factors in the Migration of Spanish from Hawaii to California*, unpublished M. A. thesis, Stanford University, 1940; also, *Hearing on Immigration into Hawaii Before Committee on Immigration*, U. S. Senate, 67th Congress, 1st Session.

[47] In Bullón Fernández, *Emigración*, Appendix, p. 76, there is a reprint of a news story that appeared in *Noticiero universal* (Barcelona), March 7, 1912; it states that forty children and three adults died on the *Willisden* en route to Hawaii.

Once these settlements had been established, later contingents of Andalusians came directly from Spain to California to join relatives and friends.

Florida. Florida has long been a center for Spaniards, particularly in Tampa and vicinity. This movement has been influenced by the proximity of Cuba and the cigar industry. The *tabaqueros* of Spain—almost all of whom were Asturians originally—migrated to Cuba in considerable numbers during the latter half of the nineteenth century. Eventually some of the cigar-makers established themselves in Key West; in 1886, following labor difficulties, a number of establishments moved to Tampa with thousands of employees. The concentration of Spaniards in this vicinity has remained strong since that time with a population from 3,000 to 5,000. Ybor City, a district east of Tampa's business section, has been the center of the Spanish community, featuring such organizations as Centro Asturiano and Centro Español.[48]

Mountain West. In the mountainous range country of the western United States are to be found appreciable numbers of Spaniards engaged in sheep and cattle ranching along with some engaged in servicing industries in the towns and cities of the area. This clustering of Spaniards is especially characterized by a concentration of Basques in the sheep country of the northern Rocky Mountains, centering chiefly in Idaho and Nevada with some distribution in neighboring California, Oregon, and Washington. Basque sheepherders, and to some extent Spaniards from other Spanish sheepherding provinces, began coming to the United States about 1910. In some ways this has constituted one of the most distinctive of Spanish migrations. Spain is one of the nations that has been continuously engaged in sheep-raising for hundreds of years back into antiquity. It is carried out in its most spectacular fashion in the mountains of northern Spain—the Basque provinces, Santander and Navarre: a region of incredibly steep pasturelands of green grass, rounded off into pinnacles by deep valleys. To see a herd of sheep under the care of a Spanish shepherd in the mountains of Idaho is one of the most ancient of old-world scenes, transferred to an American setting.

Boise, as the urban community in the center of the Idaho-Nevada sheep ranges, has become the Basque capital of the United States, as some have described it. There is a sort of Boise-San Francisco axis in

---

[48] In *Southern Folklore Quarterly*, in the volumes for 1937, 1938, 1939, and 1941, appear a number of articles on the Spaniards in Tampa, written by Ralph Steele Boggs and others.

Basqueland U. S. A. with San Francisco serving as a great recreational capital for Basques in many states.

Industrial Midwest. In the heart of the industrial empire of the United States—in the midwest along with Pennsylvania and West Virginia—a few thousands of Spaniards have settled in the employment patterns presented by heavy industry. In 1950 there were 5,157 Spaniards resident in the industrial states of Illinois, Michigan, Ohio, Pennsylvania, and West Virginia. The most compact group consisted of a concentration of Asturian coal miners who settled in West Virginia decades ago in such numbers as to rank that state as sixth or seventh " Spanish state " in the censuses of 1920, 1930, and 1940. In addition to these, there were also metalworkers in other West Virginia locations, such as Clarksburg. In the steel cities of Ohio and Pennsylvania can be found Galicians and Vizcayans; in the rubber factories of Ohio are others of the same regions.

Assimilation. The descendants of Spanish immigrants have, of course, moved into the general courses of American life and, except for an occasional gathering such as a Spanish picnic, they are roughly cross-sectional of the citizenry of the United States. The number of Spaniards who came as immigrants, and who stayed permanently, had dwindled to 45,456 according to the census of 1950,[49] largely by virtue of the deaths of the earlier arrivals. This number will undoubtedly diminish very speedily to a very small number by 1970. Thus, the alien Spaniards coming in such tiny quotas in the last forty years will be unable to keep alive the Spanish identity in the United States.

Spaniards have demonstrated a decided tendency to cling to their Spanish roots, as indicated by the high percentage of them that have remained aliens. In the twenty-year period from 1923 through 1942, only 20,722 Spaniards became naturalized citizens of the United States.[50] A few months later, in early 1943, there were still 39,670 Spanish aliens according to the alien registration (which had just begun its now annual enumeration).[51] This figure approximated 70 per cent of all Spaniards then in the United States who claimed Spain as country of origin; further, it approximated 35 per cent of the whole net number of immigrants to the United States from Spain in modern decades. With the coming of World War II, and to some extent in the late 1930's, many

---

[49] *Historical Statistics of the U. S.*, p. 66.
[50] See *Annual Report of the Immigration and Naturalization Service, 1950.*
[51] *Ibid.*

thousands of Spaniards did become citizens, however, and in 1960 there were only 17,526 registered Spanish aliens.[52]

Concluding Observations

Speaking most broadly, the foregoing paragraphs furnish a foundation upon which to build a number of generalizations about the numerical and social impact of Spanish immigration to the United States.

In spite of the prevalence of Spanish family names in some parts of the United States, a small number of Spaniards came directly to the United States. The net number (arrivals less departures) in the period from 1900 through 1924, the period which brought most of them, would probably number less than 110,000. For the most part they came in the few years before the passage of the Immigration Act of 1924 and their numbers have been negligible since that Act.

Spanish immigration to the United States has been but a very small part of Spanish immigration as a whole. Most Spanish migrants went to Latin America, particularly to Argentina and Cuba with some smaller numbers to Brazil, Mexico, and Uruguay. Spanish immigrants to the United States are perhaps ten per cent or less of the total.

The settlement of Spaniards in the United States has resulted in five major regional concentrations: the New York City area, California, Florida (particularly Tampa), the Mountain West, and a scattered pattern in the industrial midwest. There are vast areas of the United States where few would be found, particularly the grain-producing plains states, the rural midwest, and most of the south. The settlement pattern has been largely urban with substantial rural settlement only in California and the range country of Idaho and Nevada. There are very few Spanish communities in any compact sense today; Tampa, Boise, and Gary (West Virginia) offer some aspects of this.

R. A. Gomez

University of Arizona,
Tucson, Arizona

---

[52] Courtesy of Department of Justice, Immigration and Naturalization Service, by letter.

Basque Settlement in Oregon

Ione B. Harkness

BASQUE SETTLEMENT IN OREGON

By IONE B. HARKNESS[1]

THE SOUTHEAST corner of Oregon harbors one of the strangest and most interesting people of all its diverse races. The Basques, whose origin is lost in obscurity, whose native tongue, the Escuara, is a puzzle to philologists, have answered the call of climate and settled in the semi-arid region of Malheur and Harney counties.

From the northern coast of Spain the towns of Bilboa and Viscaya sent forth the vanguard in 1889 to seek in the new world a location similar in topography and climate and adapted to their ancient occupation of sheep herding. This they found in the Nampa triangle in the vicinity of Steens Mountain. The creeks and small lakes supply water; the soil supports various varieties of grass; the climate is dry; the location is remote from the civilization that is detrimental to sheep raising. A sweep of country stretching 275 miles between Crane, Oregon, and Winnemucca, Nevada, furnishes a wide range.

The settlers, ambitious young men, entered the United States by way of Ellis Island, and quickly drifted across the continent in search of the familiar habitat for sheep herding. This they found at various points in the inland empire. Today the principal Basque settlements are at McDermitt, on the northern Nevada border; at Jordan Valley, at the intersection of the 43rd parallel with the Idaho boundary; at Andrews, 125 miles south of Crane; at Fields, 15 miles farther south; and as far north as Ontario, at the junction of the Malheur River with the Snake.

The Basques proved to be so much better herders than the Mexicans that the latter were quickly driven out. Their method was to take bands of sheep into the hills and stay for years until their accumulated wages would enable them to buy flocks or ranges of their own. Then their friends and relatives would be sent for. Usually a cousin or brother came first; then before many years the whole clan was with him. They arrived in large numbers just before and during the World War. Since the war many of the American ranchers have sold out to the Basques,

---

[1]This study was made in 1925 as part of a thesis on communistic settlements in Oregon.

either because their fortunes were made or because of the depression in stock raising.

The leading man among the Basques at McDermitt, Joe Uguesia, was worth more than $20,000. He owned large bands of sheep and the largest store in the town.

Near Westfall, Malheur County, a Basque owns one of the finest ranches, has three large bands of sheep, drives a Buick, and carries a large life insurance. He and his three children speak good English, his wife speaks Spanish and "Bosco," the colloquial name for themselves and their language. An unusual circumstance in regard to this man is that he hires only American herders, ranch hands or camp tenders. Usually the race is extremely loyal and clannish.

McDermitt is strictly a Basque town; only two stores in the entire village are owned by Americans.

At Fields there are five families, while around Andrews there are some 50 or 60 single men. The pioneers of this section were Felix Urisar, Angel Egurolla, Eusabio Asuerey and Henri Suedagasta. Jordan Valley is a strong Basque settlement. At Ontario a "Bosco" boarding house accommodates 20 or 30 young people.

The pioneers among the Basques kept rather closely to sheep herding; very few became naturalized, as they expected to return to Spain when they had accumulated sufficient fortune. The second generation, however, has taken up various occupations, becoming auto mechanics, chauffeurs, merchants or hotel proprietors. So more relatives were sent for from Spain to carry on the ancestral occupation.

They are a thrifty, energetic, peaceable people and make good citizens. In Jordan Valley and Ontario many of the leaders in community enterprises are Basques. In the county track meets, declamatory contests and county fairs their children are creditably represented and they win their share of the honors. All of them are more or less educated, speaking Spanish besides their own Escuara and quickly learning English. A large proportion of the children attend high school and many enter college. The Catholic faith is their religion, but as they become Americanized they drift away from the faith of their fathers.

Brilliant colors are used in their costumes. Many of the young men wear a bright kerchief or sash. They are attractive in appearance and make a favorable impression on the sojourner among them.

The typical Basque has a clear, olive complexion, dark eyes, perfect teeth and very red lips. They are socially inclined and are fond of gathering in the plaza or around the stores, where some will play the accordian or guitar, while others of the group stand in a circle with their hands on each other's shoulders and sing. They dance the American dances, and have also their own Spanish and folk dances. Though they play cards they do not gamble, and though they drink they do not become boisterous or vulgar.

In the remote districts where American influence is less pronounced the houses are of the Spanish Basque type, low stone houses, divided into many small rooms, insuring warmth in winter and coolness in summer.

The cases of racial intermarriage is confined to Basque men marrying American girls; there is not a single case of marriage between an American man and a Basque girl.

The Spanish Basques in California

Julia Cooley Altroochi

THE SPANISH BASQUES IN CALIFORNIA

By Julia Cooley Altrocchi

IT has required the Spanish cataclysm to bring the isolated Basques from the purple ravines of the Pyrenees and the seaward slopes of Biscay into the forefront of world attention. For hundreds of years these inexplicable people have lived unobtrusively, self-sufficiently, quite as proudly as their own mountains, constituting a mystery which has remained more or less unelucidated since the days of Strabo and Livy. At intervals, intrepid bands of Basque whalers making their expeditions as far as Newfoundland in pre-Columbian, possibly pre-Viking days, or Basque corsairs darkening the waters of the world with their sail-shadows, or individual liberators like Simon Bolivar or saints like Francis Xavier have issued out of the Biscayan Gulf to participate for better or worse in world affairs. But otherwise little has been heard of the Basques except in the charming interpretations of Pierre Lhande, George Borrow, Rodney Gallop, Eleanor Mercein and Dorothy Canfield Fisher.

That there are, for instance, thousands of Basques living as artisans in the cities and as shepherds along the golden slopes of California is a fact realized by exceedingly few Californians. Yet the exodus of Basques from Europe towards the pampas of the Argentine, where they first learned to be successful shepherds, and then upward towards the slopes of California so much resembling their own slopes, has been going on steadily for almost a hundred years. For the most part, the Spanish Basques have settled north of San Francisco Bay, along the Sacramento Valley and the beautiful foothills of the Coast Range, while the French Basques have settled south of the Bay in the San Joaquin Valley, especially in the vicinities of Fresno and Bakersfield. So quietly and successfully have the Basques merged with their background that it requires a definite venture to discover them.

I well remember the day when, having learned, after living in California for nine years, that there were Basque shepherds in the Sacramento Valley, we struck out from San Francisco to find them. It was an April day, when the California hills were still green, not stubble-gold as they become when the hot summer sun has poured down upon them. But as we drove northeast of San Francisco, at the outer edge of the Sacramento Valley, the Vaca Hills turned from green to sea-blue, the grass became deeper in color and blade, with white cranes making oriental panels here and there; and great lakes of flowers appeared along the foothills, blue lakes of brodiæa, golden lakes of California poppies and "meadow sunshine." It was such scenery as demanded picturesque inhabitants—and provided them.

Very soon, flocks of sheep appeared and white ranch-houses, riotous with roses and bordered with jonquils. It was time to ask questions. We stopped at a ranch-house and inquired for Basques. An American rancher's wife answered the bell.

"Yes, I believe there *are* Basques around here," she replied to our question. "The Marcos are Basques, aren't they, Will? Yes, they're Basques. High class. As nice as anybody" (implying at least a potential deprecation of the foreigner).

"Yes, nice people," supplemented the rancher. "You might have a little difficulty getting under their skin. Kind of quiet, you know. Keep to themselves. Mrs. Marcos is a high-class woman. The Basque women, especially, are mighty nice, good-looking and well-educated."

To my question as to whether the Basques seemed in the least musical, whether, for instance, they ever sang in the fields or while tending their sheep, the rancher's wife answered:

"Oh, a little, I guess. Now and then you hear 'em. But for singing you ought to hear the Italians when they're picking fruit in the orchards. Sing? All the time!"

"What do they sing? Opera?"

"Oh, yes. Especially from that opera—you know—*Allegro*—and, and—lots of others!"

This incredible remark put an amusing end to our questions and sent us in search of the Marcos family. A circuitous ride along a country road under the hills led us to the remote Marcos ranch. Green hills, white sheep, rain-pools, blue brodiæa, a white farm-house under poplar trees. Not a house of stone, as in the Basque country in the old days, "whose height must not exceed that of the upraised lance of a mounted horseman" and whose "beams were stained with bullock's blood," but a house of wood, balconyless, porchless, dull white, splashed with the lovely shadows of trees, and somehow melting into the landscape. The setting was not unlike that which Rodney Gallop gives as typical in his charming *Book of the Basques:*

"Those blue mountains and green valleys, those golden maize-fields and poplar-bordered streams are to be found elsewhere. But one could never mistake the aspect of the villages, clusters of whitewashed houses with chocolate beams and shutters and the scarlet gash of red peppers drying on the balconies ..."

As soon as we had let down the pasture-bars and driven into the enclosure, the alien feeling shut down around us completely. There, in a sheep-pen a few rods from the house, five men were working, Marcos and his assistants. Foreigners in every line. Squat, square-shouldered, square-hipped, square-browed men, strong and agile, with dark hair, eagle-keen dark eyes and large, well-formed noses. Some one has spoken of their "Egyptian-statue shoulders." I could not help remembering also one of the more or less discarded theories that the Basques may be descendants of the ancient Etruscans. Certainly there is more than a passing resemblance between these strong, stocky, keen-faced people and the wonderful statue of the Etruscan peasant couple in the museum at Volterra and the many magnificent tomb-figures from Corneto-Tarquinia and Arezzo and Populonia.

The five Basques were conducting the rattle-brained sheep up a runway into a truck through the leadership of a white goat (cousin, no doubt, to those "Judas goats" that lead the sheep to slaughter in the

Chicago and Kansas City stock-yards). The sheep were to be driven, by truck, for summer grazing to the Sutter By-Pass, twelve miles away. "In the old days," said Marcos, "it would have taken two days to drive them, on the hoof."

Before driving away, M a r c o s courteously took time out to step over to his house and to call his wife into the yard, under the poplar trees, to meet us. No wonder Mrs. Marcos had elicited eulogies from the neighboring rancher. She was a superb-looking woman, tall, hand-some, with the same square set to the shoulders, a proud lift of the chin, a fine forehead, high cheek-bones, dark, waving hair and the greenest eyes that were ever seen. The word "Minerva" slipped not al-together inconsequently into my mind. Mrs. Marcos wore no toga, but a shining-clean, leaf-patterned (laurel?) green gingham dress, a white lace apron and a dark green sweater. She was very amiable and willing to answer questions, though a little eager that her husband should be off to the Sutter By-Pass.

In the course of conversation, we learned that Mrs. Marcos came from Navarra, and that she was naturally worried about the Spanish war sit-uation.

"Yes, my father is there. My relatives are there. We write and receive no answer. Many of our young men went over to get Spanish wives and have remained in Spain to fight. Yes, we are all Loyalists."

It was interesting to see how far the Spanish situation had reached, stretching its shadow out over all these Basque shepherd-families on the California hills. We changed the subject, to lift the sadness from Mrs. Marcos' face. Through her an-swers to our questions, we learned

of the Basque festivals that are held now and then at Bakersfield, Fresno, Los Gatos and Richmond, of the old Basque costumes worn at the festi-vals, of the wine drunk out of pig-skin containers, of the lambs barbe-cued whole in Homeric style, of the music of the guitars and the flutes and the cornets, of the dances, the Spanish fandango or the jota, from Andalusia, and of the *purusalda*, the genuine Basque dance, and of the old songs that are sung. When we asked our question about singing in the fields, Mr. Marcos succinctly made answer:

"In our country we sing. Not here much. We sing no more."

The answer reminded us of other things we had heard, about the Mexicans who, only a little while ago in California, were still singing their Spanish songs as they sheared the sheep or rounded up the cattle, about the Italians who have been joshed by their fellow-workmen out of singing their *"allegros"* unless they are deep in the orchards and vineyards away from other people, about the Japanese "who were the politest people you ever saw when they first came over," and who can only be seen at very rare intervals now, far away in the almond-orchard aisles, bowing to each other low from the waist when they think no one else can possibly see them. .

Why is it that our American civi-lization silences the music and the graciousness in all these people? Singing they come, and silent they stay. Is it still the cold clutch of the Puritan on our spirits that mutes the song—even here in Cali-fornia, where the tradition should be the guitar - strumming, singing Spanish tradition?

"In our country we sing. Not here much. We sing no more."

From the Marcos home, we drove to another lonely ranch, as alien and remote as the first, the sheep ranch of Nate Yanci. A gray house, unpainted barns, the silver Mediterranean mist of olive trees about the house, gnarled apple trees and giant eucalyptus trees.

Mr. Yanci was decidedly suspicious of us. He came out of his house and leaned with his elbows against the pickets of his unpainted fence, never unlatching the gate for us to enter his dooryard. He gave the same impression of Etruscan strength and secrecy that the other Basques had given. A sturdy, square figure, an egg-shaped face, bushy eyebrows, a shrug-shoulder air, a reluctant smile, and luminous gold-brown eyes. That deep light in Basque eyes, as of sunlight reflected back from fathomless seas. Whether the eyes are green or brown, that same strange luminosity is there. An old, old light guarded through thousands of years? The oldest race in Europe? "At the foot of the Pyrenees they witnessed the arrival in Europe of our Aryan ancestors." Plausible indeed seems the theory that the name by which the Basques call themselves, Eskualdunak, means—"people of the sun."

Even in their simple, Americanized clothes, the Basques seem to have a feeling for the picturesque and for the consonances of color. Mr. Yanci wore blue overalls, a blue shirt, a blue sweater and a white, green-spotted cap. The jaunty Basque beret had been discarded. "They wear the beret when they come—and when they die. *They insist on being buried in it,*" a neighbor told us later. "They dress American after they get here."

Nate Yanci leaned over his fence and talked reluctantly, with long seas of silence between the sails of his words.

"Sheep going well?" we asked.

"I try." (Noncommittally as a New Englander.)

"It's pretty here."

"Yes. So pretty as anywhere. Almost so pretty as Spain. Hills not so high."

"You come from the Spanish Basque country?"

"Navarra."

"Have you been here long?"

"Been here in California fourteen years. In America thirty years."

"Have you many sheep?"

"Fifteen hundred sheep. Rent twelve hundred acres of land."

"Are there many Basques around here?"

"Yes. Some Basques. It good here. Some *make America.*"

This phrase, "make America," interested us greatly, for it is precisely the phrase that the Italian immigrant, who makes money, is successful, uses. He also "makes America"! Witness "the grand Gennaro" in the splendid Italian-American novel of that name. It is apparently the universal immigrant ambition to "make America." A good, constructive verb, whether used transitively or intransitively!

"Do they go back after they make America?" we asked. Noncommittally again came the answer:

"I don't know. Might as well stay where make the living."

"Will you let me take your picture?"

"Sorry. I sick and dizzy to-day. Would let you take picture some other day."

"Do the shepherds sing in the fields? Do you make music?"

"We have the radio."

"Do the *shepherds sing?*"

"Once I remember on Stockton

Island, I hear a shepherd sing across the river. I no see. It was dark. I heard the song." (Stockton Island is in the marshlands of the Delta country along the Sacramento.)

These Basque shepherd-songs of the Pacific must always remain more or less of a mystery, although one precious song actually composed by a California F r e n c h Basque shepherd is preserved for us in Pierre Lhande's *L'Emigration Basque.* It is a song improvised on a lonely, foggy night on the Pacific slopes to the dubious companionship of the shepherd's makhila or pipe:

*"Reste avec moi, makhila bien-aimé!
Si j'avais le malheur de te perdre,
Comment suivrais-je mon troupeau? . . ."*

This calls to mind the bit of repartee supposed to satirize the romantic attitude towards the shepherd:

"Gentle shepherd, where is your pipe?"
"Ain't got no tobacco, mum!"

A point that Rodney Gallop frequently makes in his *Book of the Basques* is that we must not force the poetic a t t i t u d e upon the Basques. They are largely a matter-of-fact people facing life squarely with straight shoulders and level eyes. Their songs, their poems are brief, succinct, free of ornamentation, very often ending with a humorous or ironic twist. Yet several of the songs that Gallop quotes are lovely with the poignancy of true lyricism. Perhaps our California shepherds sing this old Basque favorite:

" 'Early in the morning as the day dawns
I drive my sheep out to pasture,
Then I lie stretched out in the shade.
Who is more content than I?
Mine is a happy lot.' "

Or this loveliest of the Basque love songs:

" 'White wood-pigeon, whither are you flying?
All the passes into Spain are full of snow.
To-night you will take refuge in our house.'

" 'I am not afraid of the snow nor of the darkness,
My beloved, for you I would pass through night and day,
Through night and day and through deserted forests.' "

Before the sun went down over the Vaca Hills, turning them to peacock-blue, we f o u n d one more Basque family hidden away under the slopes. The mail-box read, picturesquely: Huliane Iriarte, Milian LaCabe. Iriarte was not at home, but Mr. LaCabe came in from the barn, where he was very busy, for the lambing season was not quite over, and he and Mrs. LaCabe made us very comfortable in the huge modernized kitchen with its frigidaire, electric s t o v e and radio. There was no ornament on the walls except a large sheep-scene calendar of the Hotel Español in Sacramento ("Stock and Sheep Men's Headquarters. Bar in Connection. 114 J Street, Sacramento.") Quite evidently the LaCabes had "made America." Yet they, too, tooked like the ancient Etruscans, with that square, sturdy, proud, pre-Roman look that seemed to cling to these interesting Basque types. The La-Cabes were far more friendly than the others, possibly because their daughter was a student at the University of California and we hailed from there. They not only invited us over the forbidden threshold but proffered us, by way of quaint refreshment, a roll of spiced home-made sausage, *"losanizas."* They also offered us a bowl of chick-peas or *"garbanzos,"* a dish which they, as well as most Spanish Basques serve every Sunday. These are cooked slowly in salt water spiced with onion and garlic. "That's the old, old style," said Mrs. LaCabe.

Mr. LaCabe gave much pleasant information about the location of Basques in California and the prowess of certain individual Basques, especially a b o u t "Yudarte," the richest of them all, who "in the fifties, had sheep all over Van Ness Avenue in San Francisco, clear to the Presidio," and whom LaCabe had known as a very rich old man in Hollister in the early nineteen hundreds.

In the course of my questionings, I learned that, like many other Basques, on New Year's Eve and at Epiphany, Mr. LaCabe goes from Basque house to Basque house, singing old folk songs. But it was the word "dance" which made Mrs. La Cabe's face suddenly luminous. It was evident that she had been a merry dancer in her day and that she still tripped the light fantastic at the Basque festivals and parties, in spite of her sixty years. For a moment her joy illuminated and made clear Voltaire's description of the Basques as "those people who dwell or rather who dance at the foot of the Pyrenees."

"Oh, yes," she said, "I always dance the jota at the dancing parties. I love it!—And if I have no castanets, I snap the music with my fingers!"

It was easy to picture the mother's grace when we saw the lovely daughter dancing the jota at Casa España at the University of California a few weeks later. Charming in her black velvet jacket, white blouse, tasseled beret, black velvet breeches with silver bells jangling from the knees, white stockings criss-crossed with espadrilles of blue ribbons, and black pumps, she performed the quick bowings, facings, scrapings, head-tossings and leaping steps of the madcap jota, with all the riotous energy and charm of a true daughter of the Pyrenees.

Experts will tell you that the jota so joyously adopted by the Basques is a comparatively recent importation from Aragon. The old *purusalda* is the *real* Basque dance. "The true Basque steps," says Violet Alford in *Ceremonial Dances of the Spanish Basques,* in an article in *The Musical Quarterly,* "appear to be that triple or quadruple 'galley,' twisting the free foot in the air close to the standing foot; the little quiet steps, and the curious forward caper, throwing one foot after the other right up to face level."

Miss Alford has much to say of the misty origins of some of the B a s q u e ceremonial dances, the sword dances, the morris dances, the wine-glass dances, formalized descendants, undoubtedly, of o l d pagan rites in sacred groves. She points out many pagan aspects of these dances to prove her theory. Again, the finger of time seems to point far, far back to sturdy, mysterious ancestors of these sturdy, mysterious Basques, ancestors ever

THE SPANISH BASQUES IN CALIFORNIA

so remotely preceding the Vascones whom Strabo described as dancing to the flute and the t r u m p e t, "either together or singly, competing amongst themselves as to who should leap highest and fall on his knees with most grace."

It is pleasant to realize that on our California hillsides, these very ancient, European dances are still throbbing away, perpetuating their joy, their rhythm and their beauty, binding the old world to the new, when so much of old-world custom is going the way of all beautiful, discarded things. May the Basques long continue their lovely customs!

As we drove on that Basque-adventure day, one more brief encounter awaited us. B e t w e e n Knight's Landing and Yuba City, we came upon the lush, overflowed land between the Sacramento and the Yuba Rivers (part of the Sutter By-Pass), where the road travels along the summit of a high levee. The topaz light of evening was on the water, transforming it into a dark gold lagoon out of which the jet black trunks and branches of partially submerged trees jutted to make fantastic Gustave Doré pictures. Along a levee at right angles to the highway, a shepherd was driving home his flock. If only that golden light of evening might have hung suspended indefinitely to perpetuate the picture!

Hand-in-hand with my little boy, I ran along the levee to catch up with the shepherd. As the man turned, he presented a face of astonishing beauty, a David-the-shepherd face, with the contours of a dreamer and those Basque-luminous eyes, as blue as the deepest sea. His whole face was radiantly happy, as if from within himself were supplied all the desiderata.

"I am taking my sheep home to the camp for the night. Yes, I am from Navarra. Do I sing songs to my sheep sometimes? Yes. Spanish songs. Am I lonely? Well (with an almost Latin shrug), *I guess one gets lonely anywhere.*"

Here, undoubtedly, was a shepherd who sang to his sheep not only the old Basque songs but the songs of his own making. Though it would be difficult to hide away and hear these lovely, ungarnered songs, it is at least comforting to realize that only a hundred miles from the great city of San Francisco, Basque shepherds *do* sing their songs and Basque people dance their time-misted dances and life goes on obscurely, quietly, beautifully, as it has gone on for thousands of years in the shadow of the Pyrenees.

In San Francisco itself, there are little islands of Basques. There is even a *Salon de Pelota,* or *Juego de Pelota,* on Pacific Avenue, that is, a courtyard constructed for the playing of the great old Basque game of *pelota,* a very old game of ball in which the hand is used like a tennis-racket,—that game which made famous "bombers" out of the Basques in the Great War. There are two small hotels, which cater almost entirely to Basques, the Hotel Español and the Hotel de España, "Headquarters for Wool Sheep Cattlemen," on Broadway.

Some weeks after our country expedition, we dropped in at the Hotel de España for dinner one evening. There, at a long table, were seated some twenty Basque shepherds, the now easily recognizable type, stocky, square-set people with thick, rippled necks, b u s h y eyebrows, level, luminous, eagle-keen eyes, large noses, olive skins. There were the bright colors again, sky-blue shirts with yellow ties or grass-green shirts with red ties! And there were the gestures and the loud voices! How these Basque shepherds, down from the lonely pastures, talked and argued, as if to make up in disputatious volubility for the long silences of the hills!

Only one other American couple was present, besides ourselves, at a side-table. "I suppose t h e m Basque shepherds get pretty lonely up in the hills!" said the man, speaking our thoughts for us.

The Basque waitress, with jingling gold Spanish rings in her ears, served us a Spanish-American meal of peppery beef stew, the inevitable chick-peas enriched with a tomato-mushroom sauce, ravioli, fried chicken, Zucchini and an American apple pie. She kept apologizing, in broken English, for one of the shepherds who kept getting drunker and drunker every minute on strong red wine. "Too bad. He's really a fine man. Has very pretty daughter, very talented, who plays the accordion wonderful. But he just gets crazy drunk. Can't stop him!"

The inebriate one became more and more quarrelsome, so that we feared that, at any moment, he might knife his chief antagonist who sat across the table from him. But at last everyone left except himself. He still remained, bleary-eyed, clutching a final glassful of red wine. Catching our interested glance, he suddenly began to ad-dress us. It was easy to see that he had fallen under the influence of communist orators for his extempore speech was full of catch-phrases. He ended finally with a flourish of his large, square hands:

"We got to help each other, I say! We got to get together! Once I had $7,000. Now I have $20.00. But I tell you, some day I'll get it all back!" And over went the red wine, blood-staining the table all the way across!

This other glimpse of the shepherds, out of their more quiet setting, had served to reveal to us some of the human emotions that surge beneath their hillside silences. It served to explain something of the ancient violences for w h i c h the Basques were famous in the Dark Ages, the martyrdoms of St. Eusebius and St. Leon at their hands, and the patriotic violences that the Basques have recently displayed in their own country, even the Basque women rising and throwing their enemies over the sea walls into the Bay of Biscay!

All these had been but brief and passing glimpses into the lives of the Spanish Basques in California, but nevertheless they had served to create for us something of a pattern by which we might more easily understand the designs of that larger pattern which is weaving itself outward from Spain and across the Pyrenees and the Bay of Biscay and the whole world to-day.

Reluctant Shepherds

Pat Bieter

Reluctant Shepherds: The Basques in Idaho

by PAT BIETER

Pat Bieter comes honestly by his interest in Idaho's Basque people, since Mrs. Pat Bieter is a Basque. Mr. Bieter, an instructor in North Junior High School in Boise, thus has an unusual opportunity to learn the Basque side of the story. This article grew out of a seminar paper in the graduate division of the University of California, and eventually may grow into a book.

SOUTHERN IDAHO presents a unique problem to the student of western history. For here lives a group of people which has presented an enigma to scholars since the time of the Romans. They settled here thousands of miles from their homeland in a place which bears little resemblance to anything they ever saw before, and then took jobs which were alien to many of them. These are the Basque people of southwestern Idaho, whose history, although it begins before Christ in Europe, scarcely dates back seventy-five years in America. What brought these people to Idaho? One must look to the Basque country of Europe for the answer.

The Basque country lies in northwestern Spain where the Pyrenees Mountains jut sharply into the Bay of Biscay. The same border which divides France from Spain also separates the four Spanish Basque provinces —Guipuzcoa, Viscaya, Alava, and Navarre— from the three French Basque provinces of Labaurd, Basse-Navarre, and Soule. However, since the Basque immigration into Idaho has been nearly entirely from among the Spanish provinces, we shall consider only these.

In a section one hundred miles along the coastline and approximately eighty miles in depth live 450,000 people of one of the purest and oldest races known in Europe. The Basque history is lost in antiquity, purely a matter of historical speculation. Anthropologists are not even positive how they got into Spain. Certain facts, however, are known by historians about them.

They have lived within the same area since before the time of the Roman conquests, for:

Roman historians make frequent references to a tribe living in or near what is now the Basque country, a tribe speaking a peculiar language which their neighbors did not understand.[1]

[1] Rodney Gallop, *A Book of the Basques* (London: MacMillan, 1940), 9.

The rugged Pyrenees together with the fierce disposition of the Basque tribes themselves seem to have protected them from the ravages of the Gothic hordes. Feudalism never took hold of the Basque provinces, for the nature of the land was such that large estates were impossible. The hilly land could best be farmed in small individual plots. Besides, much of the Basque economy was directed toward the sea. For centuries they had fished the waters of Biscay and searched the North Atlantic for whale. Basque ships had reached Newfoundland and fished the Grand Banks a full two centuries before English-speaking fishermen began to take the Newfoundland cod.[2]

THE SPANISH BASQUES were probably converted to Christianity before the seventh century. In Lequeitio, in the province of Viscaya, there is a Catholic church which was built in the year 730. Early in the Basque history two important principles, which were to be carried with their sons to America, were established—a fierce love of freedom based on individual land ownership, and a deep feeling for their religion. Their political history, however, was not fortunate.

They had been unable to withstand the rising Spanish monarchy but had been conceded what we today might call dominion status. They had a representative assembly much in the model of the Greek city states with a council of elders who presided. Their liberty was symbolized by the oak tree of Guernica, later to be blotted out by the Fascists in the Spanish civil war. Thus, from the Middle Ages to the nineteenth century, the Basques remained aloof from European politics. Theirs was a small semi-independent island

in the sea of conflict during this period. They were, however, still under the Spanish sovereigns. During the Carlist Wars of the nineteenth century they saw the possibility of complete independence and became embroiled in the conflicts. Here the Basques first showed their propensity for picking the losing side in civil wars, and after 1876 lost not only their dominion status but also any hope for complete independence. The Basque language was officially suppressed, Basque enthusiasm for Spanish rule dwindled. It was during this period, just after the second Carlist War, that the Basque immigration to the United States began.

In any migration there are factors which both drive one from his native soil and attract him towards other shores. In the case of the Basques both sorts of forces were at work.

A modified form of the law of primogeniture was in effect in Euzkadi (which is what the Basques call their homeland). That is, the father would nominate after careful consideration one of his sons *or daughters* to take over the farm or business after his death. This process left the remaining children with the alternative of either staying as tenants on the family farm, or leaving.[3] Generally they stayed until conditions in Spain became such that other countries were more attractive. Another pressing factor was the compulsory service in the Spanish army, for a period of four years.[4] That service could, however, be waived for a price which, if it were paid, would allow the youth to leave the country and return without the stigma of desertion. It is significant that many Basques coming to the United States paid this fee, showing that they probably intended to return eventually to Spain.

[2] Janette Guthman, "Basque People of the Northwest," *The National Woodgrower* (December, 1945), 35:14; interview with Professor Lawrence Kinnaird, University of Oregon.

[3] Interview with Boni Garmendia of Boise, an early Basque immigrant to the Boise Valley.
[4] Interview with the late John D. Archabal, Berkeley, California, his family paid this fee when he left Spain.

Map by George Bowditch

Another factor causing many Basques to leave was poverty coupled with the imminent possibility of the despised Spaniards overrunning their hitherto isolated homeland. The stories of the wealth to be gotten in the American west were known among this practical people. News of California's gold rush and the silver riches in Nevada reached them at the time when it would appeal to them most. Consequently, many Basque youths set out to make their way to California, which to them was the American west.[5] It is significant that in this early period Idaho is nowhere mentioned as a stopping place, nor is the sheep industry (today so commonly considered attractive to the Basques) considered as a means of livelihood.

LEQUEITEO IN THE SUMMER OF 1954

WHEN THESE VANGUARDS of the Basque movement reached California they found the road to riches was a bumpy one. Gold was not in the streets. Their language presented a nearly impossible barrier to their getting work. They found themselves in a strange country, speaking a strange language, equipped to do little but farm or fish. A group made their way from California to northern Nevada looking for work. Some of them took jobs as farm laborers. These men were sturdy and fearless, accustomed to life in the outdoors. Sheep ranchers tried them as herders to replace some of their untrustworthy Indian and Mexican hands, and were pleased with the result. The bands of sheep came back fat and intact. The Basques took, if they did not welcome, these jobs because herding required no prior education—only honesty and

a strong body. They found themselves at no disadvantage because of their lack of English, for there were only the dog and the stars to talk to. But they were new at herding sheep. Few of these Spanish Basques, in contrast to their French brothers, had ever herded anything but a team of oxen or a fishing boat loaded with tuna. As one older Idaho Basque once said, though, "Dammit, we had to eat!"

The towns of McDermitt, Nevada, and Jordan Valley, Oregon, became centers of dispersal for these early immigrants.[6] They gradually worked their way into the Boise Valley, where they found employment as herders and laborers in and around Boise City, which in the last decades of the nineteenth century was becoming a rapidly growing center in the Snake and Boise River Valleys.[7] The news soon reached the people at home that there were jobs available to Basque youths as herders in Idaho and Nevada. Then the rush was on. Young Basques began to leave Spain by the hundreds, heading this time not for California, but for the fleecy gold of Nevada and Idaho. Many went to work a few days after they arrived here. One can easily imagine the feelings of these men when they first found themselves in the hills with a band of sheep. They had been accustomed to the lively communal life of the temperate Basque country—a life of feast days and dancing, of pelota games and good wine. They had worked hard and long but seldom alone. Now they found themselves in the dry desert mountains of Nevada and Idaho, alone with perhaps 2,500 sheep put in their charge for six to eight months. They had chances to go to town, but few of them went. They couldn't talk to anyone anyway, and they were unable to enjoy the laughter of the local people as they fumbled with the English language. So they remained in the hills, hoping for the day when they could send home for a wife or girl friend and run their own band of sheep. It is not easy to get a Basque to talk about his feelings during those first days of herding, because too many times they were painfully lonely and unhappy days. To those who came to town only embarrassment lay in their attempts to learn the language. Once a Basque herder

[5] Letters from Euskadi are still received addressed to persons in "Boise, Idaho, California, U.S.A."

[6] Interview with Bob Gingery, Richmond, California, who for some years ran a bar and general store in McDermitt, Nevada.
[7] Guthman, "Basque People," 35:13.

EMPTY COUNTRY AND SHEEP
WERE THE LOT OF THE HERDS-
MEN.

Photo courtesy of the author

who had been out with the sheep for several months came into Mountain Home, Idaho, and made a practice of eating in one restaurant in the hope of picking up some English words. After two or three weeks without success he confided to a friend that he could never learn to speak English. His friend told him that Chinese ran the restaurant and they couldn't speak English either!

SOME OF THE MORE ENTERPRISING Basques began through thrift and industry to acquire a few sheep of their own and eventually were in a position to help others to come to America. Among these were typical Basque names: John B. Archabal, Antone Uranga, Miguel Gabica, José Bengoechea, Joe Uberuaga, Antonio Ascuenga, and José Navarro. Stories of their thrift and skill became famous. It is said that John Archabal's total expenses for one year were $50. Basques became skillful in getting the maximum use out of range land, sometimes even illegally. The story is told of a Basque herder who took the bells off his sheep at night and ran them into the lush grass of the Idaho State Penitentiary.

This early movement of the Basques was nearly entirely male, for few, it seems, intended to stay here. Eventually, though, wives and sweethearts were sent for and Basque families began to settle in southwestern Idaho towns. Boise soon became the center of Basque immigration. Boarding houses sprang up to shelter the new arrivals who now came straight by train to Boise. Every newcomer of those days has a different story to tell of his passage over and his train ride west. As boys, they left a homeland

where a trip of fifty miles was a momentous undertaking. After crossing the Atlantic and landing in New York, they would embark by train for Boise, having no idea where to get off because they had no slightest conception of how far it was. They carried all their possessions on their back or in a battered suitcase held together with a rope. Sophisticated eastern travelers must have been both amused and abused, for often zealous mothers would pack a string of *chorizos* (Basque sausage) and some bread for the trip. They traveled in coaches for the most part, where the strong smelling *chorizos*, many times tossed over the back of a young Basque along with a guitar, must have made quite a hit with his fellow travelers.

One of them told of his mother's warning, before his departure, to be careful of his faith in that irreligious country. When he was on the train heading for Idaho he noticed many people's lips moving much like those of the women he had seen saying the Rosary in his own village church. He wrote his mother after arriving, saying she need not fear for her son's faith because many of the people on the train were praying. He later learned that these people were chewing gum, something he had neither seen nor heard of before. None of these Basques could speak English and few of them were skilled. They usually arrived by prearrangement in Boise during lambing time and often only one or two days would elapse before they were put to work. After lambing, they selected dogs and headed for the hills with an experienced herder and camp tender.

As the Basque population began to grow

a serious religious problem presented itself. They were almost to a man Catholic, and were moving into a predominantly Protestant area. They had a problem even among Catholics because none of the parish priests could speak Basque, making confession impossible. In 1911, Alphonse J. Glorieux, Bishop of Boise Diocese, arranged with the Bishop of Vittoria in Spain for the services of a Basque priest. He sent the Reverend Bernardo Arregui to attend to the religious needs of the Idaho Basques. He was rugged physically and sympathetic to the problems of the Basque herder. Father Arregui made

gotten their national game. The picture of herders sitting around Anduiza's *fronton*, drinking from *botas* of wine and shouting encouragement while betting on their favorites, brings vivid memories to Boise Basques. Three *frontons* were built in Boise and one in Jordan Valley. The latter is still in excellent condition, although a Basque there says that a game hasn't been played in it since the start of World War II.

This trait of keeping to themselves allowed slower assimilation into society and delayed the eventual influx of Basques into other occupations. Practically all of them started out

BASQUE SHEEPHERDER WITH HIS TYPICAL "SHEEP WAGON." SHEEPHERDERS FOLLOWING THEIR BANDS TAKE THESE MOBILE HOUSES WITH THEM. MODERN SHEEP WAGONS ARE SIMILAR TO THIS, ALTHOUGH THEY HAVE PNEUMATIC TIRES.

Photo courtesy of the author

frequent trips into the hills bringing the comforts of religion to the isolated herders.[3]

FOR THE MOST PART the Basques kept to themselves. They lived in the southeastern section of Boise, where several Basque boarding houses became the center of their town activity. The establishment of these boarding houses greatly aided in bringing Basque women to the United States, by providing employment as cooks and housekeepers. Pelota courts were constructed alongside them; the Basques in America had not for-

in the United States herding sheep.[9] Sheep owners did not encourage their Basque herders to learn English, for with the English language came the possibility of other jobs, and a good herder was very valuable. But twenty-five percent did stop herding as soon as other jobs became available, often within two years after their arrival.[10] Today the coin is inverted: less than five per cent of second-generation Basques are sheepherders.

The twenty years from 1900 to 1920 saw the greatest influx of Basques into the Boise

[3] Cyprian Bradley and Edward J. Kelly, *History of the Diocese of Boise* (Boise, 1953), 307.

[9] Interview with Boni Garmendia.
[10] John B. Edlefsen, *A Sociological Study of the Basques of Southwest Idaho* (Ph.D. Thesis, State College of Washington, 1948).

Valley, but it is difficult to determine exactly how many came because they were given the general title "Spanish" in the Bureau of immigration statistics. Besides, it is impossible to tell how many jumped ship! One Basque gave the number of slightly illegal entrants at close to 750 since 1948 alone.

SHEEPHERDING did not hold the Basques for long and many got into other jobs as soon as possible. Herding, it seemed, was just a method of getting to America. As one Basque got out of herding another was ready to take his place. Thus a constant stream came to the United States until 1921, when immigration restrictions began to check the movement.

In 1921 the United States made a drastic change in its immigration policy. Up to that time practically any person who was in good physical and mental health, not illiterate, of good moral character, and not racially ineligible for naturalization could enter the country. During the war a reaction set in which led to a widespread demand for restriction. It was largely due to the belief that the country had been admitting immigrants more rapidly than it could assimilate them and to the fear that following the war the country would be swamped with immigrants desiring to escape the distress in Europe.[11]

Thus the quota system was born.

For all practical purposes the quota system ended further extensive southern European immigration. However, the sheep owners began to find themselves in a difficult situation. Herders were quitting, drawn to more attractive and higher paying jobs because, as one herder told me, "there *had* to be something in the United States better than herding sheep" and so, under pressure from wool growers, Congress passed a bill to "provide relief for the sheep industry by making special quota immigration visas available to certain alien sheepherders."[12] The bill was spearheaded by Idaho and Nevada Congressmen. It allowed 250 Basque herders to be admitted, providing they were guaranteed permanent employment and were skilled herders. Many Basques have come into the United States during the last twenty years on the basis of this legislation although strangely enough, few of them are "skilled"

11 Frank L. Auerbach, *The Immigration and Nationality Act* (New York: Common Council for American Unity, 1952), 7, 20; Edlefsen, *Basques of Southwest Idaho*, 67.
12 64 U. S. Statutes at Large (1950), 306.

herders. A Basque who came in under this quota system said, perhaps none too facetiously, that he had to go to a farm in Spain to count the number of legs on a sheep because he had never seen one! These men after serving their time in the sheep camps have gotten into all forms of occupations.

The Basques, it seems, have never had an inferior position in western society. People recognized early their values of sincerity and industry. Furthermore, they entered a frontier area where labor was scarce, which made them doubly desirable as citizens. The period of enclavement for them was short.[13] Today, second generation Basque-Americans have, somewhat sad to say, been completely Americanized. Rarely do they speak accented English, but they are proud of their old-country customs and their language, and they have managed to keep them alive through such groups as Euzkaldunak, a social organization in Boise. When, for example, Juanita Uberuaga Aldrich saw that Basque children were growing up unable to dance their native dances, she organized classes through Euzkaldunak to teach them. Euzkaldunak also sponsored the Boise appearance of the Basque ballet and singing group.

FOR THE BASQUE, language and music represent their way of life. Both are an integral part of the Basque home in America as well as in Europe. The Basque language is one of the most difficult in the world. It defies anyone not raised speaking it to pronounce its mouth-puckering, tongue-trilling sounds. But, this language, which presented such a barrier to the early Basques in America is now becoming one of the major things which help to keep Basque culture alive here in a new land.

The Basque people are now Americans. Their grandchildren will probably not be able to speak Basque, and, like every other nationality, they will become amalgamated in the American melting pot. They may even lose many of their colorful old-country customs —but not if they can help it. They are today a unique part of southwest Idaho—accepted and yet different. They are proud of their heritage and at the same time proud of their new homeland, and Idaho is proud of them.

13 Edlefsen, *Basques of Southwest Idaho*.

Hispanics in the United States

An Arno Press Collection

Cortés, Carlos E., editor. **Cuban Exiles in the United States**. 1980

Cortés, Carlos E., editor. **The Cuban Experience in the United States**. 1980

Cortés, Carlos E., editor. **Cuban Refugee Programs**. 1980

Cortés, Carlos E., editor. **The Latin American Brain Drain to the United States**. 1980

Cortés, Carlos E., editor. **Latinos in the United States**. 1980

Cortés, Carlos E., editor. **Nineteenth-Century Latin Americans in the United States**. 1980

Cortés, Carlos. E., editor. **Portuguese Americans and Spanish Americans**. 1980

Cortés, Carlos E., editor. **Protestantism and Latinos in the United States**. 1980

Cortés, Carlos E., editor. **Regional Perspectives on the Puerto Rican Experience**. 1980

Cortés, Carlos E., editor. **Spanish and Portuguese Languages in the United States**. 1980

Digges, Jeremiah [pseud. Josef Berger] **In Great Waters**. 1941

Durán, Daniel Flores. **Latino Communication Patterns**. 1980

Fernández-Flórez, Dario. **The Spanish Heritage in the United States**. 1965

Ferree, William, Ivan Illich, and Joseph P. Fitzpatrick, editors. **Spiritual Care of Puerto Rican Migrants**. 1970

Gallagher, Patrick Lee. **The Cuban Exile**. 1980

Hernandez, Andres R., editor. **The Cuban Minority in the U.S. Final Report**. 1974

Kernstock, Elwyn Nicholas. **How New Migrants Behave Politically**. 1972

Lewin, Ellen. **Mothers and Children**. 1980

Miyares, Marcelino. **Models of Political Participation of Hispanic Americans**. 1980

Morrison, J. Cayce. **The Puerto Rican Study, 1953-1957**. 1958

Prohias, Rafael J. and Lourdes Casal. **The Cuban Minority in the U.S. Preliminary Report**. 1974

Redden, Charlotte Ann. **A Comparative Study of Colombian and Costa Rican Emigrants to the United States**. 1980

Ribes Tovar, Federico. **El Libro Puertorriqueño de Nueva York**. 1970

Richmond, Marie LaLiberte. **Immigrant Adaptation and Family Structure Among Cubans in Miami, Florida**. 1980

Ropka, Gerald William. **The Evolving Residential Pattern of the Mexican, Puerto Rican, and Cuban Population of the City of Chicago**. 1980

Ross, Elmer Lamar. **Factors in Residence Patterns Among Latin Americans in New Orleans, Louisiana**. 1980

United States Congress. **Immigration**. 1970

United States Congress. **Immigration 1976**. 1976

United States Congress. **Western Hemisphere Immigration**. 1975-6

U.S. Select Commission on Western Hemisphere Immigration. **Report of the Select Commission on Western Hemisphere Immigration**. 1968

Yglesias, José. **A Wake in Ybor City**. 1963